Fun Texa[...]
and Events

Jim Gramon

Cartoons by Bill Erhard

Republic of Texas Press
Plano, Texas

Library of Congress Cataloging-in-Publication Data

Gramon, Jim.
Fun Texas festivals and events / Jim Gramon.
p. cm.
Includes index.
ISBN 1-55622-886-4
1. Festivals--Texas. 2. Special events--Texas. 3. Texas--Social life and customs. I. Title.

GT4810.T4 G73 2001
394.269764--dc21 2001048511
CIP

Republic of Texas Press is an imprint of Wordware Publishing, Inc.

Printed in the United States of America

ISBN 1-55622-886-4
10 9 8 7 6 5 4 3 2 1
0110

All inquiries for volume purchases of this book should be addressed to Wordware Publishing, Inc., at 2320 Los Rios Boulevard, Plano, Texas 75074. Telephone inquiries may be made by calling:

(972) 423-0090

This book is dedicated to

Evelyn Gramon
my Mom
for all the encouragement and support
Thanx Mom

and

Bill Erhard
Dear friend and Great Artist/Cartoonist.
Thanx for your friendship
and for the use of your wonderful sketches.

Contents

Preface. vi
Acknowledgments viii
Introduction x
January 1
February. 6
March. 17
April 41
May. 70
June 103
July 127
August 151
September 163
October. 199
November 232
December 241
Webliography 251
City & Chamber of Commerce Websites. 257
Texas Towns by Region. 275
Index of Events 281

Preface

Several years ago I pulled up a chair at the Liars' Table at the Manchaca Fire Hall. A glance at the wirey guy next to me told me he had done a lot of hard outdoors work, probably down on the farm. Clarence Vogel, the jefe maitre d' proprietor of this down home roadside café/firehall, asked me if I knew Bill. We did our howdys, and Bill's slow easy drawl told me it was a Texas farm. We taled about contrary horses and had a great chat, complete with plenty of laughs. We both like to laugh, a lot.

When Bill got up to leave he tossed me a paper napkin. He said, "Here Jim, this is for you." I started to laugh at his "gift" then I looked at the back of it. On the back was an incredible cartoon sketch of a horse. I had never seen better artistry, and here it was on the back of a paper napkin.

After Bill left, I went to Clarence and showed him the incredible napkin art. He smiled and took me into his office, where he produced a large notebook, full of plastic sheet protectors, each containing two of Bill's sketches. I laughed till I cried at the wonderful cartoons.

I'm honored that Bill calls me a friend, and I was even more honored when he said he would like to do some sketches for this book. Unfortunately, Bill ran into some health problems and was unable to do the sketches. Fortunately for all of us, Bill gave me permission to use the original napkins. So, if the quality of a couple of the sketches is a little rough, you now know the rest of the story. And yes, those are real coffee stains on a couple of them!

This is the first sketch given to me by Bill Erhard.

Acknowledgments

Sally Gramon
my lovely bride (of many years)
for all her encouragement. Luv Ya Babe.

James Gramon and **Tracye Spears**
My son and his fianceé,
for all their assistance in gathering information
from all over this huge state.

Buffalo Chuck
Two-time Chili Cookoff World Champion
for the use of some wonderful pictures

Dyanne and **Javier Cortez**
SHE - authored *Hot Jams and Cold Showers*
about the Kerrverts at the Kerrville Folk Festival,
HE - is an extraordinary leather craftsman,
THEY - generously contributed some of their pictures.

Mike Annas
Great Photographer & Great Guy
Thanx for the use of some of your pictures.

To the wonderful volunteers
Volunteers run most of these festivals. Most get
paid a nice round number, zero. Yet, most do a
wonderful job out of love for their community.
Thanx to all the folks, at all the festivals, who
helped me get the best info possible.

Let's face it,
Texans love
a good party!

Introduction

I want to take you on a great adventure. No matter how long you have lived in Texas, or anywhere else for that matter, you will be amazed and amused by this book. No, not from my writing ability, but by the incredible diversity, creativity, and just plain silliness that goes into some of these events.

How else can you explain festivals to celebrate fire ants, mosquitoes, alligators, blackeyed peas, cartoon characters, shrimp, oysters, crawfish, cotton, every kind of music imaginable, famous and infamous people, trees, rivers-lakes-streams-springs, flowers, holidays from dozens of other countries, and for oatmeal?

Texans love to party and will use any available excuse!

If we don't have a couple holidays in a month, we'll just borrow a few from other countries!

I guarantee that you will find real belly laughs just reading about some of these wonderful events. Only in Texas would a classical music festival be called the Texas Toot! What about an event called the Prickly Pear Pachanga? Or a favorite of mine, the Big Stinkin' International Improv & Sketch Comedy Festival, referred to by everyone as BS. You get the picture.

No wall full of books could cover Texas. This book will cover the major events in each region of the state, while providing the reader with contact information to the towns and events. Almost every town has some events that space limitations did not allow me to include. Generally I've only included community-wide events.

Getting Good Info Is Hard To Do!

One problem is that no book can be completely up to date. Every day new events are being announced, and other events are being discontinued. Dates, locations, and even the names of events change. It's now late June 2001, and most of the annual events that occurred in early 2001 have not yet set the date for their 2002 event. Between the time I finish this manuscript and the time you buy the book, some aspects of it will be out of date.

Early on in this project I hit my first big surprise. I have some point-and-click computer background and went into this project expecting the most current information to be on the websites. Not so, world-wide-web-breath!

I found numerous websites, boldly announcing an event and prominently displaying the dates, but without showing the year. It appears that many websites haven't been updated in years!

Websites often disagree with each other; it is often hard to know who is the official organizer of the event and should have the best info.

Another caveat about websites and literature alike. Just today I checked out a website that was last updated this week. Should be current. It was. But one of the events on the website was an announcement of a festival that is to held from February 28-31. Now, I'd pay good wampum to see the 31st of February! Must have been quite a leap this year! Or, perhaps they were "doing the time warp again." More likely, it was just a typo. The bottom line is, typos happen, and it's always a good idea to:

Check BEFORE you go!

OK, you ask, how did I get "the real info" about the events?

Simple, I just made up anything I needed!

No, actually the short answer is, "Lots of work."

The long answer is "Lots of mail, email, and phone calls." Through a variety of methods, I tried to contact every event in this book. Most of them sent me the most current info about their events. An eight-foot table in my home is covered with boxes full of the responses (and some of the literature was three years old!!!).

Space limitations also prevent me from giving the reader a "complete" description of so many events. I have tried to summarize each event, giving you the flavor of it and highlighting some of the special aspects.

So, how do you get the "real" info about an event?

Fear not, dear reader, I've provided you with the tools to prevent those problems. For each event I've tried to provide several ways to check for the most current information. Wherever possible I provide phone, mail, email, and website information. But the important thing is . . . .

Check BEFORE you go!

Most events that don't happen on the same day every year (like July 4th) get their schedule ironed out about four to six months before the event happens. Sixty to ninety days before you go, using the contact info I've provided you, you should be able to get the whole lowdown on the when and where.

I Need Your Help . . . .

Yep, that's right, I need your help on gathering info. Due to a few of the laws of physics, I can't be at all the places at the same time. But I intend to get to as many as I can.

You can help me with this book (no you can't have your name on the front!). In the future, when this book is revised, I want the info to be as correct as possible. Here's how you can help. If you know of an event that should be included in this book, or if you have new info on an event, please email the info to me at Festival@onr.com or mail it to me at Jim Gramon, P.O. Box 2100 Manchaca, TX 78652-2100.

I love going to these events, and those of you who read my last book know I'm a folklorist and storyteller. I had the good fortune to grow up around John Henry Faulk, J. Frank Dobie, Ben King Green, Kinky Friedman, Cactus Pryor, Allen Damron, Roy Orbison, and my girlfriend, Liz Carpenter.

If you would like for me to judge a contest or come tell some tall tales, just drop me a line.

Organization of This Book

I sat and scratched for days, trying to figure out the best way to organize this book, to make it as easy to use as possible. It is set up as a Calendar of Events in, what else, chronological order.

Please pay close attention to the year in the date.

When I didn't have the date for their next event, I put them in under the date their event last took place. Often this is a good indicator of the time of year/month that they like to hold it.

Wherever possible I include the organizer's target date, like "the 2nd Saturday in March."

Other events hop about like fleas on a hot plate, being held at different dates each year. For these I will give the actual date, if possible.

Otherwise I'm forced to give a generalization like, "Early March" or "Mid-July." Or, worse yet, some event organizers assure me that their event is held "Each spring"! We just stand by for 90 days?

Some events are long-term, like the State Fair of Texas, taking place over many weeks. These will be introduced on the calendar when they first begin. Then they will be shown again at the start of each succeeding month in which they occur.

Some holidays or events are celebrated all over the state. Like the 4th of July, Cinco De Mayo, Texas Independence Day, St. Patrick's Day, Octoberfest, or Juneteenth. In those cases I've selected a representative selection of events that show the various ways it is celebrated. But be sure to check your locality to see what's going on.

Another organizational challenge for this book was how to properly indicate the location of regional events, like county fairs that are held at some facility located between two towns. When this occurs, the towns closest to the event will be shown with a hyphen between them, like the fictitious Austin - San Marcos Quadrennial Hoedown and Slop Sling.

Regions of Texas and Index of Events

To help you find your way around, there is a list of Texas towns by region and an index at the back of the book.

The list has all of the towns by the geographic region of the state in which they appear. Towns were assigned to the various regions based predominantly on the geographic nature of the region. I've included a map of the state, broken into the following regions:

The state of Texas, divided into geographical regions

The index includes all the events and page numbers where they are described.

One other point: I've done my best to be sure the events are described here accurately. But I haven't been able to attend all of these festivals (I'm trying to though!), and in many cases I'm forced to depend on the promoters' and publicists' descriptions of the event. Hopefully they are all accurate, but there is no way I can guarantee it.

So, without any further palaverin'...

here's where the fun is in Texas....

Your author heading off to find another festival.

January

When the weather gets bad
we put it in the box—
U-all folks do that too
don't you?

Well, here we are in the middle of the "long" (8 to 12 weeks) Texas winter! It's depressing to think that we won't be able to go water skiing or skinny dipping for at least another month! At times the temperature even plunges down around forty degrees! I joke, a little, because there are some areas like the Panhandle that do have a long cold winter, but for most in Texas it isn't bad at all.

It's the start of a new month, a new year, and another twelve months of parties, festivals, events, shindigs, jubilees, hootnannies, fairs, cookoffs, and so on. You get the picture.

You might wonder why there aren't a lot of activities in January. Well partner, here's the story. Texans know how to party, and they know they will have to pace themselves if they ever expect to be up for the whole year. So we tend to start out slow, using those blustery, forty-degree days to put together plans and provisions for everything to come.

Planning and pace are the key words. Stuck in the house, it might just be a pretty good time to fine-tune that barbecue sauce, pie recipe, or those secret chili ingredients. I wonder if Jim Bob is going to put any ginger into this year's version of his sauce? What fertilizer is Sally puttin' on those killer tomatoes she grows? Time to plan.

It's happened many times. The stories circulate at the local Liars' Tables about folks who failed to properly pace themselves and were totally partied out before Halloween.

Pace Yourself!
And always double check the dates of the events.

Fort Worth: North Central   **Southwestern Exposition, Livestock Show**
& Rodeo

January 12 – February 3, 2002   Late January, Early February

About ten days of rodeoing, country and western music, and livestock judging of critters ranging from pigeons to bulls. Will Rogers Memorial Center, 3301 W. Lancaster, (817) 877-2400, www.fwstockshowrodeo.com

Big Spring: West   **Harley Davidson Chili Cookoff**

January 13, 2001

Bikes and bowls of red, now that is fun! Held at the Howard County Fairgrounds at FM 700 and Highway 80. Tom Koger, P.O. Box 1391, Big Spring, TX 79721, (915) 263-7641, www.bigspringtx.com

Lake Jackson: Gulf   **Brazosport Run for the Arts**

January 13, 2001   2nd Saturday in January

One of the premier road races in the country. The race is designated as the Houston Area Road Runners Association (HARRA) Fall Series 10K Championship. The course is 10K out and back, flat, fast course, certified, and sanctioned. Proceeds benefit the Brazosport Center for the Arts & Sciences. 5K Run/Walk, 10K Run. Held at the Center for the Arts & Sciences, 400 College Drive. Call (409) 265-7661. www.runforthearts.com

Freeport: Gulf   **Martin Luther King Parade**

January 14, 2002   Held on the Martin Luther King Holiday

The parade goes through Freeport and features area bands, churches, and community leaders. Held on West Second Street. Call (409) 238-4342. www.freeport.tx.us

Goldthwaite: Gulf   **Mills County Youth Fair and Livestock Show**

January 18-20, 2002   3rd weekend in January

Great fair and great fun for young and old. Held at the Mills County Civic Center. (915) 648-2650, http://resources.rootsweb.com/USA/TX/Mills/

San Antonio: South   **Juice Anniversary Celebration**

January 18-20, 2002   3rd weekend in January

The Juice Anniversary Celebration brings the pages of *The Juice* magazine to life for three days in the month of January. The concerts include blues, Christian, jazz, R&B, rap, and reggae. All events are held in downtown San Antonio, at the Lila Cockrell Sunken Gardens.

Carl Booker, 10635 IH-35 North, Suite 312, San Antonio, TX 78233, (210) 655-5956, Fax: (210) 655-7057, avista@thejuiceonline.com, www.thejuiceonline.com

Port Arthur: Gulf   Janis Joplin Birthday Bash

January 20, 2001

Janis Joplin was born January 19, 1943. She died October 3, 1970. Her annual Birthday Bash includes blues and rock music and features the Southeast Texas Musical Heritage concert as a salute to successful Port Arthur and Gulf Coast area artists and musicians. Held at the Port Arthur Civic Center, Highway 73 at Ninth Avenue.

Triangle Concert Productions, Don Ball, 3319 Avenue D, Nederland, TX

Liz Carpenter and Jim do some book signing at a small country fair.

77627, (409) 722-3699, (800) 235-7822, Fax: (409) 722-2255, trianglecon-cert@webtv.net, www.portarthur.com/janis/index1.html

McAllen: South   Rio Grande Valley International Music Festival

January 23-26, 2002   Last weekend in January

This neat music festival features educational concerts, classical, and pops. Thousands of students from the Lower Valley area get to enjoy the twelve elementary concerts. All events are held at the McAllen Civic Center, located at the Harlingen Municipal Auditorium, 1300 South Tenth, Radisson Resort, SPI 500 Padre Blvd.

Rio Grande Valley International Music Festival, Inc., Scott Hollinger, Finance Secretary, P.O. Box 2315, McAllen, TX 78502, (956) 618-6085, www.governor.state.tx.us/music/tmec.main.htm

Austin: Hill Country   Mid-Winter Festival of Music

January 26 – March 3, 2002   Last weekend in Jan. till first weekend in March

This is a six-weekend music festival, celebrating the sounds of the Medieval, Renaissance, Baroque, and Early Classical repertoire as well as a few surprises! Along the way, there will be Renaissance dances, Scottish ballads, Celtic harps, and early music at the "cutting edge"—an appropriate homage to the new millennium. Events are held at the First English Lutheran Church, 30th and Whitis.

For information contact: Texas Early Music Project, Daniel Johnson, Artistic Dir., P.O. Box 4328, Austin, TX 78765, (512) 371-0099, (512) 371-7753, dmj726@aol.com, www.early-music.org

Mission: South Texas Citrus Fiesta

January 25-27, 2001   **Last week in January**

This fiesta and county fair features a free parade, a fun fair for kids and adults, food, live music, costume style show, coronation of Queen Citriana and Citrus King, Parade of Oranges, a golf tournament, arts and crafts, folklorico dancers, children's music, cloggers, live county/western, tejano, mariachi, and stage bands. Held in La Lomita Plaza, in downtown Mission.

Texas Citrus Fiesta, Barbara Pena, Director, P.O. Box 407, Mission, TX 78573, (956) 585-9724, Fax: (956) 580-9728, www.missionchamber.com

February

Y'all redy
fer sum biskits?

We're just about done with winter. Talk at the Feed-and-Seed has turned to when to plant what and in which field. How big a garden are you puttin' in this year? How many rows of what? Which calves, sheep, goats, colts, llamas, and emus are going to be ready to show at the upcoming county fair? And, who's gonna win the prizes for the best whatever?

WARNING: The events are starting to kick off, despite the unpredictable weather. During the spring and fall, always carry enough clothes that you could handle a thirty-degree change in the weather. In Texas we have what we call blue northers that blow in very quickly. In an hour I've seen the weather go from the sunny seventies, to sleeting in the thirties. So to avoid having to wear a plastic trash bag serape home, always carry some extra layers of clothing. When my son James was competing in soccer tournaments all over the state, the back of our truck looked like I sold used clothing for a living! Be prepared.

Now a word about barbecue, BBQ, bar-b-cue, or barbeque.

However you choose to spell it, we do a lot of it in Texas, and always remember that it's sacred. Folks who could care less how you vote or which church you attend, can end up squaring off over the proper technique for cooking good barbecue. What kind of marinade to use,

Barbecuin' in Texas is serious stuff. In Texas this is a typical "small" 3 grill model! Photo by Javier Cortez.

how long to smoke it, do you use a rub or not, wood, gas, or charcoal, what kind of wood, direct or indirect heat, wrap in foil or not? All that, and we haven't asked anything about what kind of sauce you use (tomato or not, sweet or not, etc.). Are you taking notes? Most Texans have opinions on most of these questions.

I love barbecue. My bride (20 years) Sally says I've never met a barbecue I couldn't enjoy. The way I figure it, by not being picky, I get to enjoy a whole lot more barbecue. One of my favorite things to do is ask folks at cookoffs what their preferences are. It's fun. It's kind of like pushing a snowball off the top of a really big hill. It's fun to watch 'em get wound up. A guaranteed icebreaker. Just don't make the mistake of asking them about their secret ingredients. That's personal!

Always double check the dates of the events.

Fort Worth: North Central   **Southwestern Exposition, Livestock Show and Rodeo**

January 12 – February 3, 2002   Late January, Early February

About ten days of rodeoing, country and western music, and livestock judging of critters ranging from pigeons to bulls. Held at the Will Rogers Memorial Center, 3301 W. Lancaster, (817) 877-2400, www.fwstockshowrodeo.com

Dallas: North Central   **Renaissance Polyphony Weekend**

February 1-3, 2002   1st weekend in February

Renaissance Polyphony Weekend is a workshop for persons wishing to sing Renaissance Polyphony. Held at the University of Dallas in Irving, Texas.

Susan Barton, 9215 Forest Hills Blvd., Dallas, TX 75218, (214) 327-6823, Fax: (214) 327-5879, www.toot.org

Navasota: North Central   **Go Texan Days**

February 1-3, 2002   1st weekend in February

This super little three-day festival features lots of good old down-home fun. There is a parade, country music, dances, auction, horseshoe, washer and domino tournaments, hay hauling competition, arts and crafts, and barbecue and chili cookoffs. The events are held at the Grimes County Fairgrounds.

Stacey Ross, P.O. Box 1479, Navasota, TX 77868, (936) 825-2020, (936) 825-6600, Fax: (936) 825-3699, www.rtis.com/reg/navasota

Wimberley: Hill Country   **The 8th Annual Wimberley Jazz at Cypress Creek Café**

February 1-3, 8-10, 2002   2nd & 3rd weekends in February

This cool jazz festival features a series of live jazz performances held in a comfortable intimate club that seats no more than 100 people. It is a nonsmoking event with the emphasis on talent, sound quality, and the customer. It is held Friday, Saturday, and Sunday on the first two weekends in February. Cypress Creek Café, 320 Wimberley Square.

Bruce Calkins, P.O. Box 76, Wimberley, TX 78676, (512) 847-2515, (512) 847-2515, Fax: (512) 847-5200, bcwimbo@aol.com, www.cccmusic.com

Goliad: South   Wild West Extravaganza
February 2, 2002   1st Saturday in February
Catch a glimpse of life in the Old West.
Goliad Chamber of Commerce, P.O. Box 606, Goliad, TX 77963. Presidio La
Bahia. (361) 645-3752, www.lnstar.com/mall/txtrails/goliad.htm

Yoakum: South   Land of Leather Days
February 2-3, 2002   1st weekend in February
Yoakum, as everybody surely knows, is the Leather Capital of the Southwest. Only leather tough Texans would face the unpredictable Texas February
weather to celebrate their main industry with a chili cookoff in the charming
streets of downtown Yoakum. The festival features the Grungiest Boot and Hat
Contest, a cow chip toss, a beer can stack, and a chili eating contest.
Yoakum Chamber of Commerce, P.O. Box 591, Yoakum, TX 77995, (512)
293-2309, www.ci.yoakum.tx.us

El Paso: West   Southwestern International Livestock Show
                                     & Rodeo
February 2-10, 2002   Starts 1st weekend in February
This annual event is fun for the whole family. Events include horse shows,
western gala, cattle drive, team roping championship, and chili cookoff. Also, a
junior livestock show and auction, a media rodeo, and a piglet roundup. Saddle
up, partner! Held in the El Paso County Coliseum.
For information call (915) 532-1401. www.elpasostockshow.com

Laredo: South   Washington's Birthday Celebration
February 2-17, 2002
Washington's Birthday Celebration is an annual citywide festival that has
been occurring for almost a century. There are parades, dances, fireworks,
mariachi music, golf tournament, 5K run, carnivals, and food. Music includes
big band, bluegrass, blues, Cajun, children's, classical, country, folk, jazz, rock,
and tejano.
Washington's Birthday Celebration Association, Melanie Hinojosa, 1819
Hillside Road, Laredo, TX 78041, (956) 722-0589, Fax: (956) 722-5528,
wbca@icsi.net, www.wbcaldo.com

San Antonio: South   San Antonio Stock Show and Rodeo
February 2-17, 2002
The San Antonio Stock Show and Rodeo showcases the music industry's
most outstanding country and adult contemporary artists in appearances held
during the 20 rodeo performances. One of the top four rodeos in the U.S., the

San Antonio Stock Show has featured Clint Black, the Doobie Brothers, and Hank Williams Jr. Events are held in Freeman Coliseum, at 3201 East Houston.

Livestock Expo, R. Keith Martin, P.O. Box 200230, San Antonio, TX 78220-0230, (210) 225-5851, (210) 225-0612, Fax: (210) 227-7932, saleadmin@sarodeo.com, www.sarodeo.com

The San Antonio Stock Show and Rodeo. Photo courtesy San Antonio Convention and Visitors Bureau, Al Rendon.

Wimberley: Hill Country   Winter Jazz Concert Series
February 4-6, 11-12, 2001

For information on purchasing tickets, call our special phone line (512) 847-5200. For information, lodging, and music lineup call (800) 460-3909. Held at the Cypress Creek Café's Club, on the square in Wimberley.

Wimberley Winter Jazz Concert, Nancie Austin, P.O. Box 1807, Wimberley, TX 78676, (800) 460-3909, (512) 847-5200 (tickets), Fax: (512) 847-2515, nanciea@earthlink.net, www.texashillcntry.com/wimberley

Lovelady: East   Lovefest
February 7-9, 2002   starting the Thurs. before the 2nd Sat. in February

You gotta love it! For 18 years the lovely little town of Lovelady has celebrated Valentine's Day with a parade, an arts and crafts fair, live local bands all day, and chili and barbecue cookoffs. The celebration also includes a 42 domino tournament.

Houston County Chamber of Commerce, P.O. Box 307, Crockett, TX 75835, (409) 544-2359, www.crockett.org/lovelady.htm

San Benito: Gulf   South Texas Youth Stockshow
February 7-10, 2002   2nd weekend in February

There's nothing more Texan than a stockshow and county fair. This four-day event features livestock showing and judging, carnival rides, lots of concession booths, a horse show, car show, steer roping, and arts and crafts displays. Held at the Cameron County Showgrounds, on Highway 510.

South Texas Youth Stockshow, Fred Garcia, P.O. Box 2070, San Benito, TX 78586, (956) 423-3542, www.san-benito.ccls.lib.tx.us

Lubbock: Panhandle   String Fling
February 8, 2001

String along with 14 secondary classical and pop music orchestras, performing in clusters, and an All-City Seventh Grade Orchestra from the Lubbock Independent School District. Listen to the 450-member LISD massed orchestra present a medley of wonderful music. Held at the Civic Center Theatre.

C. Doyle Gammill, Music Coordinator, 1628 19th Street, Lubbock, TX 79401, (806) 766-1045, Fax: (806) 766-1036, paladincdg@aol.com, www.lubbock.org

Houston: Gulf   Annual World Championship Bar-B-Que Cookoff
February 9-10, 2002   2nd weekend in February

Corporate and Go-Texas cookoff teams will feature the most creative in barbecue decor, with pits disguised as fire engines, covered wagons, airplanes, and waste disposal trucks, just to name a few. Live bands and other entertainment perform throughout the contest. Proceeds benefit their charity. This event is held in conjunction with the Houston Livestock Show & Rodeo.

For more information, call (713) 791-9000, or go to www.hlsr.com

Austin: Hill Country   Motorola Marathon
February 10, 2002   2nd Sunday in February

This ten-year-old race is one of the fastest growing marathons in the country. The course runs from far northwest Austin towards downtown, ending up on the shores of Town Lake. (512) 505-8304, (512) 472-3254, www.motorolamarathon.com

Austin: Hill Country   Texas Guitar Show
February 10-11, 2001

The Texas Guitar Show in Austin centers around the buying, selling, and trading of stringed instruments. Held at the Crockett Center.

The Crockett Center, 6301 Hwy 290 East, Austin, TX 78723, (800) 356-3347, Fax: (417) 863-7767, www.texasguitarshows.com

Odessa: Panhandle   Shakespeare Festival
Twelve days long, held between mid-February and mid-March

Enjoy the beautiful replica of the original Globe Theatre in England, where the great Bard's plays were introduced to the world. There are also carnivals, art exhibits, and trail rides to surrounding towns. Held at the Globe of the Great Southwest.

Odessa College, 2308 Shakespeare Road, Odessa, TX 79764, (915) 332-1586, www.odessa.edu

Luckenbach: Hill Country   HUG-IN

February 11-13, 2001

Cowboy poetry, fiddling contests, music festival, singing contests. The HUG-IN features a Valentine campout and dance with live country and rock music and a reunion of old and new Luckenbach regulars.

VelAnne Howle, 412 Luckenbach Town Loop, Fredericksburg, TX 78624, (830) 997-3224, Fax: (830) 997-1024, somebody@luckenbachtexas.com, www.luckenbachtexas.com

San Antonio: South   Valentine's Day Oldies Dance

February 12-13, 2001

The Valentine's Day Oldies Dance feature blues, jazz, and oldies. Top talent performers keep the music coming. Guadalupe Theatre, 1301 Guadalupe Street.

Guadalupe Cultural Arts Center, Pilar Chapa, 1300 Guadalupe Street, San Antonio, TX 78207-5519, (210) 271-3151, Fax: (210) 271-3480, guad-arts@aol.com, www.guadalupeculturalarts.org

Houston: Gulf   Houston Livestock Show and Rodeo

February 13 - March 4, 2001   mid-February to mid-March

This super event is sponsored by a nonprofit, charitable organization whose net proceeds benefit Texas youth through scholarships and educational programs. Concert entertainers appear at each of twenty rodeo appearances. Held at the Astrodome, Astrohall, and AstroArena, which is located at 2000 South Loop West at Kirby Street.

Dan Gattis, General Manager, P.O. Box 20070, Houston, TX 77225-0070, (713) 791-9000, Fax: (713) 794-9528, www.hlsr.com

Mercedes: South   South Texas Music Fest and Texas International Bull Chip Throwing Contest

February 14-18, 2001

Awards show, fiddling contests, music festival, singing contests, songwriting contests, street dance. The festival & Texas International Bull Chip Throw is held at 1000 North Texas Avenue, at the Mercedes Showgrounds. Music includes country, folk, bluegrass, western, mariachi, Texas swing, tejano, and religious. Arts & crafts plus lots of contests and workshops. Trophies, prizes. 130 acres of music. Mercedes Showgrounds, 1000 North Texas Avenue.

Paul Martinez, P.O. Box 37, Donna, TX 78537, (956) 464-7767, Fax: (956) 969-0622, musicfest@hiline.net, www.musicfst99.com

Gruene: Hill Country   Old Gruene Market Days
February thru December, 3rd Saturday and Sunday of each month

This little town is nestled on the bank of the Guadalupe River, just north of New Braunfels. The town has become a center for Texas cooks and artisans who sell their wares on the 3rd Saturday and Sunday, except in December, when it is the 1st weekend. (210) 629-5077, www.gruene.net

Don't miss the music and fun in Gruene (pronounced green; on the menus they often offer Gruene beans). Here is the historic music venue, Gruene Hall.

Tyler: East   Squatty Pines Storytelling Festival
Normally mid to late February

This event is a blast. Retreat to the East Texas Piney Woods on the shores of beautiful Lake Tyler for 3 days of stories, music, workshops, hayrides, fishing, hiking, and more, all sponsored by the East Texas Storytellers organization (800) 235-5712, www.homestead.com/EastTexasTellers, www.itellstories.com

Kingsville: Gulf   South Texas Ranching Heritage Festival
February 15-17, 2002   3rd weekend of February

This Ranching Heritage Festival features cowboy poets, storytellers, artisans, craftsmen, ranch rodeo, cowboy singers, musicians, cow camp and chuck wagon cookoffs, and ranch races for the kids. Come enjoy great live country, cowboy, and tejano music. Held at Texas A&M University-Kingsville and J.K. Northway Coliseum, at the Conner Museum and at Dickkleberg Park.

Texas A&M University Kingsville, South TX Ranching Heritage Society, Altal Ham, John E. Conner Museum, MSC 134, Kingsville, TX 78363, (361) 593-2810, (361) 593-2810, Fax: (361) 593-2112, hhham@yahoo.com, www.tamuk.edu/museum/ranching.html

Austin: Hill Country   "Chilly" BBQ & Chili
February 16-17, 2001

Held at VFW 8787 in Austin. Contact: Dee Dee Miller, (512) 365-7821 or Howard Klotz after 6 P.M. at (512) 836-8767, www.ribman.com

Galveston: Gulf

Mardi Gras Galveston

February 16-17, 23-24, 2002   The two weekends preceding Fat Tuesday

Mardi Gras Galveston is a wonderful party that includes a musical festival, seven parades, and processions over two weekends with masked balls, food, art exhibits, and tons of live entertainment. Activities are held in the Strand Entertainment Area and downtown.

Lou Muller, Executive Director, 2504 Church, Galveston, TX 77550, (409) 763-6564, (888) 425-4753, Fax: (409) 762-8911, julie.harman@galveston tourism.com, www.galvestontourism.com, www.mardigrasgalveston.com

Old Town Spring: Gulf

Frontier Days

February 17-18, 2001

Chili cookoff, cowboy camp, Indian village, Civil War reenactments, and lots of fun and food. 1-800-OLD-TOWN, www.oldtownspringtx.com

Alamo: South

Texas Independence Day Celebration

February 19, 2001

Texas Independence Day Celebration & Parade is a hometown parade with music, food booths, and crafts downtown, following the parade. Features local mariachi bands, folklorico dancers, and bands from the RV parks. Held in downtown Alamo.

Alamo Chamber of Commerce, Vickie Hargett, P.O. Box 636, Alamo, TX 78516, (956) 787-2117, Fax: (956) 782-1172, sacvb@sanantoniocvb.com

The historic Alamo, where a small band of Texans were killed during their battle for independence from Mexico.

San Antonio: South

Texas Music Educators Association Annual Convention

February 20-23, 2002

The TMEA sponsors teacher training sessions on the regional level and produces an annual clinic/convention each February that draws more than 18,000 musicians, teachers, and members of the music industry. Musical styles include children's, classical, jazz, concert bands. Held at the Henry B. Gonzalez Convention Center. Texas Music Educators Association, Robert Floyd, Executive

Director, P.O. Box 49469, Austin, TX 78765, (512) 452-0710, Fax: (512) 451-9213, rfloyd@tmea.org, www.tmea.org

Mercedes: South   **South Texas Music Festival**

February 20-24, 2002

A three-day-long festival of country, bluegrass, folk, western, religious, mariachi, tejano, Mexican Hat Dance, folkloric dancers, & clogging held at the 130-acre Rio Grande Valley Show Grounds. www.musicfst99.com

Brownsville: Gulf   **Charro Days Festival**

February 21-24, 2002   Last Thursday in February, through Sunday

Charro Days mean music, dance, parades, and fun. This festival is all of that. It includes public dances, live entertainment, a youth parade, then a twilight parade, and even a grand international parade, carnival, and Noche Mexicana, Baile Ranchero on Friday and Sabado Tejano on Saturday. Held at the Jacob Brown Auditorium, located at 600 International Blvd.

Charro Days, Michael T. Puckett, P.O. Box 3247, Brownsville, TX 78523-3247, (956) 542-4245, Fax: (956) 542-6771, www.charrodays.org

Edinburg: South   **Fiesta Edinburg**

February 21-24, 2002

Celebration featuring a midway carnival and family activities. A 3-mile run, a parade, carnival, hoop fest, grito contest, and lots of live music. There are cloggers and folklorico dancers. Events are held at the Edinburg Municipal Park, located ¼ mile south of Highway 107, on Doolittle Road.

Edinburg Chamber of Commerce, 602 W. University, Edinburg, TX 78539, (956) 383-4974, www.edinburg.com/fiesta

Plano: North Central   **Very Special Arts Festival**

February 23, 2002

Very Special Arts is an international organization that promotes art and music for all ages and celebrates the abilities and creativity of people with special needs, as well as the community in general. The festival site is at Plano Centre, located at the corner of Springcreek Parkway and Jupiter Road.

Plano Parks and Recreation Department, Joan Shopoff, P.O. Box 860358, Plano, TX 75086-0358, (972) 941-7272, (972) 941-7250, Fax: (972) 941-7182, www.planotx.org/current/event.html

Los Fresnos: Gulf   **Sombrero Festival**

February 24-26, 2001

The Sombrero Festival features a kid's day on Thursday, live music every day, and entertainment for the entire family including tug-o-war, bean cookoff, jalapeño eating contest, 10K run, waiter's race, grito contest, slam dunk contest, bread contest, street dances, best decorated sombrero contest, magicians and juggling acts roaming the park daily, and food and game booths. Held downtown at Washington Park, Brownsville.

Sombrero Festival, Molly Plitt, P.O. Box 1262, Los Fresnos, TX 78566, (956) 550-9682, (956) 550-9683, Fax: (956) 550-9678

South Padre: Gulf   Spring Break at South Padre Island
Held from late February through March

Spring Break at South Padre Island features national, regional, and local entertainment, bands, DJs, and activities booked by corporate sponsors, promoters, local clubs, and hotel resorts. The live music includes rock, country, new age, blues, rap, and reggae. Held on the beachfront on South Padre Island, Texas.

Mary K. Pollard, 7355 Padre Blvd., South Padre Island, TX 78597, (956) 761-3000, (800) 767-2373, Fax: (956) 761-3024, cvb@sopadre.com, www.sopadre.com

Austin: Hill Country   Austin Blues Family Tree Project
February 23-24, 2002   **Last weekend in February**

The Austin Blues Family Tree Project celebrates the live music component of the blues by creating a cultural history documentary on black music and musicians in Austin. Held at the Victory Grill, Antone's, and Huston-Tillotson College.

Harold McMillan, 1705 Guadalupe Street, Suite 234, Austin, TX 78701, (512) 477-9438, Fax: (512) 477-9344, darts@eden.com, www.diversearts.org

San Angelo: Hill Country   Buffalo Soldier Heritage Day
February 25, 2001

Activities include military drills, demonstrations, and a celebration of the African American troops of the western frontier. Fort Concho. (915) 481-2646

El Paso: West   Siglo De Oro Drama Festival
February 28, 2001

In its 24th year, this festival celebrates the literature and linguistic ties still shared by Spain and the border region of Mexico and the United States. The festival brings the best amateur and professional groups to the Chamizal stage, presenting works of the Spanish masters, both in English and Spanish. Participants come from as far away as Puerto Rico, Spain, and Jerusalem.

Held at the Chamizal National Memorial, at 800 S. San Marcial, in El Paso. Call: (915) 532-7273, ext. 102. www.elpasotex.com

March

Spring is here—
ain't it?

Now we are starting to really get serious about the partyin'! The crops and the critters are sproutin' up, and the folks are goin' a bit stir crazy, lookin' for some fun. The first of the livestock shows are kicking off.

There are many ethnic backgrounds in Texas. It was a bit of a surprise to me that Texas is a world center for the Irish. St Patrick's Day celebrations take place all over the state, as the rivers and beer turn green!

Texas was, and some say still is, an independent republic. March is a very significant month in the history of that Republic. Many of the festivals across Texas in March and April relate to commemoration of some of these events,

- On March 2, 1836, the Texas Declaration of Independence from Mexico was signed.
- March 6, after a thirteen-day siege, the Alamo fell to the Mexican army under General Santa Anna. Around 180 Texans died in the battle.
- March 15, 1836, in Refugio, Mexican General Urrea executed fifteen Texas prisoners.
- March 27, 1836, in Goliad, Mexican Col. José Nicolás de la Portilla, following orders from General Santa Anna, executed 342 Texan prisoners. Word got out when 28 escaped while the Mexican soldiers were reloading their rifles.

Always double check the dates of the events.

Colorado River   Riverfest
March through May

This is the Texas festivals' answer to the chain letter. The LCRA (Lower Colorado River Authority) has united a whole group of local festivals under the Riverfest umbrella. Dozens of events take place in the cities along this 500-mile stretch of the Colorado River, running from San Saba, through Austin, and all the way to the Gulf Coast. They include a spring craft fair in El Campo, the Lometa Diamondback (yes, rattlesnakes) Jubilee in late March, and the River Rendezvous in La Grange for canoeing enthusiasts in late April. (888) TEXAS FUN, www.lcra.org

Denton: North Central   Tejas (Texas) Storytelling Festival
Early March

The festival is held in Denton's Civic Center Park. Festival highlights include Hit or Myth, starring members of Denton's Storytelling Advisory Task Force, Ghost Tales: chilling, raise-the-hair-on-the-back-of-your-neck ghost tales, Late Night Liars Concert, Friday Concerts for Children and Teens: Children With Special Needs Concert, Tale Trading, and Story Swaps. www.tejasstorytelling.com

Austin: Hill Country   Star of Texas Fair & Rodeo
Every March

The Austin-Travis County Livestock Show & Rodeo has become known as a fun way for the entire family to enjoy top musical entertainers and rodeo acts. Enjoy bluegrass, blues, classical, country, rock, and Latin/tejano music. Proceeds go to a variety of youth-oriented programs.

Travis County Expo Center, 7311 Decker Lane, Linda Raven, Executive Director, P.O. Box 9876, Austin, TX 78766-9876, (512) 467-9811, Fax: (512) 467-9064, www.staroftexas.org

Glen Rose: North Central   North Texas Longhorn Show
Every March

Come and see Texas longhorns up close when top breeders of North Texas meet to display one of the oldest breeds of Texas cows. Held at the Expo Center on Hwy 67, Glen Rose, Texas. For information call the Expo Center at (254) 897-4509, www.texasoutside.com/glenrose/calendar.html

Glen Rose: North Central   Snaketales
Every March

Learn about the myth and magic of these resplendent reptiles at a day of snake presentations by the Herp Society and other friends of snakes. Enjoy storytelling, demonstrations, fun and facts ... all for the snake's sake. Held at the

Fossil Rim Wildlife Center, Hwy. 67, Glen Rose, Texas. For information, call (254) 897-2960, www.texasoutside.com/glenrose/calendar.html

Dallas: North Central   Texaspride Celebration

Every March

Features recording artists, Mexican dancers, Comanche storyteller, Buffalo Soldiers, Texas Rangers, historical exhibits, and much more. Held in the Hall of State, Fair Park, (214) 426-1959

The familiar skyline greets visitors to the numerous festivals and events held in Dallas. Photo courtesy of Dallas Convention and Visitors Bureau.

Fort McKavett: Hill Country   Annual Living History Day

Every March

Features infantry and cavalry drills by reenactors. Fort McKavett State Historic Park. (915) 396-2358, www.tpwd.state.tx.us/park/fortmcka/fort mcka.htm#tour

Corpus Christi: Gulf   Spring Roundup Celebration in Aransas County

Every March

Includes cowboy poetry and song, reenactments, food, and demonstrations. Also features a special ranching heritage exhibit at the Fulton Mansion. (361) 729-0386, www.tpwd.state.tx.us/park/fulton/fulton.htm

San Felipe: North Central   Annual Colonial Texas Heritage Festival

Every March

This event features reenactments, Buffalo Soldiers, crafts, food, and historic tours. Stephen F. Austin State Historic Park. (409) 885-3613, http://sanfelipetx.areaguides.net/

Goliad: South   Annual Goliad Massacre Reenactment

Every March

Re-creation of the occupation of Fort Defiance by Col. Fannin and the massacre, followed by a memorial service and pilgrimage to the Fannin Memorial. Presidio La Bahia. (361) 645-3563, www.lnstar.com/mall/txtrails/goliad.htm

Denton: North Central   Texas Storytelling Festival
Every March

Features storytellers from across the country, includes ghost stories, bilingual and children's concerts. Civic Center Park. (940) 387-8336, (972) 991-8871, www.tejasstorytelling.com

Hidalgo: South   BorderFest
March 2-3, 2002   1st weekend in March

BorderFest is a citywide cultural celebration that includes a parade, live continuous mariachi, Top 40, country, and tejano music, food, crafts, pageants, and more. It is the oldest and largest outdoor heritage music festival in the Rio Grande Valley. Entertainment includes folk dancing, Scottish bagpipes, and international choirs. Held on the BorderFest Grounds at 700 East Esperanza.

BorderFest Association, Joe Vera III, 611 East Coma, Hidalgo, TX 78557, (956) 843-2734, (956) 843-2302, Fax: (956) 843-2722, yesac956@aol.com

Taylor: Hill Country   Taylor Jaycees National Rattlesnake Sacking Championship
March 2-3, 2002   1st weekend in March

This small town, northeast of Austin, is rich with history. Each spring, to protect the herds and folks, it became a tradition to round up all the rattlesnakes they could find, as they come out of their dens, and before they've had time to feed and become more active. Professional snake handlers are on hand to show how it's done. Do you know whether rattlesnake tastes like chicken? Events are held in Murphy Park, out on Lake Drive, (512) 365-1988, www.pe.net/~rksnow/txcountytaylor.htm

Fulton: Gulf   Fulton Oysterfest
March 2-3, 2002   1st weekend of March

They'll be shuckin' and jivin' at the Fulton Oysterfest, which includes men's and women's raw oyster eating contests, oyster shucking contests, live country music, parade Saturday, kiddie carnival, arts and crafts fair, and food booths. Held at Fulton Navigation Park, on Fulton Beach Road.

Jimmy Hattenback, P.O. Box 393, Fulton, TX 78358, (361) 729-2338, (361) 729-2388, Fax: (361) 729-3248, www.rockport-fulton.org

Austin: Hill Country   Celebrate Texas Independence Day
1st Week of March

Our purpose is to encourage and promote the education of the general public regarding Texas Independence Day and the history of Texas and its people.

Celebrate Texas, Inc., Miz VelAnne, 3401 South Lamar Blvd., Austin, TX 78704, (512) 383-0505, Fax: (512) 462-1147, www.celebratetexas.com

Port Arthur: Gulf

Mardi Gras of Southeast Texas

1st week of March

Texas and Mardi Gras, what could be more fun? This is a traditional Mardi Gras celebration, featuring eight parades, arts and crafts, assorted foods, a children's fun zone, fireworks, carnival rides, and street entertainers. One stage features live music including blues, Cajun, Christian, country, jazz, rock, and tejano. Held in downtown Port Arthur, on Procter Street.

Mardi Gras Southeast Texas, Laura Childress, 3830 Highway 365, Port Arthur, TX 77642, (409) 721-8717, Fax: (409) 721-8700, www.portarthur.com/mardigras/index1.html

Mardi Gras and Texas, quite a combination! Here's my friend Buffalo Chuck celebrating. Photo courtesy of Buffalo Chuck.

Rainbow: North Central

Somervell County PRCA Rodeo

Usually the first week in March

Featuring live country music and a great rodeo. Held at the Expo Center.

Glen Rose Horse Show and Rodeo Association, Terry Starnes, P.O. Box 306, Rainbow, TX 76077, (254) 897-4171, Fax: (254) 897-7713

Rio Grande City: South

Starr County Fair

1st week in March

A great county fair with loads of fun. The Starr County Fair features local schools in the performance events in our stage area all throughout the fair. Livestock are exhibited and sold after the fair for premium amounts. Features two rodeos, a carnival, and commercial exhibits with lots of items. Held on the Fairgrounds.

Starr County Fair, James Peterson, P.O. Box 841, Rio Grande City, TX 78582, (956) 487-2043, (956) 487-3623, Fax: (956) 487-6227

Jefferson: East   Mardi Gras Upriver
1st week in March

Mardi Gras Upriver features family entertainment and a street dance. Friday Night is the "Doo-Dah" parade, Saturday is the main parade, and the children's parade is held Sunday. All events are held in downtown Jefferson.

Krewe of Hebe, Mary Hileman, P.O. Box 562, Jefferson, TX 75657, (903) 653-9577, (903) 665-3663, www.tnti.com/towns/jefferson

Spring: Gulf   Spring Polka Festival
1st week in March

The Regional Polka Festival includes polkas, waltzes, country music, a fried chicken dinner, and a dance. Held at the Knights of Columbus Hall at 1310 Highway 90 West.

Knights of Columbus Council #3313, B.J. Stolarski, P.O. Box 1133, Sealy, TX 77474-1133, (979) 885-6370, (979) 885-6786, kofc3313@usa.net, www.hometownusa.com/tx/Sealy.html

Kingsville: Gulf   Texas Cactus Festival
1st week in March

The Texas Cactus Festival activities include cactus cooking and tasting, an arts and crafts fair, and entertainment by tejano, country, and mariachi musical groups. Held at the Southgate Mall, at 2231 Brahma Boulevard.

Kingsville Visitors and Convention Bureau, Carol Ann Anderson, 1501 North Highway 77, Kingsville, TX 78363, (361) 592-8516, (800) 333-5032, Fax: (361) 592-3227, cub@kingsvilletexas.com, www.kingsvilletexas.com

Alpine: West   Texas Cowboy Poetry Gathering
March 2, 2001

The Texas Cowboy Poetry Gathering features traditional cowboy music in most of the poetry and storytelling sessions. All music is live and performed on acoustical instruments by working cowboys. Activities include museum gear auction, cowboy church service with music, and celebrity roping. Cowboy dancing in the Alpine Civic Center. Held at Sul Ross State University on Highway 90 East.

Texas Cowboy Poetry Gathering Committee, JJ Tucker, P.O. Box 395, Alpine, TX 79831, (915) 837-8191, (915) 837-8191, Fax: (915) 837-5516, klgleen@sul-ross-1.sulross.edu, www.cowboypoetry.org

Dallas: North Central   North Texas Irish Festival
March 3-4, 2001

The North Texas Irish Festival in Fair Park is one of the largest Irish festivals in the U.S. The festival offers continuous Celtic folk music on seven stages and a complete children's area, making the event fun for the whole family. Featured acts include Altan and the Christy O'Leary Band and more. Events are held at Fair Park.

Southwest Celtic Music Association, Harold Rolle, 4340 North Central Expwy., Suite 104, Dallas, TX 75206-6550, (214) 821-4173, (214) 821-4174, ntif@yahoo.com, www.ntif.org

Austin: Hill Country   Austin Music Awards
1st week in March

Whatever style you like, this show has got it! It also serves as the official opening of the South by Southwest Music and Media Conference (Mar. 8-17, 2002). Held at the Austin Music Hall, located downtown at Third Street and Nueces.

Austin Chronicle, Margaret Moser, P.O. Box 49066, Austin, TX 78765, (512) 454-5766, Fax: (512) 458-6910, mail@auschron.com

Lubbock: Panhandle   Texas Tech Jazz Band Festival
1st week in March

The Texas Tech Jazz Band Festival features jazz performers from around the nation. Allen Theatre at Texas Tech University, 18th Street and Boston Avenue, Texas Tech University Jazz Department, Alan Shinn, P.O. Box 42033, Lubbock, TX 79409-2033, (806) 742-2270 ext. 256, Fax: (806) 742-2294, nzads@ttacs.ttu.edu

Woodville: East   Bluegrass and Gospel
1st week in March, May, July, and September

There's bluegrass and gospel music. There will also be an 1840-1920 early East Texas farming village with railroad museum, wagon museum, and an 1860 country store. Events are held at the Woodville Heritage Village Museum, on Highway 190 West.

Woodville Heritage Village Museum, Ofeira A. Gazzaway, P.O. Box 888, Woodville, TX 75979, (409) 283-2272, (800) 323-0389, Fax: (409) 283-2194

Alpine: West   The Annual Texas Cowboy Poetry Gathering
March 2-4, 2001

In the mountains of Texas, in the Big Bend country, the practitioners of this wonderful artform gather on the campus of Sul Ross State University. There is plenty of poetry, music, storytelling, dancing, great food, and the trappings of Texas are all a part of the second oldest cowboy gathering in the United States. A Western Art and Custom Cowboy Gear Exhibit is the oldest in the United States and features the best of the best saddlemakers, braiders, silver engravers, artists, and more. Learning about making gear and ranch history are all part of this exciting weekend. For more information call (915) 837-2326. www.tourtexas.com/alpine/alpine.html

Walnut Springs: North Central   Rattlesnake Hunt
March 3, 2001

The Rattlesnake Hunt features food, arts, crafts, a Saturday night country music street dance, carnival, helicopter rides, snake shows, hunts, and demonstrations. Continuous entertainment all day. Additional information phone number is (817) 797-4019. All proceeds go to benefit crippled children. Events are held in downtown Walnut Springs.

Walnut Springs Lions Club, Kelly Olson, P.O. Box 174, Walnut Springs, TX 76690, (254) 797-4801, Fax: (254) 797-8201, www.pe.net/~rksnow/txcounty-walnutsprings.htm

Luckenbach: Hill Country   Texas Independence Celebration
March 4, 2001

Don't miss the Texas Independence Celebration featuring K.R. Wood's "Fathers of Texas," a history of the Texas Revolution in song. Be sure to meet the sheriff. All events are held in scenic downtown Luckenbach.

VelAnne Howle, 412 Luckenbach Town Loop, Fredericksburg, TX 78624, (830) 997-3224, Fax: (830) 997-1024, somebody@luckenbachtexas.com, www.luckenbachtexas.com

Victoria: South   Victoria Livestock Show & Auction
March 7-11, 2002

Whatever you want, it's here. A county fair, a parade, an auction, a rodeo, singing contests, and plenty of fiddlers. The Livestock Show & Auction features a dance in which several country and polka bands perform. The livestock show lasts over four days and concludes with the auction on Monday. Held at the Community Center.

Things are busy down at the Livestock Auction barn.

Victoria Jaycees, Bill Fisher, P.O. Box 2255, Victoria, TX 77902-2255, (361) 576-4300, (512) 502-0822 (pgr.), www.victoriachamber.org/cgi-bin/calendar/calendar.pl

Sweetwater: Panhandle   Jaycees Annual Rattlesnake Roundup

March 8-11, 2001

This is the biggest rattlesnake roundup in Texas; this event has taken place every year since 1958. Weeklong festivities center around the annual gathering of thousands of Western diamondback rattlesnakes. Festivities include Miss Snake Charmer Contest and awards for the most and biggest snakes caught.

Sweetwater Chamber of Commerce, P.O. Box 1148, Sweetwater, TX 79556, swater@camalott.com, (915) 235-5488, Fax: (915) 235-1026, www.rattlesnakeroundup.com

Refugio: Gulf   Refugio County Fair & PRCA Rodeo

March 8-12, 2001

Texans always have trouble pronouncing the name of this neat little town! This super County Fair & PRCA Rodeo covers five days with many events and contests such as a chili cookoff, hot sauce contest, livestock show, arts and crafts, and live dances. Held at Refugio County Fairgrounds.

Harvey Dierschke, P.O. Box 88, Refugio, TX 78377, (361) 543-4508, Fax: (361) 543-5112, www.uscounties.com/Texas/Refugio-County/index.html

Austin: Hill Country   South by Southwest Music and Media Conference

March 8-17, 2002

One of the most significant music events in the nation. I've watched South by Southwest Music and Media Conference grow from a few bands playing on a couple of nights, to a four-day conference attended by both international and national music industry professionals. The five-night music festival features more than 900 bands, with every type of music represented. The Conference takes place at the Austin Convention Center. The bands play at a wide variety of locations, so call ahead for a schedule.

South By Southwest, Inc., Roland Swenson, P.O. Box 4999, Austin, TX 78765, (512) 467-7979, Fax: (512) 451-0754, sxsw@sxsw.com, www.sxsw.com

Austin: Hill Country   Zilker Kite Festival

March 9, 2002   2nd Sunday in March

One of the oldest kite-flying contests in the U.S. Held in beautiful Zilker Park, located in downtown Austin. See hundreds of colorful, handmade kites catch the March winds. Anyone can come and fly their kite, but there is also organized competition. Categories includes the smallest kite, the strongest-pulling kite, the highest, and the most creative kite, but everyone's favorite is the largest kite. Events take place at Zilker Park, 2100 Barton Springs Rd.

Bunnie Tidwell, 8400 Jamestown Dr. #406, Austin, TX 78758, (512) 339-0412, Fax: (512) 471-3696, Bunnie@mail.utexas.edu, www.zilkerkitefestival.com

Cotulla: North Central   La Salle County Fair and Wild Hog Cookoff

March 9-12

The La Salle County Fair & Wild Hog Cookoff is a four-day event filled with activities. Events include a livestock show, cookoffs, parade, children's contests, arts and crafts, science fair, races, and more. Entertainment includes folk and tejano music and a country western dance. Held at the La Salle County Fairgrounds on Highway 97.

La Salle County Fair Association, Peggy Hillje, P.O. Box 553, Cotulla, TX 78014, (830) 879-2852, (830) 879-2852, Fax: (830) 879-2852, cotullatx.areaguides.net

Mesquite: North Central   Steel Guitar Jamboree

2nd week in March

Learn some hot new guitar riffs at the Steel Guitar Jamboree in Irving. Folks come from all over the nation to see and hear legendary performers and other great talents and visit with instructors, instrument manufacturers, and suppliers. Held at the Harvey Hotel, just off Highway 121.

Charlie Norris, President, 500 North Galloway, Mesquite, TX 75149, (972) 285-1251, (888) 208-9709, Fax: (972) 285-1378, www.steelguitar.com/webpix/showpix/dal01pix/dal01in.html

Austin: Hill Country   Texas Bach Festival

March 9-20, 2001

Wear you boots and listen to some great classical music. The Texas Bach Festival commemorates the anniversary of the death of Johann Sebastian Bach. Artists and ensembles performing at the festival include the Austin Civic Chorus, the Austin Vocal Arts Ensemble, the Orchestra of St. David's, the Austin Children's Choir, and guest artist cellist Phoebe Carrai and organist Faythe Freese. Concert locations vary, so please call (512) 719-3300 for information.

Chorus Austin, Jonna Robertson, P.O. Box 354, Austin, TX 78767-0354, (512) 719-3300, Fax: (512) 719-3339, www.chorusaustin.org

Zapata: South   Zapata County Fair

March 9-12, 2001

Don't miss all the live music, arts and crafts, exhibits, livestock show and auction, carnival, and a Saturday morning parade. Street dance takes place on Friday and Saturday nights. Live entertainment throughout the festivities includes a variety of tejano and country western music. All events are held at the Zapata County Fairgrounds, at 23rd Street and Fresno.

Zapata County Fair Association, Janie de la Garza, P.O. Box 872, Zapata, TX 78076, (956) 765-8361

Buna: East   Redbud Festival

March 10, 2001

The best parts of a county fair, parade, and music festival. The Redbud Festival features live entertainment on two stages, arts and crafts, well over 200 booths, and a parade. Entertainment by local bands and admission is free.

Buna Chamber of Commerce, Margaret Holmes, P.O. Box 1782, Buna, TX 77612, (409) 994-3315, (409) 994-3882, www.hometownusa.com/tx/Buna.html

Houston: Gulf   Bayou City Art Festival - Downtown

March 10-11, 2001   **2nd weekend in March**

The Bayou City Art Festival features over 300 artists displaying their work. There is live music and lots of food. This festival occurs twice a year, in October and March. Held on the Hermann Square, located at 900 Smith.

Art Colony Association, Lynette Wallace, P.O. Box 66650, Houston, TX 77266-6650, (713) 521-0133, Fax: (713) 521-0013, artfest@swbell.net

Dublin: North Central   Saint Patrick Festival

Weekend closest to St. Patrick's Day - Thursday through Sunday

St. Patrick's Day and the world's largest dairy (the Aurora Dairy), both in downtown Dublin. This three-day celebration features a parade, a Miss Dublin Pageant, a dance, contests, arts and crafts, a stage show, and food booths. You'll find a variety of games, including hog calling, milk drinking, ice cream eating, hay throwing, and a cow chip toss.

Dublin Chamber of Commerce, 213 E. Blackjack, Dublin, TX, 76446, (817) 445-3422

Corpus Christi: Gulf   St. Patrick's Day Parade and Irish Festival

March 10, 2001

The St. Patrick's Day Parade begins Saturday at 11 A.M. traveling from the Coliseum, down Shoreline, and disbanding at the Irish Culture House on Chaparral and Fitzgerald. Msgr. Patrick Higgins is the Parade Marshall. Other events take place at the Irish Culture House and Moravian Hall, at Fitzgerald and Chaparral.

Irish Culture Society, Mary K. Whitmire, Lacey Sparks, 742 Bradshaw Drive, Corpus Christi, TX 78412, (361) 225-2719, (361) 865-2301, Fax: (361) 937-0597

San Antonio: South   Tejano Music Awards

March 10, 2001

The Tejano Music Awards presents some of the best performing artists, musicians, and composers. The ceremony is taped for national television and radio distribution. Held at the Alamodome.

Texas Talent Musicians Association, Robert Arellano, 1149 East Commerce, Suite 105, San Antonio, TX 78205, (210) 222-8862, Fax: (210) 222-1029, ttma@isci.net

Texarkana: East   Pickin' Around the Campfire

Mar 13-18, 2001   2nd week in March

Enjoy a centuries-old tradition of Pickin' Around the Campfire. This neat festival features fun, food, crafts, and craft workshops, and plenty of bluegrass jamming. Events are held at the Strange Family Bluegrass/RV Park, on Highway 59 South to 3244.

Sharon Strange, Route 2, Box 327 B-2, Texarkana, TX 75501, (903) 791-0342, (903) 792-2481, sfbgtxk@juno.com

Belton: North Central   Texas Polka Music Awards Festival

March 11-12, 2002   2nd weekend in March

Three fun days of polka music and dancing deep in the heart of Texas. From all over the nation polka fans gather at the Belton County Expo Center. Besides music and dancing, visitors will find a polka mass Sunday morning, arts and crafts, and plenty of food.

Texas Polka Music Association, 11511 Katy Frwy., Suite 423, Houston, TX 77079, (713) 556-9595

Mercedes: South   Rio Grande Valley Livestock Show

March 14-18, 2001

A wonderful event that features a county fair, rodeo, and lots of tejano and country music. Chartered in 1940, the show is a nonprofit organization. Festivities are held at the Rio Grande Valley Livestock Show Pavilion, located at 1000 North Texas.

RGVLS Special Events Committee, Jim Beale, P.O. Box 867, Mercedes, TX 78570, (956) 565-2456, Fax: (956) 565-3005

San Antonio: South   Alamo Irish Festival

March 15-17, 2002

The 11th annual Alamo Irish Festival features live music, food and beverages, arts and crafts, a children's section, cultural displays, singing, and dancing. Live music is offered in the Arneson River Theater just off the San Antonio River and includes Celtic (of course), country, jazz, pop, and tejano.

La Veillita, Darryl Britten, 19843 Encino Brook, San Antonio, TX 78259-2323, (210) 938-5931, (210) 497-8435, Fax: (210) 497-1131, www.harpandshamrock.org

Conroe: East   Montgomery County Fair
March 16-25, 2001

This wonderful county fair offers a rodeo on the opening weekend, livestock shows, adult and junior home economics, livestock auction, homemaking auction, a variety of rock and country bands, and much more. The final weekend features a barbecue cookoff and a "Tejano Day" with carnival rides and live bands. Held at the Montgomery County Fairgrounds, located on FM 1484.

Montgomery County Fair Association, Beth Traylor, P.O. Box 869, Conroe, TX 77305, (936) 760-3631, (936) 760-FAIR, Fax: (936) 760-1568, www.mcfa.org

Dallas: North Central   National Accordion Convention
Usually mid-March

2000 was the "Year of the Accordion Orchestra." The emphasis of the convention and the concert was on the accordion orchestra. The Festival Orchestra provides an opportunity for players of all levels to work with the guest conductor and perform on the Saturday evening concert. Held at the Holiday Inn, located at 700 East Central Parkway in Plano, Texas.

Accordion Assoc., Norman Seaton, 11240 Drummond Drive, Dallas, TX 75228, (972) 270-3791, nseaton1@ibm.net, www.accordionusa.com

Freeport: Gulf   Annual Joy Ride Rod Run
March 16-17, 2002

A wonderful two-day classic car show and rod run. Fans have a chance to mingle with fellow auto lovers and cruise around the area. It is held in the Freeport Municipal Park, 500 N. Brazosport Blvd. Call (281) 444-8680.

Dublin: North Central   St. Patrick's Day Festival
March 17, 2001

Where better to celebrate St. Patrick's Day than Dublin? Of course this is Dublin, Texas. This three-day Irish celebration has something for everyone. Festivities include a downtown parade, a carnival, pageants, contests, cookoffs, crafts, games, and more. Entertainment includes square dancing demonstrations and a variety of country music. Saturday night features a country western dance. Other activities include a blind tractor race. Held at Dublin City Park, located at 216 Highland Ave.

Chamber of Commerce, Jeanette Word, 213 East Blackjack, Dublin, TX 76446, (254) 445-3422, (800) 9-DUBLIN, Fax: (254) 445-0394

Moulton: South   Moulton Polka Waltz Celebration

March 17, 2002   3rd Sunday in March

The Moulton Annual Polka Waltz Celebration helps raise money to benefit the Moulton Fire Department. Three bands provide continuous polka waltz music from noon until 7 P.M. All events are held at the Knights of Columbus Hall, which is located on Highway 532 West, 10 miles south of IH-10, halfway between Houston and San Antonio.

For information contact the Moulton Fire Department, Timothy Koncaba, P.O. Box 31, Moulton, TX 77975, (361) 596-4033, (361) 596-7609

San Antonio: South   St. Patrick's River of Green

March 17, 2002

The Riverwalk with green water? You bet! This event is just part of a city-wide celebration of St. Patrick's Day. Along with street and river parades, a 5K run, and a ceremony at the Alamo, San Antonians celebrate by dyeing the San Antonio River green and renaming it the River Shannon for one day. Festivities start at 12:30 P.M. at the theatre with Irish dancing, music, and clogging. The Alamo Irish Festival also features numerous musical acts, including country, folk, jazz, and R&B groups. www.sachamber.org

San Antonio celebrates St. Patrick's Day with a green river. Photo courtesy San Antonio Convention and Visitors Bureau, Al Rendon.

St. Patrick's Day Parade in San Antonio. Photo courtesy San Antonio Convention and Visitors Bureau, Al Rendon.

Shamrock: Panhandle   St. Patrick's Day Celebration

March 17, 2002

Enjoy the luck of the Irish, Texas style! This festival includes the Miss Irish Rose pageant, a parade, food, Irish Donegal beard competition (I should enter that one), bullriding, three-day carnival, dancing, TRA roping, kick-off banquet, chuck wagon cookoff, and ministerial alliance program. Events are held at the Shamrock Area Community Center, on South Main.

St. Patrick's Day Association, P.O. Box 588, Shamrock, TX 79079, (806) 256-2501

Corpus Christi: Gulf   Czech Heritage Festival

March 17-18, 2001

I'll refrain from saying Czech it out! But, you should. This neat festival features live polka music, dancing, arts and crafts, costumes, country store, Czech dinner, kolaches, Czech imports, and more. There is always plenty of live entertainment. Held at the Bayfront Plaza Convention Center, located at 1901 North Shoreline Drive.

Czech Heritage Society of South Texas, Al Prochaska, P.O. Box 1974, Corpus Christi, TX 78403, (361) 882-9226, (361) 387-4391, Fax: (361) 883-0676, czechheritage.org

Houston: Gulf   Houston Children's Festival

March 17-18, 2001

A fun event, to benefit a great cause. This is Houston's official celebration of children benefitting child advocates. The festival features twelve adventure zones and four stages of family-oriented musical and variety entertainment. Held in downtown Houston, at 500 Walker.

Connie Mims Pinkerton, 1915 Commonwealth St., No. 100, Houston, TX 77006-1841, (713) 522-9723, (713) 522-9723 ext 10, Fax: (713) 522-5766, cpinkerton@jwprod.com, www.poweroffreedom.com/hcf.html

Luckenbach: Hill Country   Mud Dauber Festival

March 17-18, 2001

More silliness in a legendary Texas town. Hondo's legend lives on. The Mud Dauber Festival features games, food, entertainment, and a dance. A celebration of the mud daubers' return, which signals the beginning of spring in the Texas Hill Country, features Luckenbach's Original One-Hole-Golf-Tournament. Held in scenic "downtown" Luckenbach.

VelAnne Howle, 412 Luckenbach Town Loop, Luckenbach, TX 78624, (830) 997-3224, Fax: (830) 997-1024, somebody@luckenbachtexas.com, www.luckenbachtexas.com

Nederland: Gulf   Nederland Heritage Festival

March 20-25, 2001

Tons of fun in small town Texas. This festival is a six-day block party. Every civic organization is involved. This is one of the last free festivals in Southeast Texas. Different music every night: Cajun, R&B, country, rock and roll. Booths, crafts market, chili cookoff, petting zoo, car show, free entertainment, carnival, and the best homemade food around. The events are held on Main Street.

Heritage Festival Foundation, Wanda Hollier, P.O. Box 1176, Nederland, TX 77627, (409) 724-2269, Fax: (409) 724-1645, nhf@pernet.net, www.nederlandhf.com

College Station: North Central   North By Northgate Music Festival

March 22-24, 2001

This is a neat annual rock music festival designed to build the local music scene in College Station, by showcasing local and national talent. With over 100 bands appearing in nine different venues! Held in the Northgate district of College Station.

North by Northgate, Amy Polk, P.O. Box 4419, College Station, TX 77844-4419, (979) 680-9282, apolk@tamu.edu, www.nxng.com

Lometa: Hill Country   Lometa Diamondback Jubilee

Mar 23, 2002   4th Saturday in March

The Lometa Diamondback Jubilee features a carnival, arts and crafts, street dance, flea market, beauty contest, barbecue cookoff, three live bands during the day, plus a dance band at night. Events are held in scenic downtown Lometa.

Lometa Lions Club, Dave Smith, Route 1 Box 223A, Lometa, TX 76853, (512) 752-3106, www.lampasas-tx.com/diamondb.htm

Newton: East   Wild Azalea Days

March 23, 2002   4th Saturday in March

A beautiful springtime drive, north of Newton on State Highway 87, then 6.7 miles east on FM 1414, then 1.8 miles south on unpaved roads. Watch for the signs along the way. The breathtaking concentration of wild azaleas that beautify Newton County's wild azalea canyons is the largest known in Texas and one of the largest in the South. The trails are open during the spring and summer months. chamber@newton.txnetwork.com

Palestine: North Central   Texas Dogwood Trails

March 23-24, 30-31, 2002   Last two weekends in March

Tours of the area are offered when the beautiful white-flowered dogwoods are in bloom. Activities are centered in the 400-acre Davey Dogwood Park, which has over five miles of roads and trails to explore. Included are an arts & crafts fair, many live music performances, and a fun run.

Texas Dogwood Trails Festival, 400 North Queen, Palestine, TX 75802, (903) 729-7275, www.palestinechamber.org/calendar.html

Dallas: North Central   Dallas Video Festival

March 23-26, 2001

This neat event is one of the largest and most diversified video festivals in the U.S. It provides a showcase for new works by national, international, and regional independent artists. More than 250 screenings, installations, panel discussions, workshops, and exhibits are presented simultaneously in multiple areas within the Dallas Theater Center, which is located at 3636 Turtle Creek.

Video Association of Dallas, Bart Weiss, 1405 Woodlawn Ave., Dallas, TX 75208-2433, (214) 651-8600, Fax: (214) 651-8896, bart@onramp.net

Jasper: East   Azalea Festival

March 24, 2001

Don't miss the springtime flowers in Texas. This annual festival features live country, Christian, Cajun, and blues. There is plenty of music during the arts and crafts festival. Events are held on the Courthouse Square.

Jasper Chamber of Commerce, Diane Domenech, 246 East Milam, Jasper, TX 75951 (409) 384-2762, Fax: (409) 384-4733, jaspercc@inu.net www.jaspercoc.org

Sherman: North Central   Texomaland Junior Fiddlers Contest

March 24, 2001

The Texomaland Junior Fiddlers Contest features age groups 0-12 and 13-18. It is the only totally junior fiddlers contest that we know of. Open to junior fiddlers everywhere. Events are held at the Loy Lake Park Stockgrounds.

Texoma Exposition and Livestock Show Association, Stanley Oakley, 1706 FM 697, Sherman, TX 75090, (903) 892-8816

Granbury: North Central   General Granbury's Birthday Party and Bean Cookoff

March 24-25, 2001

This salute to Civil War Gen. Hiram B. Granbury features a parade, bean cookoff, rib cookoff, chicken cookoff, brisket cookoff, live entertainment all day, food booths, outhouse races, arts and crafts, children's area, and games. Entries in the cookoff may be any variety of bean; they've even had pink beans. Held on the Granbury Square.

Granbury Convention and Visitors Bureau, P.O. Box 277, Granbury, TX 76048, (817) 573-5548, www.granbury-tx.com

Colorful floats & participants in parade in Lake Granbury.
Photo courtesy Lake Granbury Convention & Visitors Bureau.

Old Town Spring: Gulf   Spring Fest

March 24-25, 2001

A Texas-style art and wine festival. 1-800-OLD-TOWN, www.ohwy.com/tx/o/oldtowsp.htm

Hallettsville: North Central   South Texas Polka and Sausage Festival

March 24-25, 2001

Nuthin' better than good food and good music. The South Texas Polka and Sausage Festival includes lots of live polka music, a polka mass, food, dancing, polka and waltz contests, and a hobo band concert. Events are held at the Knights of Columbus Hall, on Highway 77 South.

Knights of Columbus, Bobby Pavliska, P.O. Box 46, Hallettsville, TX 77964, (361) 798-2311, (361) 798-3288, www.hallettsville.com

Kingsville: Gulf   Tamuk Jazz Festival

March 24-25, 2001

Like to listen to high school bands? This festival is for you. The Tamuk Jazz Festival is a competition drawing more than 20 high school bands that compete all day, concluding with a night performance. All events are held at the Jones Auditorium.

Texas A&M University at Kingsville - Music Department, Paul Hageman, P.O. Box 174, Kingsville, TX 78363, (361) 593-2803, (361) 593-2806, Fax: (361) 593-2816, www.tamuk.edu/music/calendar.html

Arlington: North Central   Texas Indian Market and Southwest Showcase
March 24-26, 2001

This fun event is praised as America's premier festival of Indian, Southwest, wildlife, and Western arts, crafts, song, dance, and culture. Live entertainment from Indian music and dance to western acts to Aztec dancers and wild bird shows. Events are held at the Arlington Convention Center, located at 1200 Ballpark Way.

Texas Indian Markets, Randy Wilkerson, 4205 Kingston, Amarillo, TX 76109, (806) 355-1610, Fax: (806) 355-1610 call first, txindmkts@tcac.net, www.indianmarket.net

Austin & Luckenbach: Jerry Jeff Walker Birthday Weekend
Hill Country
March 24-27, 2001

Don't miss Jerry Jeff's annual birthday celebration. The celebration continues Saturday with a concert starring Jerry Jeff and friends. Events are held in Austin and scenic downtown Luckenbach.

Tried & True Music, Susan Walker, P.O. Box 39, Austin, TX 78767, (512) 477-0036, Fax: (512) 477-0095, jerryjeff@jerryjeff.com, www.jerryjeff.com/

Belton: North Central   Annual Texas Western Swing Fiddling
Showcase
March 25, 2001

Fiddlin' and Texas, there's nothing better. Come and enjoy this annual event. Events are held at the Bell County Expo.

Nan Ray, Route 4 Box 418, Belton, TX 76513, (254) 939-8390, (254) 939-8390, AWells5144@aol.com, www.westernswing.com/Events.html

Brenham: South   Spring Fling - A Flower and Garden Show
March 25, 2001

Come to Brenham and help celebrate the arrival of spring with arts, crafts, food, entertainment, a pet parade, and fun for the entire family. There are continuous live country, classical, and polka bands playing on the courthouse square.

Brenham Downtown Association, P.O. Box 2294, Brenham, TX 77834, (979) 277-0913, Fax: (979) 277-9292, lynnreyn@comwerx.net, www.brenhamonline.com

Dallas: North Central   Greater Southwest Guitar Shows - The Dallas Guitar Show

March 25-26, 2001

The world's oldest and largest guitar show! The Dallas Guitar Show is two full days of the finest vintage, custom, hand-crafted, acoustic, electric, new and used guitars, banjos, mandolins, amps, effects, straps, cases, and accessories. Events are held at the Auto Building at Fair Park.

Mark Pollock, Producer, 2720 Royal Lane, No. 100, Dallas, TX 75229-4727, (972) 243-4201, (972) 260-4201, Fax: (972) 243-5193, dallas@guitarshow.com, www.guitarshow.com

Sabinal: Hill Country   Sabinal Lions Wild Hog Festival and Craft Fair

March 25-26, 2001

This neat festival features wild hog catching, arts, crafts, food games, and live country, bluegrass, cowboy, and folk music. Events are held at the Sabinal City Park and at Yellow Jacket Stadium.

Sabinal Lions Club, Ross Burris, P.O. Box 55, Sabinal, TX 78881, (830) 988-2709, (830) 988-2010

We cussen it now - but we'll be prayen fer it in August!

You just gotta keep the spring rains in perspective.

Liberty: East   Liberty Jubilee

March 30-31, 2002   **Last weekend in March**

A great festival that features a wide array of activities for the whole family. Activities include live music (country, rock, Christian, and bluegrass), a street dance, sporting events, an antique show, a children's area, a parade, clowns, jugglers, a barbecue cookoff, and more. All events are held on the square, at the Humphreys Cultural Center, in downtown Liberty.

City of Liberty, Dianne Koen, 1829 Sam Houston, Liberty, TX 77575, (936) 336-3684, Fax: (936) 336-9846, www.imswebs.com/libertyjubilee

Natalia: Hill Country   Bluebonnet Festival

March 30-31, 2002   **Last weekend in March**

The Natalia Bluebonnet Festival features a grand parade down Main Street, live music, entertainment, and food in Mustang Park. We're one big happy family!

Mustang Park, Natalia Ex-Students, Peggy Hibbon, P.O. Box 84, Natalia, TX 78059, (830) 665-5439, (830) 665-5439

Glen Rose: North Central   Bluegrass Jamboree

March 30 - April 2, 2001

Welcome to Oakdale Park, the Bluegrass Capital of Texas, and the Bluegrass Jamboree. This event has four great days of traditional bluegrass music by professional and amateur bands. Held at Oakdale Park, on Highway 144 South.

Pete May, P.O. Box 548, Glen Rose, TX 76043, (254) 897-2321, www.oakdalepark.com/calendar.htm, www.texasoutside.com/glenrose/calendar.html

Kingsville: Gulf   International Young Performers Musical Competition and Isabel Sconti Piano Solo Competition

March 30 - April 1, 2001   **3-day competition**

The International Young Performers Musical Competition and Isabel Sconti Piano Solo Competition events include: piano (concerto), orchestral instruments, bowed instruments (strings), and non-bowed instruments. Events are held at Texas A&M University Kingsville campus.

Kingsville Visitors and Convention Bureau, James and Mary Tryer, 1501 North Highway 77, Kingsville, TX 78363, (361) 592-8516, (800) 333-5032, Fax: (361) 592-3227, cub@kingsvilletexas.com, www.kingsvilletexas.com

Burnet, Marble Falls, Llano, Buchanan Dam, Kingsland and Lampasas: Hill Country — Highland Lakes Bluebonnet Trail

Usually late March to mid-April

Springtime flowers in Texas. This is a fun filled event for you and your family. Activities for all ages, including: a bicycle decorating contest, a 5K/10K run, chariot races, a visit from the Confederate Air Force, and a parade. Live music fills the air, while arts and crafts booths and food vendors fill the square. The festival ends Saturday with a street dance and begins Sunday with country gospel music. Events are held on the town square.

Bluebonnet Festival Committee, Dorothy James, 703 Buchanan Drive, Burnet, TX 78611-1742, (512) 756-4297, (512) 756-6066 Fax: (512) 756-2548, (512) 756-7764, info@burnetchamber.org

Temple: North Central — Temple Jazz Festival

March 30-31, 2001

Listen to a wide variety of quality jazz performers. All concerts and clinics are in the Mary Alice Marshall Fine Arts Auditorium on the Temple College campus.

Thomas Fairlie, 2600 South First Street, Temple, TX 76504, (254) 298-8555, Fax: (254) 298-8226, t.fairlie@templejc.edu www.templejc.edu

Santa Fe: Gulf — Galveston County Fair and Rodeo

March 30 - April 7, 2001

The festivities include a carnival with midway, live music, livestock shows, auction, rodeo for three nights, a parade, trail ride, talent show, jackpot bullriding, jackpot barrel racing, petting zoo, pony rides, and an arts and crafts show. Events take place at Jack Brooks Park, at 12006 Highway 6.

Galveston County Fair and Rodeo, Melondy Bender, P.O. Box 889, Santa Fe, TX 77510, (409) 986-6010, Fax: (409) 986-6490, www.galvestoncountyfair.com

Huntsville: East — Walker County Fair

March 30 - April 7, 2001

The Walker County Fair is a 10-day event featuring live country and western bands, livestock shows, rodeos, and special events, also a barbecue cookoff. Held at the Walker County Fairgrounds, 3 miles west on IH-45/Highway 30.

Walker County Fair Association, Carol Smith, P.O. Box 1817, Huntsville, TX 77342-1817, (936) 295-5448, www.chamber.huntsville.tx.us/calendar.html

Killeen: North Central   Killeen Festival

March 30 - April 1, 2001

This festival celebrates with a carnival, international food, live entertainment, arts & crafts, softball and horseshoe tournament. (254) 526-0550 www.killeen-cvb.com

Watauga: North Central   Pacific Islander Watauga Fest

March 30, 2002   Last Saturday in March

Attendees will experience the traditions and cultures of the Pacific Isles featuring traditional foods and crafts. Other activities will include an auto show and a fire knife dance finale. Local vendors and entertainment will also be included in the event activities. Children will enjoy the Keiki Korner activities and carnival rides.

7101 Whitley Rd., Watauga, TX 76148, Judy Allen, Interim Director, judyallen@ci.watauga.tx.us, (817) 514-5891, www.ci.watauga.tx.us

Houston: Gulf   Texas Beer Festival

March 31 - April 1, 2001

I'll drink to that! This neat event brings together the best of Houston's brew pubs and Texas's micro breweries for two days of music, fun, and refreshments. You get to be the taste tester.

Garden in the Heights, 3926 Feagan, Houston, TX 77007, (713) 880-1065, Fax: (713) 880-1586, underway@hal-pc.org

April

Here Comes Them
'Mater Bugs Again!!!

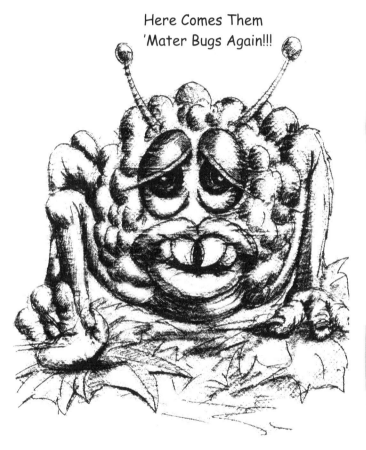

Spring gardens are comin' up,
but so are the bugs!

E verything is sprouting right up, including the flowers, critters, fruit, and vegetables. Spring brings sunshine, and the flowers are now in full bloom. The bluebonnet is the Texas State Flower, and by April they are one of many species of flowers putting on an incredibly colorful show throughout the state. Just driving to events can be a wonderful experience. Always plan a little extra time to allow you to stop and look at the flowers and creeks that are almost everywhere. All along the road you'll see folks pulled over to take pictures of the family and friends in the fields of flowers.

Livestock shows are poppin' up all over the calendar. The spring critters are gettin' big enough to show. Lambs, calves, chicks, kids, and colts are all growing like crazy, and the livestock shows soon follow.

And so does the search for fun. There are rodeos and the first of the many water related events. Since the crops are starting to come in, there are also lots of festivals honoring them—watermelons, cantaloupes, peas, beans, you name it!

There are also more events tied to Texas history. On April 21, 1836, in a place not far from Houston, called San Jacinto, the Texans defeated the Mexican army. In an 18-minute battle, General Sam Houston and about 1,000 Texans defeated the 1,400-man army of Antonio Lopez de Santa Anna, president of Mexico, and captured him. Perhaps there were problems getting the Mexican army mobilized to fight the Texans because El Presidente was "busy" with Emily West Morgan in his tent and none of his generals wanted to disturb him. Legend has it that Emily was a loyal Texian and did "everything she could" for their cause.

Few people know Emily's name. But everyone knows the song "The Yellow Rose of Texas." Makes a good story.

Always double check the dates of the events.

Mesquite: North Central   Mesquite Championship Rodeo

April through September, every Friday and Saturday night

From home-cooked barbecue to live Texas music to pro-cowboy competition, the Mesquite Championship Rodeo gives you a full night of real Texas fun—affordably and just 15 minutes from downtown Dallas, any Friday or Saturday night April through September. Events include bull riding, bronc riding, calf roping, and more.

118 Rodeo Drive, off the Military Parkway exit from I-635. (214) 285-8777, (800) 833-9339, www.mesquitetexas.com

Manchaca: Hill Country   Wheel Roundup

Each April (folks at the elementary school never returned my calls)

The Wheel Roundup never fails to please kids and the kid in their parents. On the grounds of the elementary school in Manchaca, hundreds of unique vehicles are set up for folks to go through them, and there are folks to explain how they work. Each year there are different types of vehicles. In the past there have been firetrucks, helicopters, a street sweeper, drilling rigs, TV remote truck, electric company snorkel trucks, bulldozers, and armored personnel carriers. Events are held at the elementary school in Manchaca, at the intersection of FM 1626 and Manchaca Road.

I grew up, sort of, in Manchaca (pronounced man-shack) and over the years I've watched this uniquely fun and educational event grow. I really wanted to be able to give you the date for spring 2002; unfortunately the folks at the elementary school never returned any of my numerous calls and notes left for them. Check with the friendly folks at the Manchaca Fire Hall in the spring. Not only do they have great food, I guarantee they will call you back.

Austin: Hill Country   Spamarama

April 1, 2001

Spam, Spam, Spam, Spam ... ala Monty Python. It says a lot about me, that I love this event. It's loads of fun and creativity. Spam cookoff, music of all sorts, arts and crafts booths, Spamalympics athletic competition, Spam Jam live music this year by local bands. Events occur on Auditorium Shores, at South First and Riverside Drive.

Potentate of Potted Pork Parties/Whole Hog Productions, Norman Kieke, 9027 Northgate Blvd., No. 101, Austin, TX 78758-6453, (512) 834-1960, Fax: (512) 834-9504, DArnsberge@aol.com, www.spamarama.com

Austin: Hill Country   The Capital 10,000

April 2, 2001

This is a really fun 10K race. You need to go just to see the humorous outfits worn by some of the contestants. But it is also a serious race for some and is listed among the top 100 road races in the country by *Runner's World* magazine. There are as many as 20,000 competitors and thousands of spectators. The course changes every year but always ends on the shores of Town Lake.

Don't miss it! (512) 445-3596, www.runnertriathletenews.com/news/cap10k1_2000.html

Brazosport: Gulf   Annual Migration Celebration

Held every spring, date varies

Texas is blessed with wildlife, particularly different species of birds. The Migration Celebration features field trips to numerous birding hotspots in Brazoria County. Field trips are scheduled each day and activities are included for children.

The base of operations is the Center for the Arts & Sciences, 400 College Drive. Call: Brazosport Convention & Visitors Council, 1-888-477-2505. www.gcbo.org

Austin: Hill Country   The Texas Relays

April 6-7, 2002   **1st weekend in April**

Held at the University of Texas Memorial Stadium, for more than 70 years top high school and college athletes have come from across the nation to participate in this extraordinary event. Usually scheduled for the 1st weekend in April, sessions begin on Friday morning and end Saturday afternoon.

Events are held at Texas Memorial Stadium, San Jacinto Street at Manor Road. (512) 471-3333, (800) 982-BEVO, www.texassports.com

Round Top & Winedale: Winedale Spring Festival and
North Central   Texas Crafts Exhibition

April 6-7, 2002   **1st weekend in April**

Texas's leading artists show their work at Winedale in a juried crafts show. You'll find wood workers, potters, basketweavers, jewelry makers, metal workers, and others, all in Winedale's restored pioneer building complex. There are also weaving, soapmaking, fireplace cooking, corn shucking, and rawhide chair making. Other events include a German play, hands-on pottery demonstrations, and music. There's a dance, folk, jazz, and classical music performances, and an outdoor dinner.

Winedale Historical Center, Box 11, Round Top, TX 78954, (409) 278-3530, www.cah.utexas.edu/divisions/Winedale.html

Buda: Hill Country   Buda Country Fair

April 20-21, 2002   **3rd weekend in April**

Another great country fair in the great little town of Buda (pronounced byou-da). I'm sure it will be fun for the whole family based on the success of their other festival, Budafest, which is held the first weekend in December.

Watch their website for details. Held in scenic downtown Buda, just off of IH-35, south of Austin.

For information: Thomas Crouse, 1-800-99-4-BUDA (994-2832), tom@budatx.com, www.budatx.com/BudaCalendar.htm

Johnson City: Hill Country   Cowboy Songs and Poetry
Early April

This gathering of cowboys at the Johnson Settlement presents lighter moments of the Old West. At the cabin where President Johnson's grandparents lived and ran a cattle business, modern cowboys meet to sing traditional songs, talk about the old days in poetry, and spin tales the equal of any that were told when the west was really wild. This is 1860s entertainment you can't afford to miss. Events are held at the Lyndon B. Johnson National Historical Park, Johnson Settlement, Johnson City, Texas.

Lyndon B. Johnson National Historical Park, P.O. Box 329, Johnson City, TX 78636-0329, or call (830) 868-7128 ext. 244. www.nps.gov/lyjo/visit.htm

Kingsland: Hill Country   Kingsland Bluebonnet Festival
April 6-7, 2002   1st weekend in April

Join the fun in the flowers. Activities include a 10K volksmarch, bluebonnet trails, bicycle tour, bicycle rodeo, music, children's games, chili cookoff, horseshoe pitching, arts and crafts, washer pitching contest, martial arts exhibition, and barbecue dinner.

Kingsland/Lake LBJ Chamber of Commerce, P.O. Box 465, Kingsland, TX 78639, (915) 388-6211, www.touringtexas.com/events.htm

Luling: Hill Country   Roughneck Chili and Barbecue Cookoffs
April 6, 2002   1st Saturday in April

The Roughneck Chili and Barbecue Cookoffs benefits the Central Texas Oil Patch Museum and features entertainment, live country and bluegrass music, arts and crafts, and a dance in the evening. Everything happens at the Central Texas Oil Patch Museum, 421 East Davis Street.

Luling Area Oil Museum Assoc., Jerry Kidd, P.O. Box 710, Luling, TX 78648, (830) 875-3214, Fax: (830) 875-2082, lulingcc@bcsnet.net, www.bcsnet.net/lulingcc/events.html

Burnet, Marble Falls, Llano,   Highland Lakes Bluebonnet Trail
Buchanan Dam, Kingsland
and Lampasas: Hill Country

Usually late March to mid-April

This Bluebonnet Festival is a fun-filled event for you and your family. Activities for all ages, include a bicycle decorating contest, a 5K/10K run, street dance, chariot races, a visit from the Confederate Air Force, and a parade. Live music fills the air, while arts and crafts booths and food vendors fill the square. Held on the town square.

Bluebonnet Festival Committee, Dorothy James, 703 Buchanan Drive, Burnet, TX 78611-1742, (512) 756-4297, (512) 756-6066, Fax: (512) 756-2548, (512) 756-7764, info@burnetchamber.org

Lampasas: Hill Country   Bluebonnet Fair

April 6, 2002   **1st Saturday in April**

The wonderful fair features a fish fry, antique car show, live music, food booths, a bike and tricycle decorating contest, and an arts and crafts fair.

Lampasas County Chamber of Commerce, P.O. Box 627, Lampasas, TX 76550, (512) 556-5172, www.lampasas-tx.com/celebratp1.htm

Bay City: Gulf   Heritage Day

April 6, 2002   **1st Saturday in April**

Bay City greets spring with activities at the town square and old railroad depot. They have a mini-parade, historic crafts demonstrations, food booths, and live entertainment all day. Demonstrations include butter churning, square dancers, cloggers, and ballet. Also a pie-eating contest, carriage rides, a wildflower exhibit, and kids games.

Bay City Chamber of Commerce, P.O. Box 768, Bay City, TX 77414, (409) 245-8333, www.baycity.org

Stanton: Panhandle   Old Sorehead Trade Days

April 7-8, 2001

Located halfway between Fort Worth and El Paso on I-20, in the Texas Panhandle Plains region. Laid-back family atmosphere with entertainment, arts and crafts (400 vendors), antiques, historic tours, tradin' lot. Largest trade show in West Texas draws a crowd of 20,000. Free admission. For more information, call (915) 756-2006. www.stantonfolks.com

Bellville: North Central   Country Livin' Festival

April 13-14, 2002   **2nd weekend in April**

Bellville attracts thousands of people with this spring festival, which includes a dance, self-guided bluebonnet trails, antique show, craft demonstrations, and horseshoe tournament. There's also a hayride, an arts and crafts fair, tours of the county jail museum, Little Mr. and Miss Bluebonnet pageant, and a biergarten.

Bellville Chamber of Commerce, P.O. Box 670, Bellville, TX 77418, (409) 865-3407, www.bellville.com

Dallas: North Central   Deep Ellum Arts Festival

April 5-7, 2002

An "arty party" held on the historic eclectic side of downtown Dallas. Since the turn of the century (the last one!) Deep Ellum has attracted those folks that liked a different approach to using their skills. This is a cool celebration featuring a mosaic of visual artists, continuous music on four stages, an exposé of wild and entertaining Art Cars, spontaneous street performers,

Another festival lights up the Dallas skyline. Photo courtesy of the Dallas Convention & Visitors Bureau.

and other surprises. Muralists paint canvases on site. Artists sell one-of-a-kind decorative wares. Slam poets and meandering musicians add to the creativity-in-motion.

Held on Main Street, in the 2600 to 3300 blocks. Stephen Millard, 2200 North Lamar, Suite 104, Dallas, TX 75202, (214) 855-1881, Fax: (214) 855-1882, mei@meifestivals.com, www.meifestivals.com/deepspr.html

Deep Ellum Association, 2932 Main Street, Suite 101, Dallas, TX 75226, (214) 748-4332, info@deepellumtx.com, www.deepellumtx.com

Snook: North Central   ChiliFest

April 6-7, 2002   1st weekend in April

This cool event moves around the state. The location hasn't been announced for 2002, so please check the website for information. The first ChiliFest, in 1991, and the ones that have followed consist of a chili cookoff and live performances by top entertainers. ChiliFest has featured such acts as Charlie Daniels' Band, Mark Chesnutt, John Conlee, David Allan Coe, Johnny Lee, Waylon Jennings, The Bellamy Brothers, Gary P. Nunn, and Jerry Jeff Walker. www.chilifest.org

Dripping Springs: Hill Country   Old Settlers Music Festival

April 6-8, 2001

This bluegrass festival was formerly held in Round Rock. There are four stages of live music comprised of national and international award-winning singer-songwriters, folksingers, gospel, and acoustic jazz and blues artists. Bring a lawn chair, blanket, sunglasses, and sunscreen. Held at the Stone Mountain Event Center in Dripping Springs, located on Highway 290 West, 3 miles west of Highway 12.

Old Settlers' Bluegrass Festival, Randy Collier, P.O. Box 28187, Austin, TX 78755, (512) 346-0746, (512) 346-1629, Fax: (512) 346-2705, randy@computility.com, www.bluegrassfestival.com

Poteet: South   Poteet Strawberry Festival
April 12-14, 2002

This wonderful festival is recognized as one of the oldest and most popular events in the state. There are 10 areas of continuous entertainment, featuring outdoor concerts with nationally known country/western and tejano stars. In addition to two nightly dances, a parade, the famous strawberry judging and auction, various contests, special children's entertainment, rodeo performances, and quality exhibits are only some of the many events featured during the festival. Held at the Poteet Strawberry Festival Grounds on Texas Highway 16 (20 miles south of San Antonio).

Poteet Strawberry Festival Assoc, Nita Harvey, P.O. Box 227, Poteet, TX 78065, (830) 742-8144, (830) 276-3323, Fax: (830) 742-3608, mharvey@texas.net, www.strawberryfestival.com

Fort Worth: North Central   Texas Christian University Jazz Festival
April 7-8, 2001

A neat jazz festival that features performances by top jazz musicians and outstanding high school jazz bands. Events are held at the Ed Landreth Auditorium, on University Drive and Cantey Street.

Texas Christian University, Curt Wilson, TCU Box 297500, Fort Worth, TX 76129, (817) 257-7640, Fax: (817) 257-5006, frogjazz@aol.com

Austin: Hill Country   Austin Fine Arts Festival
April 8-9, 2001

This Fine Arts Festival features 180 of the nation's finest artists, an eclectic mix of music (bluegrass, folk, jazz, rock, tejano), hands-on art activities, and culinary delights. Events are held at Republic Square Park, located at 4th and Guadalupe.

Austin Museum of Art Guild, Jacqui Schraad, Executive Director, P.O. Box 5705, Austin, TX 78763, (512) 458-6073, tafaf@amoa.org, www.austinfineartsfestival.org

Chappell Hill: North Central   Bluebonnet Festival
April 7-8, 2001

The Bluebonnet Festival features arts, crafts, food, live music (folk, country, jazz, polka, Cajun, bluegrass, and pop), museum tours, hayrides, demonstrators, children's area, and dancing. Held in downtown Chappell Hill.

Historical Society of Chappell Hill, LaDonna Vest, P.O. Box 211, Chappell Hill, TX 77426, (979) 836-6033, www.brenhamtx.org

Corpus Christi: Gulf   Folklife Celebration

April 7-8, 2001

Folklife Celebration honors and encourages traditional folk arts still being passed on in families, among friends, and within communities. Sit with the artists and learn how to make quilts, guitars, furniture, piñatas, horseshoes, and much more. Separate stage areas showcase storytelling, Mexican folk healing, dancing, and American Indian culture. Held at the Heritage Park, located at 1581 North Chaparral.

Chris Barnes, P.O. Box 9277, Corpus Christi, TX 78469-9277, (361) 883-0639, Fax: (361) 883-0676, chrisb@ci.corpus-christi.tx.us, www.ci.corpus-christi.tx.us

Llano: Hill Country   Bud Otto Open Fiddle Contest

April 7, 2001

Plenty of bluegrass and country music, and the Bud Otto Open Fiddle Contest is open to all age groups with no entry fees. Events are held at the American Legion Hall, located at 402 Pittsburgh.

Llano Country Chamber of Commerce, Mary Rhodes, 700 Bessemer, Llano, TX 78643, (915) 247-5354, Fax: (915) 247-5611, llanococ@telstar.net, www.llanochamber.org

Alvin: Gulf   Rice and Crawfest

April 6, 2002   1st Saturday in April

The Rice and Crawfest features old-fashioned fun and a wide variety of Cajun entertainment to please the entire family. Great crawfish, filé gumbo, and other foods are featured. Event hours are 11 A.M.-6 P.M. Held at National Oak Park on Magnolia Street.

Kiwanias of Alvin, Gwen Obert, 804 South Hood Street, Alvin, TX 77511, (281) 331-5088, Fax: (281) 331-7473, bcarter@flipper.alvin.cc.tx.us, www.jbrau.com/crawfest.htm

Tyler: East   Texas Blues Festival

April 8, 2001

The town square comes alive when the Texas Blues Festival features great music, food, and fun. Live music will jam on stage all day. Smoked sausage and Texas-style barbecue to enjoy.

Heart of Tyler/Main Street Project, Kathey Comer, P.O. Box 158, Tyler, TX 75710, (903) 593-6905, Fax: (903) 597-0699, kcomer@tylertexas.com, www.tylertexas.com

Corpus Christi: Gulf   Buccaneer Days

April 11 through May 6, 2001

Ah, the smell of salt air and Buccaneer Days bring back memories of Corpus Christi's past as a hideaway for pirates. It features 24 days of fun and festivities such as PRCA Rodeo, carnival, parades, fireworks, music festival, folklorico competition, Black Heritage Day, Senior Dance, Junior Talent Showcase, and sporting events. Events take place at the Memorial Coliseum, at 402 South Shoreline.

Buccaneer Commission, Vicky Lewis, P.O. Box 30404, Corpus Christi, TX 78463-0404, (361) 882-3242, Fax: (361) 882-5735, bucexecdir@buccaneer.org

Austin: Hill Country   Wildflowers Days Festival

April 12-13, 2001

One of my favorite places to visit. A wonderful time at a beautiful place. The festival is held at the Lady Bird Johnson National Wildflower Research Center, 4801 La Crosse Avenue, Austin, TX 78739. The research center celebrates the Hill Country spring wildflower season with a festival featuring native plant experts and authors, an arts and crafts exhibit, and live music.

The National Wildflower Research Center is at 4801 LaCross Ave. From downtown Austin, go south on Loop 1 (MoPac) and take the South Loop 1 exit. Follow the loop past William Cannon Drive and Slaughter Lane to La Crosse Avenue. A brown sign will direct you to turn at La Crosse Avenue. The Center is at the end of the street on the right. (512) 292-4100

Kerrville: Hill Country   Easter Festival and Chili Cookoff

April 12-13, 2002

The Kerrville Easter Festival and Chili Cookoff includes old-fashioned games, chili contest, live music, and dancing. Held at Schreiner College, on Highway 27 East.

Kerrville Easter Festival, Paul Hinson, 201 West Water Street, Kerrville, TX 78028, (830) 257-3992, Fax: (830) 257-3991, www.kerrvilletx.com

Burnet: Hill Country   Burnet Bluebonnet Festival

April 12-14, 2002   2nd weekend in April

Don't miss Burnet's wonderful salute to the Texas state flower featuring a parade, dances, arts and crafts, food booths, 5K and 10K runs, and a 25-mile bike race through the countryside. There's also a bluebonnet and wildflower arrangement contest and a flower photography contest. Other entertainment includes the Fort Hood Army Band and other live music, snake handlers, a domino tournament, a fly-in at the airport, a carnival, and a beauty pageant.

Burnet Chamber of Commerce, P.O. Drawer M, Burnet, TX 78611, (512) 756-4297, www.burnetchamber.org

Dew: North Central — Plum Creek Bluegrass Music Festival

April 12-15, 2001

The Plum Creek Bluegrass Music Festival is a family-oriented bluegrass music festival that features bluegrass, old-time country, and gospel music by nationally recognized groups as well as regional and local talent. Held in Dew, TX, Exit 189 off Highway 179 (six miles east on FM 489).

Karl Shiflett, P.O. Box 576, Groesbeck, TX 76642, (254) 729-3702

New Ulm: North Central — New Ulm Art Festival

April 13, 20 & 27, 2002   The last three Saturdays in April

The New Ulm Art Festival features craft and food booths, live German polka music, barbecue cookoff, talent show, singing contests, auto show, and a raffle. Polka dancers, square dancers, and concert by Sara Hickman on the last weekend. Held at the New Ulm Firemen's Park.

For information contact Pam Cernoth, P.O. Box 55, New Ulm, TX 78950, (979) 992-3391, www.newulm- tx.com

From one Hare to Another,
How does Easter & Eggs go together?

Fredericksburg: Hill Country   Easter Fires Pageant

April 13-14, 2002   Easter Weekend

A cast of 600 presents a story of Fredericksburg's origins, in which a mother convinces her children that signal fires lit by Comanches actually came from the Easter Bunny's kitchen, while she was boiling eggs.

Gillespie County Fairgrounds, three miles south of town on TX 16, (210) 997-6523, www.fredericksburgtexas.net

Georgetown: Hill Country   Easter Pageant

April 13-14, 2002   Easter Weekend

This popular outdoor pageant is held in the Sunken Garden at San Gabriel Park, a beautiful setting in Georgetown's major city park. The pageant, featuring a large cast and many live animals, is a musical drama telling the life of Jesus Christ. There are three free performances. (512) 930-4649

Magnolia: East   Depot Day

April 14, 2001

This is an all-day festival with live entertainment provided by the Bobby Croft Show, a carnival, food, and arts and crafts booths. Events are held at the Old Depot, which is located downtown.

Magnolia Area Chamber of Commerce, Anne Sundquist, P.O. Box 399, Magnolia, TX 77353-0399, (281) 356-1488, (281) 356-1488, Fax: (281) 356-2552, macctx@juno.com, www.magnoliatexas.org

Stephenville: North Central   Texas Gospel Singing Convention

April 14-16, 2001

Good old down-home Texas gospel singing. This event takes place the 3rd weekend in April each year. Group and specialty singing is scheduled for Friday, group singing on Saturday and Sunday. Gospel singers from Texas and the Southeast U.S. have gathered in Stephenville for more than 60 years for this event. Events take place at the Stephenville High School Auditorium, 2650 West Overhill.

Texas State Gospel Singing Association, Linda McElroy, 2643 West Washington, Stephenville, TX 76401, (254) 968-2994, www.ci.stephenville.tx.us, www.stephenvilletexas.org

Deer Park: Gulf   Totally Texas

April 14-16, 2001

The name says it all. Activities include a country music show, beauty pageant, contests, kid's rodeo, classic car show, bike rodeo, armadillo races, Kids Go Country Music Contest, Lone Star Showcase-Talent Contest (all ages), parade, fireworks, live music (country, jazz, rock, bluegrass), golf tournament, and pet show. Events are held at the Burke Activity Center at 500 West 13th St. Deer Park Parks and Recreation, Jean Riggs, P.O. Box 700, Deer Park, TX 77536, (281) 478-2050, Fax: (281) 479-8091, www.deerparktexas.com

Llano: Hill Country   Crawfish Open

April 14-15, 2001

Crawfish Open features live music, games, arts, crafts, and food. This year's event hosted a clay pigeon shoot. Call for location information.

Llano Chamber of Commerce, Mary Rhodes, 700 Bessemer, Llano, TX 78643, (915) 247-5354, Fax: (915) 247-5561, llanococ@tstar.net, www.llano-chamber.org

Waxahachie: North Central   Scarborough Renaissance Faire

April 14 through June 3, 2001

Texas meets Renaissance Europe at the Scarborough Faire. This is a 16th-century English Renaissance village. Music, arts and crafts, food, and games are all taken from around life in England in the 1550s during the reign of King Henry VIII. Spread over 35 tree-covered acres, the village features live classical and folk music, dancing, juggling, magic, craft demonstrations, games of the period, and succulent food. The Faire is held every weekend near Waxahachie, FM Road 66 off IH-35 East.

Richard Holeyfield, P.O. Box 538, Waxahachie, TX 75168, (972) 938-3247, Fax: (972) 938-1890, www.scarboroughrenfest.com/faire.shtml

Terrell: North Central   Terrell Heritage Jubilee

April 14-15, 2001

The Jubilee is a two-day event featuring arts and crafts, prettiest baby contest, chili cookoff, rodeo, live entertainment, a carnival, food, game booths, gunfighters, tribal dancers, fishing pond for the kids, a fiddler's contest, car show, historic home tour, and a melodrama. Events take place at Ben Gill Park on Highway 80.

Terrell Chamber of Commerce, Noreen Walker, P.O. Box 97, Terrell, TX 75160, (972) 563-5703, Fax: (972) 563-2363, trledc@swbell.net, www.terrell-texas.com/calendar.htm

Luckenbach: Hill Country   Bluebonnet Ball

April 15, 2001

Everybody is somebody, and everything is fun in Luckenbach. This wonderful old Texas town has been forever touched by the sense of humor of Hondo Crouch. Enjoy the fun and the Hill Country flowers. Each year there are top entertainers.

Luckenbach, VelAnne Howle, 412 Luckenbach Town Loop, Fredericksburg, TX 78624, (830) 997-3224, Fax: (830) 997-1024, somebody@luckenbach-texas.com, www.luckenbachtexas.com

Beaumont: Gulf   Neches River Festival
April 15-28, 2002

This festival celebrates both the Neches River and the school students of Beaumont, with many activities centering around educational accomplishments. The 2nd weekend of the festival is probably the best for visitors with its downtown parade, boat show, and chili cookoff. You'll also find a costume contest, a bicycle race, a flower show, a flotilla, and an arts and crafts show. There's plenty of music and other entertainment. Most festival activities are at the city's Riverfront Park.

Beaumont Convention and Visitors Bureau, P.O. Box 3827, Beaumont, TX 77704, (409) 880-3749, or 1-800-392-4401

Texarkana: East   Pickin' Around the Campfire - Trade Days
April 17-22, 2001

An old-time tradition comes to life in this festival. Pickin' Around the Campfire features fun, food, crafts, jamming, jamming, and more jamming with Trade Days held on Friday and Saturday 10 A.M.-4 P.M. to sell crafts, needlework, antiques, musical instruments, and treasures to trash of all sorts. Events take place at the Strange Family Bluegrass/RV Park, at Highway 59 South to 3244, just follow signs to park.

Sam and Sharon Strange, Route 2, Box 327 B-2, Texarkana, TX 75501, (903) 791-0342, (903) 792-2481

Huntsville: East   General Sam Houston Folk Festival
April 19-20, 2002

The General Sam Houston Folk Festival features historical characters in authentic costumes telling tales of Sam Houston and his friends. Demonstrations of pottery making, quilting, woodworking, weaving, candlemaking, heritage exhibits, Civil War reenactments, and tours of Sam Houston's home and offices. Live entertainment features a variety of ethnic and regional music, including German singers, fiddle, and acoustic musical acts. Events are held at the Sam Houston Memorial Museum, located on 1836 Sam Houston Avenue.

East Texas Folk Festival Inc, Shelley Solow, P.O. Box 628, Huntsville, TX 77342-0628, (936) 294-1832, (936) 293-1962, Fax: (936) 294-3670, clover@lcc.net, http://www.shsu.edu/~smm_www/FolkFest/index.html

Troy: North Central   Fun-Fest & BBQ Cookoff

Apr 19-20, 2002   3rd Friday & Saturday in April

Loads of fun, parade, and plenty to eat. Help judge the BBQ cookoff held downtown. (254) 938-7468 www.ribman.com

Meridian: North Central   Texas Music Festival and Chili Cook-Off

April 19-21, 2001

Texas has produced some of the greatest country singers and songwriters in the music industry, and Larry Joe Taylor is one. The Texas Music Festival pays tribute to some of these talents. Two jam-packed days and nights feature legendary performers and star bound newcomers.

Sherry Taylor, Route 4, Box 212-AA, Stephenville, TX 76401, (254) 968-8505, ljt@2-cool.com

Fort Worth: North Central   Main St. Fort Worth Arts Festival

April 19-21, 2001

Downtown Fort Worth comes alive during this four-day celebration of the visual and performing arts. Outstanding musical and artistic talents of every variety (bluegrass, blues, country, folk, jazz, R&B, rock, and tejano) are showcased on historic, red-bricked Main Street. More than 400,000 people attend each year to hear more than 120 live performances. Hundreds of artists line a 10-city-block area with a national fine arts exhibition and competition, international foods, and special events.

Downtown Fort Worth, Inc., Stephen M. King, Director, 306 West Seventh Street, Suite 400, Fort Worth, TX 76102, (817) 336-2787, Fax: (817) 334-0970, stephen@dfwi.org, www.msfwaf.org

San Antonio: South   Fiesta San Antonio

Apr 19-28, 2002   3rd and 4th weekends in April

Fiesta San Antonio is a 10-day celebration featuring exciting carnivals, spectacular sports, fantastic fireworks, lively entertainment, ethnic feasts, art exhibits, and sparkling parades that glide down San Antonio's river and streets. More than 150 unique events satisfy every taste and interest, drawing some 3.5 million participants and spectators.

Fiesta San Antonio Commission, Chuck Wascom, Executive Vice President, 122 Heiman, San Antonio, TX 78205, (210) 227-5191, (877) SA-FIESTA, Fax: (210) 227-1139, julie@fiesta-sa.org, www.fiesta-sa.org

Fiesta San Antonio River Parade. Photo courtesy of the San Antonio Convention & Visitors Bureau.

Fiesta San Antonio / Market Square. Photo courtesy of the San Antonio Convention & Visitors Bureau.

Bastrop: Hill Country   Yesterfest and the Salinas Art Festival
April 20, 2002   3rd Saturday in April

Several historic buildings line Main Street of this lovely little town, and that is where the art festival takes place on the 3rd Saturday of the month. Out at the city park, the locals celebrate their pioneer past with historical exhibits, reenactments, craft demonstrations, music, and food. Native American dancers perform, cloggers and banjo players entertain, pipes & drum corps members join in Civil War reenactments, a Main Street dance at night, and a campfire stew dinner. (512) 321-6283

Lufkin: East   Downtown Hoe Down
April 20, 2002   3rd Saturday in April

A BBQ cookoff, games, bed races, and much more. Held in downtown Lufkin.

Contact Lufkin Convention and Visitors Bureau, 1615 S. Chestnut, Lufkin, TX 75901, (800) 409-5659, lufkintx@lcc.net

Alpine: West   Texas Mountain Western Heritage Weekend
April 20, 2002   3rd weekend of April

The Texas Mountain Western Heritage Weekend activities include a bit and spur show at the Civic Center, chuck wagon supper, cowboy music, poetry, storytelling, chuck wagon cookoff, ranch rodeo at Dusty's Arena, and cowboy church services. Held at the Civic Center.

Western Heritage Group, Mr. Skinner, 106 North Third, Alpine, TX 79830, (915) 837-2326, (915) 364-2440, Fax: (915) 837-3638, chamber@alpine-texas.com

Irving: North Central   **Rockin' '50s Day and Car Show**

April 20, 2002   3rd Saturday in April

Irving Heritage Park, 200 S. Main St., Irving, Texas. Come back to the '50s with this festival along Main Street in the Irving Heritage District.

"K" Downs, Irving Preservation, kdowns@ci.irving.tx.us, (972) 721-3636, www.ci.irving.tx.us

Snook: North Central   **Snookfest**

April 20, 2002   3rd Saturday in April

Snookfest features a parade at 10 A.M., antique farm equipment exhibits, an arts and crafts fair, games, and horseshoe, washer, and domino tournaments. You can hear Czech and country music in the park all day while you sample some of the Mexican, Czech, and other foods for sale. A children's barnyard and an evening dance at the fire station complete the schedule.

Snookfest, P.O. Box 10, Snook, TX 77878, call City Hall at (409) 272-3021, www.texas-on-line.com

Burton: North Central   **Burton Cotton Gin Festival**

April 20-21, 2002   3rd weekend in April

Honoring their long history, the Burton Farmer's Cotton Gin Festival pays homage to the National Landmark 1914 cotton gin and features antique cars and farm machinery, tractor pull, sausage cookoff, ice cream and pie eating contests, tours of the historic gin, arts and crafts, folk life demonstrations, events for kids, continuous live entertainment, tractors, operations of cotton gin, and a Main Street parade. There is live country, folk, bluegrass, Cajun, and polka music. Events are held on Main Street.

Burton Cotton Gin and Museum, Todd Stockpile, P.O. Box 98, Burton, TX 77835, (979) 289-3378, (979) 289-FEST, Fax: (979) 289-5308

Operation Restoration Inc., P.O. Box 132, Burton, TX 77835, 409-289-5102, www.cottonginmuseum.org

Humble: Gulf   **Good Oil Days**

April 20-21, 2001

This cool festival blends art and oil, entertainment and education, history and destiny. The 50-acre festival site is transformed into an oil boomtown in the early 1900s. Music includes country, cowboy, jazz, pop, reggae, and rock. All events are held at the Humble Civic Arena, at 8233 Will Clayton Blvd.

Humble Area Chamber of Commerce, Janet Hayes, P.O. Box 3337, Humble, TX 77347, (281) 446-2128, Fax: (281) 446-7483, jhayes@humblearea-chamber.org, www.goodoildays.org

Harlingen: Gulf   RioFest

April 20-22, 2001   2nd or 3rd Weekend in April, depending on Easter

Fair Park hosts RioFest's Annual Celebration of the Arts, a 21st-century Renaissance! The festival provides a rich variety of performing arts, cultural arts, family and children's activities. Events take place at Casa de Amistad and at the 40-acre Fair Park, on Highway 77 North.

For information, Kathy Preddy, Executive Director, P.O. Box 531105, Harlingen, TX 78553-1105, (956) 425-2705, (956) 412-2787, Fax: (956) 440-0476, riofest@aol.com, www.riofest.com

The Texas Coast   The Great Texas Birding Classic

April 20-29, 2001

This is a competitive birdwatching tournament sponsored by Texas Parks & Wildlife and Texas Partners in Flight. The top three teams at the end of the week earn the privilege of deciding which habitat conservation projects will be funded by the Conservation Cash Grand Prizes. For more information call 1-888-TXBIRDS. www.tpwd.state.tx.us/gtbc/dates

Houston: Gulf   Houston International Festival

April 20-29, 2001

Seven outdoor zones spotlight more than 1,500 performers over the 10-day festival, featuring a mix of jazz, country, blues, Cajun/zydeco, Latin, gospel, rock, and popular music. Held in downtown Houston.

Houston Festival Foundation, Kathi Austin, Director, 1221 Lamar Street, Suite 715, Houston, TX 77010-3015, (713) 654-8808, Fax: (713) 654-1719, houintfest@hif.org, www.hif.org

Stonewall: Hill Country   Wildflower Day in the Spring

Any weekend during the spring. Special events on the 3rd weekend of the month.

Stroll through the flower filled meadows of President Lyndon B. Johnson's ranch. These beautiful flowers inspired Lady Bird Johnson to a lifetime of work to educate and beautify America. Don't miss these beautiful scenes as you drive through the historic Texas Hill Country.

Events take place at Lyndon Baines Johnson State Park, on U.S. Hwy 290. (830) 644-2252, www.fredericksburg-texas.com/events.htm

Dripping Springs: Hill Country   Founder's Day and Chicken Cookoff

April 20-21, 2002   **3rd weekend in April**

This celebration includes a parade, chicken cookoff, street dance, arts & crafts, contests, live music, fiddler's contest, horseshoe & washer pitch contests, car show.

Dripping Springs Founders Day, P.O. Box 578, Dripping Springs, TX 78620, (512) 858-4740

Mauriceville: East   Mauriceville Crawfish Festival

April 20-21, 2002   **3rd weekend in April**

Crawdads and Texas! That's about as good as it gets! The Mauriceville Crawfish Festival is an annual event featuring a parade on Saturday, a carnival, arts and crafts booths, a beauty pageant, live entertainment, and a crawfish-eating contest. Events take place at the Mauriceville Fairgrounds on Highway 62.

Mauriceville Crawfish Festival Committee, Sybil Jenkins, P.O. Box 683, Mauriceville, TX 77626, (409) 745-1202

Somerville: North Central   Spring Festival

April 20-21, 2002   **3rd weekend in April**

Lots of fun in the sun. The boat parade visible from Welch Park at Lake Somerville makes this festival unique. Decorated boats of all shapes and sizes plow the waves between the mainland and an island. There's also a dance at night, a variety of games, food booths, horseshoe pitching, a chili cookoff, an arts and crafts fair, live entertainment, and bingo. Don't miss it! Somerville Chamber of Commerce, P.O. Box 352, Somerville, TX 77879, (409) 596-2383. Honey Dowdy, hdowdy@startel.net, www.rtis.com/reg/somerville

Kirbyville: East   Magnolia Festival

April 20-21, 2002   **3rd weekend in April**

The tallest pyramid magnolia in the United States grows near Kirbyville, at the edge of Newton County. There is a parade, a dance, contests, an arts and crafts fair, live entertainment, a pancake breakfast, a 5K run and walk, food booths, and a carnival.

Kirbyville Chamber of Commerce, P.O. Box 417, Kirbyville, TX 75956, (409) 423-5827, www.kirbyville.txnetwork.com/banner

West Columbia: Gulf   San Jacinto Festival

April 20-21, 2002   **3rd weekend in April**

Great fun, honoring a great victory. For history buffs, West Columbia was the first capital of the Republic of Texas and the meeting place of the Columbia Congress, which elected Sam Houston president and signed the constitution.

This festival pays tribute to the Texian victory over the Mexican army at San Jacinto in 1836, when Texas won its independence from Mexico. There are tours of historic sites, Belle of the Brazos pageant, a volleyball tournament, helicopter rides, a parade, a dance, contests, arts and crafts, entertainment, and food booths.

West Columbia Chamber of Commerce, P.O. Box 837, West Columbia, TX 77486, (409) 345-3921, www.tgn.net/~columbia

Portland: Gulf   Windfest

April 20-21, 2002   **3rd weekend in April**

For 28 years Portland has been hosting this four days of fun in the sun, including a carnival, parade, arts and crafts, street dance, 5K/10K run & 2-mile walk, beauty pageant, golf tournament, tennis tournament, chili/bean/rib cook-off, jalapeno-eating contest, and a horseshoe tournament. Held in downtown Portland.

The Portland Chamber of Commerce, 2000 Billy G. Webb Drive, P.O. Box 388, Portland, TX 78374, (361) 643-2475, Fax: (361) 643-7377, jena@portlandtx.org, www.portlandtx.org

Dayton: East   Dayton Old Tyme Days

April 20-21, 2002   **3rd weekend in April**

This neat festival features live country folk music, dancing, classic car show, and a barbecue cookoff. Artisans demonstrate how it was done in the old days. Crafts and artisan booths are located in the Dayton downtown area where all events take place.

Dayton Retailers Association, Kleve Kirby, 1911 North Winfree St., Dayton, TX 77535-1702, (936) 258-3553, (936) 258-5268, www.oletymedays.com

Lubbock: Panhandle   Lubbock Arts Festival

April 20-22, 2001

This super festival is an annual two-day celebration of the arts, offering people the opportunity to explore a rich variety of performing, visual, and culinary arts, children's activities, along with numerous cultural activities. Musical styles include tejano, blues, bluegrass, Christian, classical, country, folk, jazz, rock, and rockabilly. Event are held at the South Plains Fairgrounds at Broadway & Avenue A.

Lubbock Arts Alliance, Deborah Bigness, 2109 Broadway, Lubbock, TX 79401, (806) 744-2787, Fax: (806) 744-2790, arts@nts-online.net, www.lubbockarts.org/laat001.htm

Portland: Gulf   Portland Pioneer Days
Mid-April (depending on Easter)

This neat town hosts a crowd of about 25,000 people who come for the parade, outdoor music, a street dance, games, arts and crafts, and food booths. There's also a fajita cookoff, style show, a golf tournament, a carnival, and an auction.

Portland Chamber of Commerce, P.O. Box 388, Portland, TX 78374, (512) 643- 2475, www.portlandtx.org

Smithville: Hill Country   Smithville Jamboree
April 20-21, 2002   Weekend after Easter

The jamboree features two downtown parades, dances at night, an arts and crafts fair, a fireworks display, and horseshoe and washer pitch tournaments. The festivities take place at Crockett River Bend Park on the Colorado River just outside Smithville. There's plenty of food for sale, so bring your folding chair, picnic basket, and enjoy.

Smithville Chamber of Commerce, P.O. Box 716, Smithville, TX 78957, (512) 237-2313, www.ci.smithville.tx.us

Denton: North Central   Fry Street Fair
April 21, 2001

A neat one-day music festival, held between Fry Street and Hickory Oak Delta Lodge.

Brian Woodruff, 1001 Alice Street, Denton, TX 76201-2874, (940) 383-3486, www.discoverdenton.com/events

Seguin: South   Texas Ladies State Chili Championship
April 21, 2001

Y'all come on down and watch these great ladies cookin' up the red. Ladies over 18 years old may enter (entry fee required) to compete for the title of "Texas Ladies State Chili Champion." Top three places qualify for the International Chili Championship Cookoff held in November 2001 in Terlingua, Texas. Things are cookin' at Starke Park East.

For information call Ken Rodd (210) 887-8827 or email: txladies-state@aol.com, hometown.aol.com/txladiesstate

Austin: Hill Country   The Annual Austin Rugby Tournament
April 21-22, 2001

Since 1968 this tournament has grown into a national event and is the oldest and largest rugby tournament in the Southwest. The competition takes place in beautiful Zilker Park, 2100 Barton Springs Road. Several divisions compete over the two-day event, which is capped off with a party on Sixth Street.

Alan Sharpley, sharpley@dynastat.com, Home: (512) 288-3384, Work: (512) 476-4797, Fax: (512) 472-2883, Austin RFC, P.O. Box 12932, Austin, TX 78711, www.austin360.com/community/groups/austinrugby

Houston: Gulf   Houston International Jazz Festival
April 21-22, 2001

Enjoy one of the coolest music festivals anywhere. Saturday and Sunday's events are held at Herman Square/Reflection Pool at 900 Smith.

Jazz Education, Inc., Bubbha Thomas, P.O. Box 8031, Houston, TX 77288, (713) 839-7000, Fax: (713) 839-8266, jazzed@neosoft.com, jazzhouston.com

Athens: North Central   PRCA Stampede Rodeo
April 26-28, 2001

Come rodeo in the town that invented the hamburger. The PRCA Stampede Rodeo is a three-day professional rodeo with top contestants and rodeo stock. Included in the events are professional acts (trick riding, clowns, etc.) and a golf tournament with a professional cowboy on each team. Held at the Henderson County Fairpark Complex, Highway 31 East.

Athens Chamber of Commerce, Tere Lawyer, P.O. Box 2600, Athens, TX 75751, (903) 675-5181, (800) 755-7878, Fax: (903) 675-5183, athenscc@flash.net, www.athenscc.org

Houston: Gulf   Art Car Ball
April 26-28, 2001

Talk about creativity, color, and fun! They even have eleven categories for you to enter your creation in. The Art Car Ball is the funniest fundraiser and the best party in Houston. Art Car Weekend is the nation's largest and oldest Art Car Parade. Events take place at the Allen Center Garage, located at 300 Clay Street.

The Orange Show Foundation, Jennifer McKay, 2402 Munger, Houston, TX 77023, (713) 926-6368, (713) 926-CARS, Fax: (713) 926-1506, orange@in-sync.net, www.orangeshow.org

Cameron: North Central   Dewberry Festival
April 27, 2002   Last Saturday in April

Lots of entertainment and fun, including a parade, BBQ cookoff, carnival, and of course, tons of dewberries. (254) 697-4979, camerontx@tlab.net

Austin: Hill Country   Eeyore's Birthday Party
April 27, 2002   Last Saturday in April

Another unique Austin event. Remember hippies? Well they come from far and wide to help Eeyore the donkey, of Winnie the Pooh fame, celebrate his birthday. Free spirits set flight in dress, music, and fun. There are bands, painted faces, jugglers, and all are free from mid-morning till sunset. Don't miss it!

Pease Park, Parkway St. off W. 12th St. (512) 448-5160

Liberty Hill: Hill Country   Liberty Hill Festival
April 27, 2002   **Last Saturday in April**

This small town pulls out all the stops with this old-fashioned celebration that features a pet parade, a cute baby contest, horseshoe and washers tournament, arts and crafts stalls, a carnival, and a barbecue at the VFW Hall. On Sunday afternoon there is a gospel singing and covered-dish dinner at Foundation Park.

Downtown Liberty Hill (512) 515-5075, www.libertyhillchamber.com

Wimberley: Hill Country   BreastFest
April 28, 2002   **4th Sunday in April**

BreastFest is a fundraiser for Prevention of Breast Cancer in Low Income Women. All proceeds benefit the Karen Prince Fund, a directed fund through the St. David's Foundation. BreastFest features popular musicians and celebrities.

Steven Prince, 1070 Box Canyon Road, Wimberley, TX 78676, (323) 646-8988, steve@wnbo.com, www.texashillcntry.com/wimberley

Littlefield: Panhandle   XIT Bluegrass Festival
April 28-29, 2001   **Last weekend in April**

The legendary XIT Bluegrass Festival will have bluegrass groups from all over the country performing on indoor/outdoor stages. RV hookups available. Arts and crafts, concessions, and food booths. Events are held at Lamb County Fairgrounds, located at 17th and Hwy 385.

Littlefield Arts & Heritage Committee, Emil Macha, 720 East 14th, Littlefield, TX 79339, (806) 385-3870, Fax: (806) 385-6229, www.littlefield-texas.org

Hallettsville: North Central   Texas State Championship Fiddlers Frolic
April 25-28, 2002

This super event features more than 80 contestants competing in age divisions for the top cash prize and state championship trophy. The events include a jam session for early arrivals, Cajun and bluegrass music, Cajun food, dance contests, barbecue, sausage, chili cookoffs, induction of worthy fiddlers to the Hall of Fame, fun run, and the State Championship Fiddler contest finals. Held at the Knights of Columbus Hall, on Highway 77 South.

Texas State Championship Fiddlers' Frolics Inc., Frank Zaruba, P.O. Box A, Hallettsville, TX 77964, (361) 798-2311, arj09286@cvtv.net, www.fiddlersfrolics.com

Glen Rose: North Central   Spring Bluegrass and Gospel Festival
April 25-29, 2001
Bluegrass artists gather from all over America, performing old-time favorites, great gospel, and new traditional toe-tapping music. Grassroots music is for all ages so bring the family 'cause it's that kind of festival and that kind of park. Free cornbread and beans on Wednesday and an open showcase.

RV River Resorts and Campground, 2322 County Road at Highway 67 Tres Rios, Machelle Ralls, 2322 County Road 312, Glen Rose, TX 76043, (254) 897-4253, Fax: (254) 897-7613, www.texasoutside.com/glenrose

Denton: North Central   Denton Arts and Jazz Festival
April 26-28, 2002
This is a three-day arts festival in the park featuring the best in professional jazz and pop music on outdoor stages. There are bands, orchestras, dance, theatre, storytelling, and puppet shows. There are fine artists and craftsmen, games, activities, and a large children's art tent. Roving musicians include Dixieland, brass and chamber music, and bagpipes. Events take place at the Denton Civic Center Park at 321 East McKinney.

Denton Festival Foundation, Carol Short, P.O. Box 2104, Denton, TX 76202, (940) 565-0931, (940) 383-4418, Fax: (940) 566-7007, www.dentonjazzfest.com

Athens: North Central   TRCA Stampede Rodeo
April 27-29, 2001
TRCA Stampede Rodeo is held April 27-29. The event is held at the Henderson County Fairpark Complex.

Athens Chamber of Commerce, Stephanie, 1260 South Palestine, Athens, TX 75751, (903) 675-5181, ssamonebyrd@aol.com, www.athenscc.org

Glen Flora: Gulf   Wharton County Youth Fair and Exposition
Late April through early May
The Wharton County Youth Fair and Exposition events include a rodeo, country music, dances, livestock show, carnival, arts and crafts, and a barbecue cookoff. Held at the Wharton County Fair Youth and Exposition, FM 960 and FM 961.

Cynthia Osterloh, P.O. Box 167, Glen Flora, TX 77443-0167, (979) 677-3350, Fax: (979) 677-3371

Cleburne: North Central   Cleburne Springfest BBQ
April 27-28, 2001

Held in downtown Cleburne. Rick Holden, (817) 558-6108, www.rib-man.com

Hughes Springs: East   Wildflower Trails of Texas
Last full weekend in April

Wildflower Trails is a celebration at the start of the wildflower blooming season. The Wildflower Trail consists of Highways 49, 155, and 11 between Avinger, Linden, and Hughes Springs. There are literally thousands of different varieties of wildflowers naturally occurring in the area. Activities during the weekend include a treasure hunt, arts and crafts, a passion play, live entertainment, country & western dances, carnival, and 5K run. Events are held at Spring Park, at Second and Ward Streets.

Wildflower Trails of Texas, George Fite, P.O. Box 805, Hughes Springs, TX 75656, (903) 639-7519, Fax: (903) 639-3769, chughesspr@aol.com

Turkey: Panhandle   Bob Wills Day
April 26-28, 2002

Bob Wills Day events include a fiddlers contest, arts and crafts, dances, a parade, concessions, a midnight breakfast, and a barbecue dinner. Featured musical performances include the Texas Playboys and Jody Nix and the Texas Cowboys. Live concert Saturday afternoon, featuring the Texas Playboys. Held at the Bob Wills Center, a block west of Highway 70.

Bob Wills Foundation, Gary Johnson, P.O. Box 372, Turkey, TX 79261, (806) 423-1033, (806) 423-1151, suziej@caprock-spur.com. Contact Theresa Clinton at City Hall at (806) 423-1033. www.turkeytexas.com/bobwillsday.htm

Euless: North Central   Arbor Daze
April 27-28, 2002   **4th weekend in April**

For twelve years the city of Euless has sponsored this festival. Arbor Daze was selected as a White House Millennium Event, which receives special recognition from the president of the United States. Arbor Daze offers nightly musical entertainment from favorite oldies acts and various opportunities during the day such as arts and crafts, business exposition, plant sale, tree giveaway, concerts, youth community stages, specialty foods, and much more. Arbor Daze was selected as the Best Festival in the Nation. Held at the Bear Creek Parkway and Fuller Wiser Road.

For information, call (817) 685-1821, or check out www.ci.euless.tx.us.

Muenster: North Central   Germanfest

April 27-29, 2001

Germanfest activities include food, games, contests, 15K and 5K fun run, a bicycle rally, and live music. On Friday, Saturday, and Sunday the Texas stage will feature Vince Vance and the Valiants, and Alpenfest of Houston Polka Band will be featured in the German tent/stage. Events are held at City Park, located at the intersection of Highway 82 and Maple Street.

Muenster Chamber of Commerce, Margie Starke, P.O. Box 479, Muenster, TX 76252, (940) 759-2227, Fax: (940) 759-2227

Port Arthur: Gulf   Pleasure Island Music Festival

April 27-29, 2001

Pleasure Island Music Festival provides continuous musical entertainment during the weekend with local and regional talent along with nationally known entertainers. Also, arts and crafts, festival cuisine, youth activities tents, musical contests, treasure hunt, and a carnival. Held at the Logan Music Park on Pleasure Island, MLK Parkway.

Service League of Port Arthur, Margo Martin, P.O. Box 3134, Port Arthur, TX 77643, (409) 962-6200, Fax: (409) 962-6200

Galveston Island: Gulf   International Kite Fest

April 28, 2001

A spectacular, colorful event for the family. Don't forget your camera. There are power parachutes, kite surfing, and tons of kites featuring demonstrations by internationally known aerial kite performers. There is a kids' area for kite making and flying. Events take place at R.A. Apffel Beach (East Beach) Galveston Island.

MCM Communications, M.J. Naschke (409) 762-3930, Chris Woolwine (409) 766-7774, www.kitetrade.org/NationalKiteMonth/event_sched.shtml

Austin: Hill Country   Annual Louisiana Swamp Romp and Crawfish Festival

April 28-29, 2001

The annual Louisiana Swamp Romp and Crawfish Festival features the best in Louisiana cuisine along with tons of jumbo crawfish. There's a voodoo village with magic shops, dancers, and juju mamas, a traditional funeral procession, and lots of beads and tokens. Cajun and zydeco music by local and national entertainers. Events are held at Waterloo Park in downtown Austin.

French Smith, 1710 South Lamar Blvd., No. B-C, Austin, TX 78704-8963, (512) 441-9015, Fax: (512) 441-9016, pop@mail.roadstarproductions.com, www.roadstarproductions.com

Cisco: Panhandle   Folklife Festival and Frontier Jubilee

April 28-29, 2001

This cool festival features musical entertainment (folk and country), different arts and crafts demonstrations, bread making, food vendors, and an antique tractor show. Events are held on the Cisco Junior College Campus.

Cisco Civic League, Emma and Melodee Watts, P.O. Box 411, Cisco, TX 76437, (254) 442-2537, (254) 442-2567, (254) 442-3478, Fax: (254) 442-2546

Salado: North Central   Gospel Festival

April 29, 2001

The Gospel Festival features various local groups and artists performing original and public domain works. Directed by Tom Taylor. Events take place at Tablerock Amphitheater on Royce Street.

Tablerock Festival of Salado, Tom Taylor, Director, P.O. Box 312, Salado, TX 76571, (254) 947-9205, Fax: (254) 947-5269, tomabtaylor@hotmail.com

Lufkin: East   Angelina Benefit Rodeo

April 27, 2002   **Last weekend in April**

One of the finest small rodeos in Texas. An official stop on the PRCA circuit, which normally attracts more than 25,000 folks. Held at the Angelina County Exposition Center.

Contact Lufkin Convention and Visitors Bureau, 1615 S. Chestnut, Lufkin, TX 75901, (800) 409-5659, lufkintx@lcc.net

Crystal Beach: Gulf   Texas Crab Festival

April 27-28, 2002   **Last Weekend in April**

The Texas Crab Festival features live music, food and crafts, crab-dish cookoffs, trip raffle, live crab races, crab legs contest, carnival, treasure hunt, school poster contest, and cloggers. Music ranges from gospel to zydeco. We had Ezra Charles last year. Something for everyone. Held at Gregory Park, on Highway 87.

Boliver Peninsula Chamber of Commerce, Ann Willis, P.O. Box 1170, Crystal Beach, TX 77650, (409) 684-3017, (800) SUN-FUN 3, Fax: (409) 684-5940, cofcbolivar@yahoo.com, www.cityofbeaumont.com/psurr.htm

Catfish Time Ain't It?

Freer: South   Freer Rattlesnake Roundup

April 27-28, 2002   **Last Weekend in April**

The event is a weekend salute that celebrates the area's most famous resident. Fun for all ages, the Freer Rattlesnake Roundup includes indoor concerts featuring tejano music stars, a parade, carnival, arts and crafts fair, dances, stage shows, strolling grounds entertainment, daredevil snake shows, and traditional rattlesnake hunt and contest. Fried rattlesnake and other foods available. Held at the Freer Cactus Corral, at East Highway 44, 2 miles east of Freer.

For more information, contact the Freer Chamber of Commerce at (512) 394-6891. Freer Chamber of Commerce, Nancy Deviney, P.O. Box 717, Freer, TX 78357, (361) 394-6891, (361) 394-6891, Fax: (361) 394-5672, freertx@yahoo.com, members.nbci.com/Papa1/

La Porte: Gulf   Sylvan Beach Festival

April 27, 2002   **Last Saturday in April**

Since 1956 La Porte has celebrated its seashore, Sylvan Beach, with this festival that draws about 25,000 people. Events include a parade, dance, live entertainment, music, a chili cookoff, and a variety of games. There's also a Miss Sylvan contest.

La Porte-Bayshore Chamber of Commerce, P.O. Box 996, La Porte, TX 77572-0996, (713) 471-1123, www.laportechamber.com

Houston: Gulf — Annual Houston Pod Chili Cookoff
April 27-28, 2002

Now we're really cookin' up the red!!! Don't miss this fun event. This is actually several events including Chili Cookoff & Show Teams, Junior Cookoff, Jackpot Beans, Mexican Potluck Fiesta Dinner, Tonk Tournament, 42 Tournament, Breakfast Casserole-Off, Gumbo Cookoff, Hot Wing Fry-Off, silent auction, chili tasting cups for sale, live music both days. Events are held at the Traders Village, 7979 N. Eldridge Parkway, Houston, TX.

For more information, contact Beverly Caldwell, (281) 334-0403. www.tradersvillage.com

Cleburne: North Central — Springfest Barbecue Cookoff
April 28, 2001

The Springfest Barbecue Cookoff features great food, arts, crafts, sidewalk sales, a classic and antique car show, firefighters' hose-off, RV and boat show, mousetrap extravaganza, live entertainment, and more. Events are held in downtown Cleburne.

Cleburne Chamber of Commerce, Roy Christian, P.O. Box 701, Cleburne, TX 76033-0701, (817) 641-4562, www.cleburne.com, www.cleburnechamber.com/springfest_2001.htm

San Antonio: South — Bowie Street Blues
April 29, 2001

Bowie Street Blues is an open-air concert featuring traditional blues artists from around the state, allowing the public to savor the grass roots of Texas blues tradition. Held at HemisFair Park, on the grounds of the Institute of Texan Cultures.

UT Institute of Texan Cultures, Laurie Gudzikowski, 801 South Bowie Street, San Antonio, TX 78205, (210) 458-2300, Fax: (210) 458-2380, lgudzikowski@utsa.edu, www.texancultures.utsa.edu/new/tff/bowie_blues.html

San Antonio: South — Fiesta Around the World
April 29, 2001

Fiesta Around the World is an annual event during Fiesta Week in San Antonio. Proceeds help St. James The Apostle and area schools offset their annual budgets. Entertainment. Held at Rosedale Park, at 340 Dartmouth.

John J. Gutierrez, 907 West Theo Avenue, San Antonio, TX 78225, (210) 924-1201, Fax: (210) 924-0201

May

Where's Da Food?

The partying is really gettin' going now. Spring rolls on into another month of flowers, festivals, and fun. Texas is more culturally diverse than most nations of the world, and the month of May starts off with Cinco de Mayo, which pays homage to the Mexican soldiers who defeated the French army at Puebla, Mexico.

Do you know what a bowl-o-red is? Well you better find out, 'cause it's an important part of the lives of Texans and Texas festivals! That's right, it's chili. And, like barbecue, it's sacred too. There are as many chili recipes as there are cooks. The red color is about the only thing they all have in common. What do you like, thick or thin, what kind of meat, do you even use meat, what size chunks, a little sweet or not, hot or not, big tomato chunks or tomato sauce, and what about the spices? Taking notes? Most Texans have strong opinions on these questions, too.

Go and try the chili at the cookoffs; most of it is wonderful. Just remember to always have a cool drink handy BEFORE you start sampling.

Always double check the dates of the events.

Mesquite: North Central   Mesquite Championship Rodeo

April through September, every Friday and Saturday night

From home-cooked barbeque to live Texas music to pro-cowboy competition, the Mesquite Championship Rodeo gives you a full night of real Texas fun—affordably and just 15 minutes from downtown Dallas. Any Friday or Saturday night April through September. Events include bull riding, bronc riding, calf roping, and more.

118 Rodeo Drive, off the Military Parkway exit from I-635. (214) 285-8777, www.mesquitetexas.com

Mesquite Chamber of Commerce, 617 N. Ebrite, Mesquite, TX 75149, (972) 285-0211, www.mesquitechamber.com

Kerrville: Hill Country Cowboy Artists of America Roundup

Early May

Annual "Art Stampede" show and sale. Cowboy Artists of America Museum. (830) 896-2553, www.caamuseum.com

Iraan: West Alley Oop Day

May or June of odd-numbered years

V.T. Hamlin, the creator of the Alley Oop cartoon strip, lived in Iraan, Texas. He had worked there as a geologist for an oil company and became inspired by the prehistoric nature of the terrain in Pecos County. Enjoy the parade, dance, golf cart races, pet shows, and even a chili cookoff. There's also an arts and crafts fair and live entertainment provided by musicians and dancers.

Iraan Chamber of Commerce, P.O. Box 153, Iraan, TX 79744, (915) 639-2528

Georgetown: Hill Country Mayfair

Held each May

San Gabriel Park is one of the prettiest settings in Texas and is the site of the annual Williamson County Mayfair. The weekend is filled with family-oriented fun including arts and crafts, a 5K run/walk, car show, family fun area, live entertainment, a dance, and lots of food and drinks. For more information call (512) 930-3535.

Granbury: North Central Annual Old-Fashioned Fair

Held each May

Features pioneer demonstrations at the Hood County Senior Center. (817) 573-5548, (800) 950-2212. www.granbury-tx.com

Ingleside: Gulf Roundup Days

Early May

Ingleside, on the edge of Corpus Christi Bay, holds a parade, a dance, a bike-a-thon, a bean cookoff, and a horseshoe tournament. There's also an arts and crafts fair, beauty pageant, carnival, talent show, and music.

Ingleside Chamber of Commerce, P.O. Box 686, Ingleside, TX 78362, (512) 776-2906

Newton: East Newton County Fair

May 1-6, 2001   1st week in May

Fun, food, and entertainment. chamber@newton.txnetwork.com

San Marcos: Hill Country   Viva! Cinco de Mayo Celebration
May 3-5, 2001

Viva! Cinco de Mayo Celebration pays homage the Mexican soldiers who defeated the French army at Puebla, Mexico. Hays County Civic Center, IH-35 North and Clovis Barker.

This is a fun get-together, and when you are in town, look in on my old buddy Rob Robinson at the Hill Country Humidor, on the square. He can fill you in on "everything else" that's going on in town.

Richard Cruz, Chairman, P.O. Box 953, San Marcos, TX 78667, (512) 353-8482, webmaster@vivacinodemayo.org

Helotes: North Central   Helotes Cornyval
May 3-6, 2001

The Helotes Cornyval is designed to please the entire family. Top local entertainers perform on two stages, featuring bluegrass, Cajun, country, polka, rock, Latin/tejano music, dancing, and specialty acts. A parade on Saturday and three nights of rodeoing. Enjoy the amusement rides and carnival games. Held at the Helotes Festival Grounds, located at 12210 Leslie Road.

Helotes Festival Association, Elaine Ryan, P.O. Box 376, Helotes, TX 78023, (210) 695-2103, (210) 688-3537, ElaineRyan@Txsonline.com

Fort Worth: North Central   Mayfest
May 3-6, 2001

Mayfest is a celebration of the Fort Worth community, featuring live performances by the Fort Worth Symphony and many other local talents. Mayfest features six stages, all with live entertainment. Music styles include children's, classical, country, folk, jazz, R&B, rock, Latin/tejano. Events take place at Trinity Park.

Junior League of Fort Worth, Lisa O'Connor, 1110 Penn Street, Fort Worth, TX 76102, (817) 332-1055, Fax: (817) 332-3902, mayfest@flash.net

Alice: South   Fiesta Bandana City Celebration
May 3-8, 2001

The Fiesta Bandana has food, arts and crafts, toys, games, and a carnival. Nightly entertainment with live country and tejano music, talent show, and on the first night, a Queen's Contest, Prince and Princess, and baby photo contest. Held at Plaza Park on Alto Street.

Alice Chamber of Commerce/Fiesta Bandana Committee, David Gaza, P.O. Box 1609, Alice, TX 78333, (361) 664-3454, Fax: (361) 664-2291, jsleight@alicetx.org, www.alicetx.org

Howe: North Central   Founder's Day

May 4, 2002   **1st Saturday in May**

Howe Founder's Day includes a parade, bicycle rally (10K, 35K, and 60K) horseshoe pitching and other contests, an arts and crafts fair, live entertainment, and food booths.

Howe Chamber of Commerce, P.O. Box 250, Howe, TX 75059, (903) 532-6012

Sabinal: Hill Country   Lonesome Dove Days

May 4, 2001

Lonesome Dove Days features the following festivities: arts and crafts, games, live music, square dancers, folklore dancers, and food booths. The event also includes a dance, a rodeo, and lots of fine country and cowboy music. Held in the City Park, north off Highway 90 at Highway 187.

Sabinal Chamber of Commerce, David Flores, President, P.O. Box 55, Sabinal, TX 78881, (830) 988-2010, (936) 336-6643

Goliad: South   Cinco de Mayo Festival

May 4, 2002   **Saturday closest to May 5**

Goliad has a special connection with May 5, the date of the Battle of Puebla, since the Mexican general in the battle, Ignacio Zaragosa, was from Goliad. Mexico wasn't a strong country back then, in fact, the French invaded because Mexico owed them money. Zaragosa led a ragtag army into battle with the French and won. Attractions include a dance, an arts and crafts fair, ballet folklorico, Miss Zaragoza Coronation, a commemorative mass, appearances by international dignitaries, and food booths.

Goliad Chamber of Commerce, P.O. Box 606, Goliad, TX 77963, (512) 645-3563

Beaumont: Gulf   Beaumont Cinco de Mayo Festival at Riverfront Park

May 4-5, 2002   **Weekend closest to May 5**

Beaumont's remembrance of the Battle of Puebla includes a parade, a queen's pageant, a jalapeno-eating contest, a pinata party, arts and crafts, and plenty of Mexican food. You'll be entertained by mariachis and folk dancers.

Beaumont Convention and Visitors Bureau, P.O. Box 3827, Beaumont, TX 77704, (409) 838-6581, Fax: (409) 833-6718, www.bmtcoc.org

Dallas: North Central   Cinco de Mayo Celebration

May 4-5, 2002

The Cinco de Mayo Celebration includes these major attractions: education expo, family resource center, health care pavilion, career fair, Plaza de Niños, carnival rides and games, fan fair, sampling and demonstration opportunities, and family-oriented activities. Held at Fair Park, located at 3809 Grand Avenue.

Marcos Rincon, 6060 North Central Expwy., Suite 670, Dallas, TX 75206, (214) 750-0670, (214) 800-5220, Fax: (214) 750-1038, mary@rinconcommunication.com

Ennis: North Central   National Polka Festival

May 4-5, 2002   1st weekend in May

This large Czech festival starts Saturday with a parade, followed by street entertainment including gymnastics, folk dancing, and a 10K run.

You'll also find regional arts and crafts for sale, plenty of Czech food, such as kolaches (pastry) and klobase (sausage). Some of the best polka bands in the state play in four halls around Ennis for polka and waltz lovers.

Ennis Chamber of Commerce, P.O. Box 1177, Ennis, TX 75119, (214) 975-2625

Falfurrias: South   Fiesta Ranchera

May 4-5, 2002   1st weekend in May

This is a bigtime festival in small town Texas, which features a western dance, a trail ride, arts and crafts, entertainment, and food booths. There's also a carnival, a rodeo, live music, and games.

Falfurrias Chamber of Commerce, P.O. Box 475, Falfurrias, TX 78355, (512) 325-3333

Navasota: North Central   Nostalgia Days

May 4-5, 2002   1st weekend in May

Step back to the turn of the century in Navasota during Nostalgia Days, when townspeople dress in clothing typical of that period. Well-restored Victorian buildings provide a rich backdrop for this event, which features a parade, a street dance, live music, and home tours. Among the types of music you may hear are Dixieland jazz, western swing, and folk. There's plenty of entertainment by cloggers, square dancers, and others. Activities include a juried arts and crafts show, hayrides, a carnival, a quilt show, and theater performance.

Grimes County Chamber of Commerce, P.O. Box 530, Navasota, TX 77868, (409) 825-6600, www.rtis.com/reg/navasota

Orange: East   International Gumbo Cookoff

May 4-5, 2002   1st weekend in May

The International Gumbo Cookoff in Orange, paying tribute to that spicy delicious Cajun stew we call gumbo, has three tent dances featuring Cajun, zydeco, and country and western music. You'll also find a parade, plenty of food, arts and crafts, a children's area, storytelling, a fun run, and plenty of other entertainment. There will also be a Country Music Singers Amateur Talent Contest. This year's festival will include water activities plus a boat show. Held in downtown Orange, between Fifth and Third Street on Front Street.

Greater Orange Area Chamber of Commerce, Ron Sigler, 1012 West Green Avenue, Orange, TX 77630, (409) 883-3536, (800) 528-4906, Fax: (409) 886-3247

Rosenberg-Richmond: Gulf   Fort Bend Czechfest

May 4-5, 2002   1st full weekend in May

Music, dancing, food, and crafts give visitors a thorough view of Czech culture in Texas. You'll see people in traditional Czech festival costume, Czech imports, and Czech dance performances. The event also offers a kolache bakeoff, children's games, and a carnival.

Rosenberg-Richmond Chamber of Commerce, 41200 Ave. H, Rosenberg, TX 77471, (713) 342-5464

Vernon: North Central   Doan's May Picnic

May 4-5, 2002   1st Saturday in May

This community picnic has been held every May Day since 1884 in Watt's Grove on the Red River. A local school sells barbecue, but most people bring a picnic lunch, spread a blanket on the ground, and relax for the day.

Vernon Chamber of Commerce, P.O. Box 1538, Vernon, TX 76384

Gladewater: East   East Texas Gusher Days

May 4-5, 2002   1st full weekend in May

Gusher Days, begun in 1986, looks back to the East Texas oil boom of the 1930s. Activities include a parade, chili cookoff, street dance, a two-act musical comedy, arts and crafts, food booths, a carnival, and a variety of games. Held in Downtown Gladewater.

Gladewater Chamber of Commerce, John Paul Tallent, P.O. Box 1409, Gladewater, TX 75647, (903) 845-5501, Fax: (903) 845-6326

Lamesa: Panhandle   May Fun-Fest

May 4-5, 2002   1st full weekend in May

Come join the fun. There is a bicycle parade, food booths, arts and crafts, cakewalks, pie and watermelon eating contests, dog shows, and baby contests.

Lamesa Area Chamber of Commerce, P.O. Drawer J, Lamesa, TX 79331, (806) 872-2181

Austin: Hill Country   Cinco de Mayo Festival: Lo Nuestro
May 4-5, 2002

This event is a celebration of Hispanic culture featuring live country, tejano, mariachi, and conjunto music. Food, arts and crafts, game booths, plus the Mighty Thomas Carnival will provide family fun for everyone. Held at Fiesta Gardens, located at 2101 Bergman Ave. For more information: (512) 867-1999

Richardson: North Central   Cottonwood Art Festival
May 4-5, 2002   **1st weekend in May**

This wonderful festival is a showcase of fine art and fine crafts that transform Richardson's Cottonwood Park into a gallery every spring and fall! Sculpture, painting, fiber, ceramics, glass, jewelry, photography, and more grace the rows and rows of more than 200 artists who exhibit their work in what has become one of the best fine art festivals in the country. Satisfy your taste buds with fine cuisine offered in our culinary arts area. (972) 669-0912, www.cor.net/specialevents/cottonwood/homepage.html

Post: Panhandle   BBQ Cookoff
May 4-5, 2002   **1st weekend in May**

A WTBA sanctioned barbecue cookoff and loads of fun in a small town with a ton of history. Events take place at 208 N. Avenue F.

Danny Cooper, (806) 495-1252, Cooperdv@aol.com, www.posttexas.com

Marlin: North Central   Marlin Festival Days
May 4-5, 2002   **1st weekend in May**

Marlin Festival Days includes a parade, 5K run, fun run, dancing, arts and crafts, food booths, a carnival, horseshoe pitch, volleyball tournament, Little Miss and Mr. Contests, and barbecue cookoff. Country, polka, and tejano music. Marlin City Park, P.O. Box 854, Marlin, Texas 76661

Marlin Festival Association, Inc., Freddie Walker, P.O. Box 854, Marlin, TX 76661, (254) 883-2451, (254) 883-5888

Cedar Park: Hill Country   Cedar Chopper Festival
May 4-5, 2001

This is one of my favorites. The festival has included fun, food, and entertainment for the past 20 years. Throughout the day on Saturday there are arts and crafts, food and beverage booths, tournaments, a carnival, hot air balloons, airplane fly-overs, and much more. The festival site is located on New Hope

Road under the Cedar Park water tower, which is one mile north of 1431. For more information, contact the Cedar Park Chamber of Commerce,

Harold Dean, Executive Director, 350 Discovery Blvd., Suite 207, Cedar Park, TX 78613-2268, (512) 258-8007, (512) 260-4260, Fax: (512) 260-4265, deanl@cedarparkchamber.org, www.cedarparkchamber.org

Mineola: East   Mineola May Days Bean Fest

May 4-5, 2002

The Mineola May Days Bean Fest features live entertainment, arts and crafts, carnival, three-on-three basketball, children's play area, bean cookoff, recipe contest, and a treasure hunt. Tap your foot to bluegrass, country, and rock. Held in downtown Mineola, on Commerce Street.

Mineola Chamber of Commerce, James Banks, P.O. Box 68, Mineola, TX 75773-0068, (903) 569-2087, (800) 646-3652, Fax: (903) 569-5510

Amarillo: Panhandle   Greater Southwest Music Festival

May 4-6, 2001

Amarillo Convention Center and Polk Street United Methodist Church, Greater Southwest Music Festival features competition for jazz bands, show choirs, concert bands, concert choirs, and orchestras from elementary schools, middle schools, and high schools. Free live concerts featuring jazz and classical music.

Margaret Scales-Peacock, 1000 South Polk, Amarillo, TX 79101, (806) 373-5093, (800) 444-4763, Fax: (806) 373-5656, gswmf@aol.com

Spring: Gulf   Texas Crawfish Festival

May 4-6, 11-13, 2001

This cool festival features family entertainment, petting zoo, activities, arts and crafts, commercial vendors, exhibitors, carnival rides, live music, delicious Cajun food, and shopping. Over the six days of festivities, festivalgoers learn the art of peeling crawfish and enjoy the sounds of a great group of musicians on four stages. Held at the Old Town Spring Preservation Park, which is one mile east of I-45N on Spring Cypress Road.

Barbara Metyko, 119 East 20th Street, No. 103, Houston, TX 77008, (713) 863-9994, (800) 653-8696, Fax: (713) 868-3383, bmetyko@gte.net, 1-800-OLD-TOWN, www.texascrawfishfestival.com

Levelland: Panhandle   Country Fest, Rock Fest, R&B Fest and Bluegrass Fest

May 4-6, 2001

The Country Fest on Monday evening the first at 6 P.M. kicks off the show. Rock Fest is on the second and the R&B Fest on the third keeps the beat going Wednesday evening with performances starting at 6 P.M. Saturday evening three of the world's best bluegrass instructors take the stage with their ensembles to perform bluegrass favorites.

Levelland Chamber of Commerce, Sandy Parker, 1101 Avenue H, Levelland, TX 79336, (806) 894-3157, (806) 894-2228, Fax: (806) 894-4284, levellandcoc@door.net

Fort Bend: Hill Country   Czech Fest
May 4-6, 2001

Texas's largest Czech festival opens to the public in May. Includes authentic Czech food and genuine Czech costumes, polka and country music, dancing, Czech, German, and Polish singers, choirs, and dancers, children's events and games, arts and crafts. Held at the Fort Bend County Fairgrounds, at 4310 Highway 36.

Fort Bend Czech Alliance, Vickie Matocha and Pat Parma, P.O. Box 1788, Rosenberg, TX 77471, (281) 342-4898, (281) 342-5934, parma@nstci.com

Bryan/College Station: Annual POPS Concert - Bright Lights!
North Central   Broadway!
May 5, 2001

The Annual POPS Concert featured "Bright Lights! Broadway!" as the Brazos Valley welcomed back the phenomenal cast of Michael Herzlin Productions performing Broadway's best-loved composers and their greatest hits. This fabulous POPS concert concluded with a spectacular fireworks display over Lake Bryan. Held at Lake Bryan Park.

Brazos Valley Symphony Orchestra, for ticket information (979) 779-6100, bvso.org

Caldwell: Panhandle   Burleson County Cinco de Mayo Celebration
May 5, 2002

Burleson County Fairgrounds Caldwell Parade at 10 A.M. Downtown Caldwell on the square. Festival starts 12 noon, with food, crafts, games, and various entertainment during the day. Dance from 8 P.M.-12 A.M.

Martin Revilla, reva@tamu.edu, (979) 862-7768, www.angelfire.com/tx4/CincoDeMayoFestival/

Denton: North Central   Cinco de Mayo Celebration
May 5, 2002

This wonderful Cinco de Mayo music festival celebration kicks off at the Civic Center Park with a parade starting at 10 A.M. There are live bands, vendors, children's arts and crafts, and a dance. Held at the Civic Center, 321 East McKinney. City of Denton, Teresa Salazar, 321 East McKinney, Denton, TX 76201, (940) 349-8289, Fax: (940) 349-8384, tmmilan@cityofdenton.com

Fort Stockton: West   Cinco de Mayo Celebration

May 5, 2002

Cinco de Mayo, May 5, marks the day in 1865 when the Mexican army repelled a French invasion at the city of Puebla. Cinco de Mayo in Fort Stockton features live entertainment, Tex-Mex food, fajita cookoff, arts and crafts, games, and street dances. Special performances include conjunto and tejano musica y ballet folklorico performed by the children. Live music all day and a street dance at night. Held at St. Joseph's Park, on Main Street.

Paisano Pete, World's Largest Roadrunner "lives" in Fort Stockton.

Knights of Columbus, Tony Villarreal, P.O. Box 984, Fort Stockton, TX 79735, (915) 336-5085, (915) 634-5127, Fax: (915) 336-8098, comm2pecosco@hotmail.com

Brookshire: Gulf   Cinco de Mayo

May 5, 2002

City of Brookshire Cinco de Mayo Celebration will feature live music, folklorico dancers, mariachi bands, food, crafts, and games. The celebration will be from 10 A.M. until 5 P.M. with a dance held afterward. It's a fun-filled day for the whole family. Held in downtown Brookshire.

City of Brookshire, Ms. Lemos, P.O. Box 459, Brookshire, TX 77423, (281) 934-2222, (281) 934-2465

San Saba: Panhandle   Cow Camp Cookoff

May 5, 2002

The Cow Camp Cookoff features local bands performing throughout the day with a dance from 9 P.M.-1 A.M. Other activities include arts and crafts booths, competition for the best brisket, pork ribs, chicken, and pinto beans, horseshoes, and washer pitching. Held at Risien Park, Highway 190 East.

San Saba County Chamber of Commerce, 302 East Wallace, San Saba, TX 76877, (915) 372-5141

Seymour: North Central   Festival in the Park
May 5, 2002

Festival in the Park includes a farmer's market, arts and crafts, food, fireworks, an antique car show, horseshoe and volleyball tournaments, a field day, and live country and gospel music. Events are held at City Park, in the Portwood Pavilion, located at the intersection of McLain Street and Park Road.

Seymour Chamber of Commerce, James D. Colthamp, Executive Director, P.O. Box 1379, Seymour, TX 76380, (940) 888-2921, Fax: (940) 888-3800, scoc@wf.quik.com

Beaumont: Gulf   Boys Haven Crawfish Festival
May 5, 2001

Another great Crawdad Festival! Catch the live music from several great bands. Visitors can also enjoy a Texas-Meets-Louisiana feast of crawfish, boudain, gumbo, barbecue, and beverages as they enjoy the silent auction, door prizes, and a ceremony recognizing the supporters of Boys Haven. Held on the South Texas Fairgrounds, on Gulf Street, just off IH-10.

Boys Haven, C.A. "Pete" Shelton, P.O. Box 5815, Beaumont, TX 77726-5898, (409) 866-2400, (409) 866-5292, Fax: (409) 866-7976

Lubbock: Panhandle   Cinco de Mayo Celebration
May 5, 2001

The celebration starts off with a luncheon and is a one-day outdoor concert with food, games, and public information. There are also many booths.

Lubbock Hispanic Chamber of Commerce, Chuck Heinz, P.O. Box 886, Lubbock, TX 79408-0886, (806) 762-5059, (807) 747-2555, Fax: (806) 763-2124

Breckenridge: Panhandle   Frontier Days
May 5-6, 2001

Frontier Days takes place at City Park and features a ranch rodeo, cowboy poets, crafts, fiddlers contest, chuck wagon cookoff, live entertainment, and a street dance.

Breckenridge Chamber of Commerce, Bob Donnell, P.O. Box 1466, Breckenridge, TX 76424, (254) 559-2301, Fax: (254) 559-7104

Austin: Hill Country

Old Pecan Street Spring Arts Festival

May 5-6, 2001

The Old Pecan Street Spring Arts Festival includes arts and crafts, food, beverages, street performers, and more than 70 acts on five outdoor stages. You will be able to find some music you enjoy from country, folk, jazz, rock, tejano, and even some children's acts. Held on East Sixth Street, between Congress and IH-35.

Crowds come from far and wide to enjoy the fun at the Old Pecan Street Spring Arts Festival.

French Smith, 1710 South Lamar Blvd., No. B-C, Austin, TX 78704-8963, (512) 441-9015, Fax: (512) 441-9016, pop@mail.roadstarproductions.com, www.roadstarproductions.com

Sanderson: West

Cinco de Mayo Celebration

May 5-6, 2001

Sanderson Cinco de Mayo Celebration features arts and crafts, food, and live music, with a dance in the evening on both Friday, May 5 and Saturday, May 6. There is also a baseball tournament that draws Texans from all over the state. The tournament starts on Friday and can run through Sunday. Fun for the whole family!! Events are held on the courthouse square.

Terrell County, Terry Tex Toler, P.O. Drawer 4890, Sanderson, TX 79848, (915) 345-2275, (915) 345-2324, Fax: (915) 345-2250, cactuscapital@sandersontx.net

Seymour: North Central

Fish Day

May 6, 2002   **First Monday in May**

Gone Fishin'!!! This annual three-day event commences on Monday when everyone closes up shop and heads out to Lake Kemp for games and food. They have a dance, a fish fry contest, fishing, boating, volleyball, a log roll, a tug of war, a queen contest, and arts and crafts. They've been holding this event for more than 60 years.

Seymour Chamber of Commerce, P.O. Box 1379, Seymour, TX 76380, (817) 888-2921

Woodville: East   Bluegrass and Gospel

May 6, 2001

The jammin' begins at 5:30 P.M. with the stage show scheduled for 7 P.M. Bluegrass, Cajun, country, folk, and gospel music. There is an 1840-1920 early East Texas farming village with railroad museum, wagon museum, 1860 country store, and more. Musical acts have included Cajun and host band Yeller Dawg. Held at Woodville Heritage Village Museum, Highway 190 West.

Woodville Heritage Village Museum, Ofeira A. Gazzaway, P.O. Box 888, Woodville, TX 75979, (409) 283-2272, (800) 323-0389, Fax: (409) 283-2194

Bandera: Hill Country   Silver Dollar Downs Crawfish Race
                                            and Festival

May 6, 2001

The annual "Cowboy Crawdaddy" Crawfish Race and Festival was originally organized simply to throw a great party for those who love crawfish and live away from the coastal region. It has become one of Bandera's premier annual events, starting at 3 P.M. and ending either when the crawfish are gone or the partygoers fall over! EAT A BUG, CUT A RUG! We don't claim to be "Cajun," we just love to party and eat crawfish. There are fiddlin' contests, a street dance, and even some great cowboy poetry. This event is B.Y.O.B. Held at Mansfield Park, which is 3.5 miles north of Bandera on Highway 16.

Dusty Britches, P.O. Box 1977, Bandera, TX 78003, (830) 460-8198, (830) 796-3045, Fax: (830) 460-8198

Houston: Gulf   Houston Heritage Chapter Cajun Music
                                            Festival

May 6-7, 2001

Back to the wonderful music of the bayou. Don't miss the fun.

Cajun French Music Association - Houston Heritage Chapter, Nancy Schexnayder, President, P.O. Box 77292, Houston, TX 77792, (713) 682-2436

San Antonio: South   Tejano Conjunto Festival

May 8-13, 2001

Great music and great fun, this festival pays tribute to the unique hybrid sound that blends Mexican mariachi music, Latin American cumbias, and rancheras, polkas, waltzes, schottisches, country, blues, and jazz. The button accordion reigns supreme in the conjunto ensemble. If you ain't got that squeezebox, you ain't got conjunto music. More than thirty-two acts are scheduled to appear. Held at the Guadalupe Theatre, Rosedale Park, located at the intersection of 340 Dartmouth and North General McMullen.

Guadalupe Cultural Arts Center, Pilar Chapa, 1300 Guadalupe Street, San Antonio, TX 78207-5519, (210) 271-3151, Fax: (210) 271-3480, guadarts@aol.com

Tejano Conjunto Festival in San Antonio. Photo courtesy of the San Antonio Convention & Visitors Bureau.

Jasper: East   Jasper Rodeo

2nd week in May

Jasper is the "Jewel of the East Texas Forest." Each year top rodeo talent and top country music stars perform at each night's events, and the largest PRCA rodeo is held. It attracts top-ranked cowboys and cowgirls nationwide. Held at the Jasper Lions Club Rodeo Grounds, out on Fletcher Street.

Jasper Lions Club, Larry Dickerson and Russ Pulliam, P.O. Box 415, Jasper, TX 75951, (409) 384-4322, (409) 384-2651, Fax: (409) 384-3140, www.jasper-tx.org

Brenham: South   Maifest

May 9-11, 2002   **Thursday, Friday, and Saturday before Mother's Day**

The 108-year-old Maifest is a celebration of the German community. Includes food booths, arts and crafts, two stages with continuous music for three days, two downtown parades, two elaborate coronations involving more than 1,000 young people, plus community-related homecoming activities. There's German music in the beer garden Friday night and Saturday and Sunday from noon till midnight. Other attractions include a variety of games, a carnival, coronations of kings and queens, food booths featuring German and other foods, and an arts and crafts fair. Held at Fireman's Park, North Park St. and Highway 36 North.

Brenham Maifest Association, Bill Berts, P.O. Box 1588, Brenham, TX 77834-1588, (979) 836-0721, (979) 836-3695, Fax: (979) 836-3657

Abilene: Panhandle   Western Heritage Classic

May 10-11, 2002   2nd Friday and Saturday in May

Western Heritage Classic celebrates the traditions of the great ranching life-style featuring working cowboys from famous ranches! Features live music on Friday night with cowboy poets. Other events include a chuck wagon cookoff, trade shows, ranch rodeo, and a benefit dinner dance with Rhinestone Round-up. Held at the Taylor County Expo Center, at 1700 Highway 36.

Western Heritage Classic, Phil Guitar, President, 1700 Highway 36, Abilene, TX 79602, (915) 677-4376, Fax: (915) 677-0709, expoabilen@aol.com, www.westernheritageclassic.com

Marble Falls: Hill Country   Spring Fest

May 10-13, 2001

Spring Fest events include a carnival, craft booths, 5K run, fishing tourna-ment, washers and horseshoe tournament, parade, volleyball tournament, pageants, chili cookoff, and music in Johnson Park.

Marble Falls Chamber of Commerce, Francie Dix, 801 Highway 281, Marble Falls, TX 78654, (830) 693-4449, Fax: (830) 693-7594, brenda@marblefalls.org, www.marblefalls.org

Fredericksburg: Hill Country   Founders Day Festival

May 11, 2002   2nd Saturday in May

Don't miss the flowers and fun in beautiful Fredericksburg, Texas. This fes-tival celebrates the founding of Fredericksburg, May 1846. Focus of the festival is on local artisans, musicians, and vendors. There will be sheep shearing, stone spitting, blacksmithing, and corn grinding, and children's games, lots of great music, food, beer, and wine. This event coordinates with the Indian Pow-wow also going on in Fredericksburg the same weekend. (830) 997-2835 or gchs@ktc.com.

Weimar: North Central   Weimar Gedenke Country Fun Festival

May 11, 2002   Saturday before Mother's Day

Gedenke means "remember" in German, and the folks in Weimar recall their history with this street festival. There is a parade, a street dance, live music during the day, an arts and crafts fair, and food booths selling everything from homemade ice cream to famous Weimar sausage. There's also a Miss Weimar contest and a fun run.

Weimar Chamber of Commerce, P.O. Box 90, Weimar, TX 78962, (409) 725-8675

Richardson: North Central   Wildflower! Arts and Music Festival

May 11-12, 18-20, 2001

Wildflower! Arts and Music Festival features two days and four nights of nonstop music from local, regional, and national acts. Nightly concerts feature headlining country, pop, classic rock, and Motown artists. There is a children's area, wildflower bus tours, police motorcycle rodeo, arts and crafts, exhibits, classic car show, carnival, elephant rides, lion and tiger shows, and much more. Events take place at the Greenway Office Park, at U.S. 75 and Campell Road.

City of Richardson, Sandra Risk, 1251 Colombia, Richardson, TX 75081. For more information call (972) 680-7909, (972) 680-9567, (972) 680-7943, Fax: (972) 497-9689, sandra_risk@cor.gov, www.wildflowerfestival.com

Electra: North Central   Annual Electra Goat Cookoff

May 11-12, 2001

Electra Chamber of Commerce, Dawn Dunsmore, 112 West Cleveland, Electra, TX 76360, (940) 475-3577, www.ribman.com

Santa Anna: Panhandle   Fun-tier Days

May 11-12, 2002   **2nd weekend in May**

The folks in Santa Anna organize a wool demonstration in which sheep shearers, spinners, and weavers team up to show you how wool is processed from start to finish. Other activities include an antique tractor show, a Maypole dance, a parade, a dance, an arts and crafts fair, a stage show, food booths, and a fun run.

Santa Anna Chamber of Commerce, P.O. Box 275, Santa Anna, TX 76878. For information call (915) 348-3535

Beaumont: Gulf   Kaleidoscope Creative Arts Festival

May 11-12, 2002   **Mother's Day weekend**

The Kaleidoscope Festival features juried artists and artisans showing their work, and continuous live music including jazz, bluegrass, and barbershop quartets. Other entertainment includes poetry readings, ballet, and performances by cloggers, square dancers, jugglers, and storytellers. There's also an "art alive" area where artists demonstrate their skills in glass blowing, sketching, pottery, and other arts.

Beaumont Convention and Visitors Bureau, P.O. Box 3827, Beaumont, TX 77704, (409) 880-3749 or 1-800-392-4401

Clear Lake: Gulf   Clear Lake Greek Festival

May 11-13, 2001

This cool festival features live ethnic music and dancing, children's carnival, arts and crafts, clothing, jewelry, and food booths. Held at the Landolt Pavilion

Clear Lake Park, on NASA Road 1.

St. John's Theologian Greek Orthodox Church, Nadia Hayes, 202 North Walnut, Webster, TX 77598, (281) 326-1740, Fax: (281) 326-0475, nadiahayes@aol.com, www.clearlakearea.com/whatshap.html

Harlandale: North Central   Harlandale Festival

May 12, 2001

The Harlandale Festival is a day filled with food, refreshments, entertainment, and fun activities. This event is an all-day competition featuring students from the Harlandale Independent School District competing in mariachi, jazz group, and singing group categories, as well as competitions in literary arts and chess. Held at Memorial Stadium, at 4002 Roosevelt.

Harlandale District Office - Cultural Arts Department, Mirella Hernandez, 115 East Huff, San Antonio, TX 78214, (210) 921-4300, (210) 977-1588, Fax: (210) 977-1587

Mesquite: North Central   Annual Mayfest

May 12, 2001

A wonderful spring party in Texas, with everything you could want, including food, arts and crafts vendors, product/information vendors, remote pet adoption, antique fire truck, continuous entertainment, children's area with petting zoo, kite making, sack races, dominoes, chess and horseshoe tournaments, Mesquite police mini-Tahoe racing, and more, Held in the Opal Lawrence Historical Park, 701 E. Kearney St., Mesquite. For information call (972) 216-6468

Hillsboro: North Central   Bond's Alley Arts and Crafts Festival

May 12-13, 2001

This cool arts and crafts festival features the work of over 100 artists and craftsmen. This year's event had a carnival and loads of entertainment, including live music. Most of the music is performed by local talent from the Hill County area. Events are held around the courthouse in downtown Hillsboro.

Bonds Alley, Leann Richmond, P.O. Box 358, Hillsboro, TX 76645, (254) 582-2481, (254) 582-2481, Fax: (254) 582-3800, leann@uptg.com, www.hillsboro.net/business/chamberofcommerce

Houston: Gulf   Space City U.S.A. Guitar Show and Music Expo

May 12-13, 2001

The Space City U.S.A. Guitar Show and Music Expo features many of the top guitar and musical instrument dealers, traders, collectors, and manufacturers from all over the U.S. Held at the Houston Astrodome Astrohall.

Don Schwarzkopf, 4510 Marlboro Drive, Houston, TX 77092-7531, (713) 688-3773, (281) 480-6397, musicnew@neosoft.com

Athens: North Central   Uncle Fletch Davis Hamburger Cookoff American Music Festival & Operation Rainbow Chili Cookoff

May 12, 2001

Honoring Athens as the Home of the Hamburger! Hamburger cookoff, arts & crafts, children's area, food, and fun. A "Battle of the Bands" follows in the afternoon, and the invitation-only chili cookoff benefits Operation Rainbow. The evening ends with a concert, full light and laser show, and dancing in the streets! Events are held in downtown Athens.

Athens Central Business Association, (903) 675-2561, (903) 675-9321, ssamonebyrd@aol.com

Fort Worth: North Central   Cowtown Cinco de Mayo

May 13, 2001

Music and fun, along with a street dance. Held on Main Street in downtown Fort Worth.

Marcos Rincon, 6060 North Central Expwy., Suite 670, Dallas, TX 75206, (214) 750-0670, Fax: (214) 750-1038, mary@rinconcommunication.com, www.rinconcommunication.com

San Marcos: Hill Country   Texas Natural Festival Weekend

May 15, 2001

The Texas Natural Festival Weekend in San Marcos offers a variety of music including Texas western swing, cowboy poets, and country. Other events planned are a chili cookoff, Texas marketplace, a trail ride, Texas heritage craft demonstrations, dutch-oven cookoff, and more. Held on the historic downtown

The beautiful Courthouse Square, in San Marcos.

Courthouse Square. Shuttles run from Bobcat Stadium on Aquarena Springs Blvd.

Main Street Project, Kelly Franks, 630 East Hopkins, San Marcos, TX 78666, (512) 393-8430, Fax: (512) 396-2770, www.78666.com

Copperas Cove: North Central   Rabbit Fest

May 16-19, 2002

Things are hoppin' at the Rabbit Fest. (Sorry, I just couldn't resist it!) Hop on down to Copperas Cove and enjoy a colorful parade, live bands, the Rabbitfest Queen and her court, a lively midway of food and carnival rides, lots of arts and crafts, and flea market items. And yes, there will be rabbits galore! Held at City Park, on FM 1113.

Copperas Cove Chamber of Commerce - Rabbit Fest Division, Patricia Landon, 204 East Robertson Avenue, Copperas Cove, TX 76522, (254) 547-7571, covechamber@n-link.com

Garner State Park: Hill Country   Songwriters Festival

May 17-20, 2001

Join us for 4 days of fun and enjoy the talents of some well-known songwriters like Sonny Throckmorton, Johnny Duncan, Bruce Channey, and Rock Killorge. There will be open mike sessions and arts and crafts for all. Held at Garner State Park.

Friends of Garner, Frank Roberts, Route 70, Box 599, Concan, TX 78838, (830) 232-6132, (830) 232-6132, froberts@hctc.net

Vernon: North Central   Santa Rosa Roundup

May 18-19, 2002   **3rd weekend in May**

What is more Texas than a roundup and rodeo? There are also arts and crafts, food booths, and a barbecue cookoff. The rodeo runs Wednesday through Saturday.

Vernon Chamber of Commerce, P.O. Box 1538, Vernon, TX 76384, (817) 552-2564

McKinney: North Central   Mayfair Art Festival

May 18-19, 2002   **3rd weekend in May**

Join us on the Historic Downtown McKinney Square. Fabulous parade kicks off Mayfair, Sat. 10 A.M. Fine artist pavilion hosts artists from three states. Maypole dancing like you've never seen. ArtCars on exhibit, two stages of entertainment, storytelling festival, carnival, petting zoo, train rides, ponies, great fun for the entire family centered around the fine shopping of downtown McKinney. Event details and discount lodging, (972) 562-6880. For more information call (972) 562-6880.

Laredo: South   5th Annual Day Powwow Festival

May 18-19, 2002   3rd weekend in May

Features arts and crafts, inter-tribal dancing, and more. Civic Center grounds. (956) 795-2080

Pasadena: Gulf   Annual Pasadena Strawberry Festival

May 18-19, 2002   3rd weekend in May

The Pasadena Strawberry Festival will celebrate its 27th annual event at the Pasadena Fairgrounds, in the Gulf Coast Region, with continuous live entertainment, strawberries, arts & crafts, children's games, carnival rides, enormous variety of foods, beauty pageants, specialty acts, commercial exhibits, barbecue cookoff, demonstrations by various craftsmen, the State Mud Volleyball Championship Tournament, the "World's Largest Strawberry Shortcake," and MUCH, MUCH, MORE!! For more information call (281) 991-9500 or see www.tourtexas.com/pasadena/strawberryfest.html

Columbus: North Central   Magnolia Homes Tour and Live Oak Arts and Crafts Show

May 18-19, 2002   3rd weekend in May

During this festival of Columbus' heritage, girls stroll the sidewalks in ante-bellum gowns and surreys roll through streets shaded by giant oak trees. Events include an arts and crafts fair, an auction, family night on the square, surrey rides, live entertainment, performances in the opera house, and a beer garden.

Chamber of Commerce, P.O. Box 343, Columbus, TX 78934, (409) 732-5881

Bonham: North Central   Bois D'Arc Festival

May 18-19, 2002   3rd weekend in May

This festival, named after the bois d' arc (also known as the horseapple) tree, began in 1986 as part of the Texas Sesquicentennial celebration. It now includes a parade, a dance, 10K and 3K runs, historical crafts and displays, games, and an arts and crafts fair.

Bonham Chamber of Commerce, First and Center Street, Bonham, TX 75418, (903) 583-4811

Gainesville: North Central   Depot Days

May 18-19, 2002   3rd weekend in May

Gainesville raises money to preserve the old Santa Fe Railroad Depot with this festival. It starts Friday night with a street dance and continues Saturday with games, country and bluegrass music, an arts and crafts fair, a bike rally, a fun run, antique car show, and a tour of historic homes. A private museum of Coca-Cola memorabilia is open to the public during Depot Days.

Gainesville Chamber of Commerce, P.O. Box 518, Gainesville, TX 76240, (817) 665-2831

Pflugerville: Hill Country   Deutschen Fest

May 18-19, 2002   3rd weekend in May

A wonderful German community celebrating its long heritage. Events include a parade, an outdoor dance, arts and crafts, a fun run, games, music and other entertainment, plus plenty of food for sale. The live entertainment includes folk, blues, and of course, polka music. There are also activities for kids, such as a balloon man and magician.

Pflugerville Chamber of Commerce, P.O. Box 483, Pflugerville, TX 78660, (512) 251-3076

Giddings: North Central   Lee County Fair Charcoal Challenge

May 18-19, 2001

Held in downtown Giddings. Kathy Kalbas, (979) 366-2849, www.ribman.com

Groesbeck: North Central   Groesbeck Barbecue Cookoff

May 18-19, 2001

Held in downtown Groesbeck. Jean Koester, (254) 729-3291, www.ribman.com

Port Lavaca: Gulf   Port Lavaca - Calhoun County Bay Days

May 18-19, 2002   3rd weekend in May

Port Lavaca - Calhoun County Bay Days is the best little beach party in Texas and celebrates summer on the bay. Activities include live music (rock, country, polka, Latin/tejano) concerts, jet ski competition, arts and crafts, games, and lots of food and fun. Come join us! Bayfront Peninsula, Main Street and Commerce Street.

Port Lavaca Chamber of Commerce, Carolyn Adrian, P.O. Box 528, Port Lavaca, TX 77979, (361) 552-2959, Fax: (361) 552-1288, ptlcofc@tisd.net

Austin: Hill Country   Fiesta (Arts and Crafts Show and Festival)

May 18-19, 2002   3rd weekend in May

Located on the beautiful grounds of Laguna Gloria, which lead down to the banks of Lake Austin, since 1956 this event has always been fun. Leading artists and artisans from far and wide set up booths and demonstrate their wares. Puppets, watercolors, oils, carvings, castings, and many others are there. Austin Art Museum at Laguna Gloria, 3809 W. 35th Street, (512) 458-6073

Marshall: East   Stagecoach Days
May 18-19, 2002   3rd weekend in May

This wonderful festival offers a living history lesson and a ton of fun that honors the town's heritage as a transportation center for stagecoaches, the pony express, and as a train depot. There are stagecoach rides, lumberjack competition, and the Miss Loose Caboose Contest. Activities include a parade, street dance, historic homes tour, dinner theater, fiddler's contest, children's games, arts and crafts, and food booths. Events are held in downtown Marshall.

Contact the Marshall Chamber of Commerce, Phyllis Prince, P.O. Box 520, Marshall, TX 75671, (903) 935-7868, Fax: (903) 935-9982, cvd@internetwork.net

Atlanta: East   Spring Bluegrass Music Festival
May 18-21, 2001

This is a neat four-day bluegrass festival. Billie and John B. Carver, Route 1, Box 208C, Atlanta, TX 75551, (903) 796-5487

Grapevine: North Central   Main Street Days Festival
May 18-19, 2002   3rd weekend in May

Music for every taste including bluegrass, blues, children's, country, and folk. Festivities this year include exciting nonstop entertainment from three stages, street dances, live music nightly, and jazz school band competitions. Events are held in the Main Street Historic District.

Grapevine Convention and Visitors Bureau, Rick Lott, One Liberty Park Plaza, Grapevine, TX 76051, (817) 410-3189, (800) 457-6338, Fax: (817) 410-3038

Folks enjoy GrapeFest in Grapevine (where else?). Photo courtesy of the Grapevine Convention & Visitors Bureau

No matter which festivals you attend, you'll never go away hungry! Photo courtesy of Bill Erhard.

Jourdanton: South

Jourdanton Days Kactus Kick (formerly Dairy Days)

May 18-19, 2002   3rd weekend in May

This fun festival includes a chili cookoff, a parade, dances on Friday and Saturday nights, a trail ride, arts and crafts fair, Miss Jourdanton Pageant, food booths, and a 10K run. Live entertainment Saturday afternoon includes music and dancers.

By their own admission, the people in Jourdanton love to get silly, so they have the No Talent Show on Friday night, and the Anything Goes Contest Saturday afternoon. In the No Talent Show, participants get points for their lack of performance ability. Held at the Jourdanton City Park, out Highway 16.

Jourdanton Chamber of Commerce, Jerry Don Wilson, P.O. Box 747, Jourdanton, TX 78026, (830) 769-2866

Vidor: Gulf   Texas Bar-B-Q Festival

May 18-19, 2002   3rd weekend in May

A weekend of fun featuring a great tastin' and smellin' barbecue cookoff, a car show, a parade, a dance, an arts and crafts fair, food booths, a horseshoe pitching contest, a Festival Queen selection, and a tiny tot pageant for the younger set.

Vidor Chamber of Commerce, P.O. Box 413, Vidor, TX 77662, (409) 769-6339

Salado: North Central   Tablerock Spring Festival

May 18-19, 2002   3rd weekend in May

Held at the Tablerock Amphitheater, on Royal Street.

Tablerock Festival of Salado, Jackie Mills, President, P.O. Box 312, Salado, TX 76571, (254) 947-9205, Fax: (254) 947-5269, tablerock1@aol.com

Presidio: West   Onion Festival

May 18-20, 2001

The Onion Capital of the World, Presidio, honors its heritage and livelihood. Every year they celebrate for three days with menudo and onion cookoffs, recognition of the best farmer and best citizen, and onion farm tours. A parade, a dance, an arts and crafts fair, the Onion Queen contest, and plenty of food booths.

Presidio Chamber of Commerce, P.O. Box 1405, Presidio, TX 79845, (915) 229-3199

Boerne: Hill Country   Spicy Food and Music Festival

May 18-20, 2001

Be sure you have that cold drink first! Held on the square in Boerne.

Boerne Downtown Merchants Association, John Payne, P.O. Box 311024, New Braunfels, TX 78131, (830) 249-1422

Austin: Hill Country   Annual O. Henry Pun-Off World Championships

May 19, 2001   **1st Sunday in May historically**

I love this event. One of the shortest, yet most fun events in this book. Your sides will hurt from laughing and groaning at some very punny people. Sit beneath the beautiful oaks and have a great time. The Pun-Off consists of two different pun-filled competitions ... PUNNIEST OF SHOW and HIGH-LIES & LOW PUNS. Their press release reads in part: In fragrant violation of good taste, putrid puns and wretched wordplay will be the odor of the day at the 24th Annual O. Henry Pun-Off World Championships.

If you are itching for more inflammation, The O. Henry Museum is located at 409 E. 5th St., Austin TX 78701 or call (512) 472-1903, Fax: (512) 472-7102. For interviews or details, contact Gary Hallock, (512) 453-4431 or (512) 973-9929, c.hallock@mail.utexas.edu

Addison: North Central   Taste Addison

May 19, 2001

A tasty weekend blend of food, music, and family fun. The 4.5-square-mile town of Addison has more restaurants per capita than any city west of the Mississippi. Events are held in the Addison Conference and Theatre Centre, 15650 Addison Rd.

Contact Barbara Kovacevich, P.O. Box 9010, Addison, TX 75001-9010, (972) 450-6221, (800) ADDISON, Fax: (972) 450-6225, bkovacerich@ci.addison.tx.us, www.ci.addison.tx.us

Midland: West   Celebration of the Arts

May 19-21, 2001

Midland's Celebration of the Arts puts the spotlight on visual and performing arts, drawing people from all over West Texas for three days of fun. There are four stages of continuous entertainment (both local and national), 70 visual artists, a children's activity tent, a wide variety of hands-on activities, arts demonstrations, and many food booths. Saturday night there is a street concert, and Sunday there is a free family concert in Centennial Plaza. Events are held at the Midland Center, located at 105 North Main.

Arts Assembly of Midland, Linda Bond, P.O. Box 3494, Midland, TX 79702, (915) 687-1149, Fax: (915) 687-1600, artsmid@iglobal.net

League City: Gulf   Fire on the Strings Bluegrass Festival

May 19-21, 2001

The Fire on the Strings Bluegrass Festival features live music on stage with lots of space for jamming. Bring lawn chairs. Also enjoy all the attractions of the Pasadena Strawberry Festival including mud volleyball, world's largest strawberry shortcake, barbecue cookoff, etc. This year we feature a banjo contest with prizes. The festivities are held at the Pasadena Convention Center, on Red Bluff Road.

Bay Area Bluegrass Association, Stan Jones, 710 Orange Groves Lane, League City, TX 77573, (281) 332-3287, (713) 762-7554, Fax: (281) 283-0616, egig22254@aol.com

Pine Mills: East   Pickin' in the Pines

May 19-21, 2001

Pickin' in the Pines includes bluegrass, blues, country, cowboy, and folk music and is held on about 15 acres in the beautiful East Texas piney woods in Pine Mills. It is a camping weekend with campfire jams. Held in Pine Mills, at the intersection of FM 49 and 312.

Dick and Geri Miller, Route 1, Box 177-M, Mineola, TX 75773, (903) 857-2253, t-roy@lakecountry.net

Gilmer: East   Cherokee Rose Festival

Usually held in late May

This neat festival celebrates the Cherokee Indian history of the area and the Cherokee roses that bloom along an old Indian trail. Activities include guided tours of the Cherokee Trace, a quilt show, fun run, antique and classic car show, arts and crafts, stage show, and a turtle race. Visitors can participate in opossum calling and other contests.

Upshur County Chamber of Commerce, P.O. Box 854, Gilmer, TX 75644, (903) 843-2413

Austin: Hill Country   Texas Electronic Music Festival

Late May

Texas Electronic Music Festival is a Willie Nelson Picnic-style gathering featuring an electronic music festival, a dance, trade show, and convention. Our aim is to vindicate and validate electronic dance music as a viable music alternative, as well as to promote Texas-based electronic musicians and DJs as unique influences on the genre. Events are held at the Austin Music Hall, at 202 Neches.

Contact TexFest, Keith Jones, 936 East 50th Street, Austin, TX 78751-2719, (512) 834-5675 pager, txfest@eden.com

Tulia: Panhandle   Tule Creek Bluegrass Festival

Late May

The Tule Creek Bluegrass Festival held in Tulia is a family-oriented three-day bluegrass music jamboree with stage shows as well as "shade tree pickin'" around the campsites. Events are held in downtown Tulia.

Tule Creek Bluegrass Festival, Bill DeHay, P.O. Box 31042, Amarillo, TX 79120, (806) 622-3364

Dallas: North Central   Asian Music Festival

Late May

The Asian Music Festival is held every year in Dallas to celebrate Asian-Pacific American heritage month. Dallas Arts District, 2010 Flora Street, downtown Dallas.

Greater Dallas Asian American Chamber of Commerce, Irma Kusuma, 11171 Harry Hines Blvd., Suite 115, Dallas, TX 75229, (972) 241-8250, Fax: (972) 241-8270, events@gdaacc.com

Kerrville: Hill Country   Kerrville Folk Festival

May 24 - June 10, 2001   **Last week in May till nearly mid-June**

Allen Damron and Rod Kennedy founded the Kerrville Folk Festival in 1972, and a legend was born. It is the best known of all Texas music festivals. Stretching over 18 days, the festival features more than 120 accomplished international, national, and regional musicians. Held at the Quiet Valley Ranch, 9 miles south on Highway 16.

The tepees are aglow in a beautiful night view of the camping grounds at the Kerrville Folk Festival. Photo by Javier Cortez.

Kerrville Festivals, Rod Kennedy, P.O. Box 1466, Kerrville, TX 78029, (830) 257-3600, (800) 435-8429, Fax: (830) 257-8680, staff@kerrville-music.com, www.kerville-music.com

NOTE: Find out more about the Kerrverts by reading *Hot Jams and Cold Showers*, by Dyanne Frye-Cortez. She and her husband, Javier, are regulars at Kerrville.

Texarkana: East   Strange Family Bluegrass Festival
May 24-27, 2001

The Strange Family Bluegrass Festival offers live music, camping facilities, concessions, and family fun. Plenty of good music on stage with daily jamming under the trees with good fellowship. Strange Family Bluegrass/RV Park, Highway 59 south to 3244, follow signs to park

Sam and Sharon Strange, Route 2, Box 327 B-2, Texarkana, TX 75501, (903) 791-0342, (903) 792-2481, sfbgtxk@juno.com

Rusk: East   Memorial Day Fair on the Square
May 25, 2002   **Saturday before Memorial Day**

Held on the courthouse square, this event features a variety of games and contests, an ugly pickup truck contest, an arts and crafts fair, food booths, all-day entertainment, a cakewalk, and a street dance.

Rusk Chamber of Commerce, P.O. Box 67, Rusk, TX 75785, (903) 683-4242

Early: Hill Country   Ribolympics at Heartland Mall
May 25-26, 2001

Held at the Heartland Mall, U.S. 183 & U.S. 67/U.S. 377. Take your pick: spareribs, baby back, and country style ribs.

Charlotte Parrack, (915) 646-8531, www.ribman.com

Bandera: Hill Country   Funtier Days
May 25-26, 2002   **Memorial Day weekend Saturday**

Learn how to cowboy party in the Cowboy Capital of the World. A parade kicks off in the morning, followed by a full day of live entertainment, a trail ride, contests, arts and crafts fair, dances, and food booths. Don't miss this glimpse of cowboy life.

Bandera County Chamber of Commerce, P.O. Box 171, Bandera, TX 78003, (512) 796-3045

Port Lavaca: Gulf   Texas Summerfest
May 25-26, 2002   **Memorial Day weekend**

Summerfest is fun in the sun, sand, and surf. There are two dances, one on Friday and one on Saturday night. Other activities include games, an arts and crafts fair, a fishing tournament, food booths, live entertainment, a carnival, and the Miss Summerfest pageant.

Port Lavaca - Calhoun County Chamber of Commerce, P.O. Box 528, Port Lavaca, TX 77979, (512) 552-2959

Kerrville: Hill Country   Texas State Arts and Crafts Fair
May 25-27, 2002   Memorial Day weekend Friday through Sunday

Hundreds of artists and crafters come from all across Texas to gather on the fairgrounds at Kerrville's Schreiner College. This family-oriented event also offers music, food, a laser light show, old-fashioned games, and demonstrations of historic skills and crafts.

Texas State Arts and Crafts Fair, P.O. Box 1527, Kerrville, TX 78029, (512) 896-5711

Ellinger: North Central   May Festival
May 25-28, 2001

The May Festival includes a dance on Friday night, Saturday night, and Sunday during the day, a carnival all three days, homemade pit barbecue pork, beef, and sausage Sunday at noon. Held at the Chamber of Commerce, Highway 71 and FM 2503.

Ellinger Chamber of Commerce, Nancy Hoelscher, 105 East Colorado Sky, Ellinger, TX 78938, (979) 378-2315

Athens: North Central   Texas Fiddlers Contest and Reunion
May 26, 2001

The Texas Fiddlers Contest and Reunion is held on the courthouse square in Athens as a homecoming for many people. In 1932 the Bethel community started staging a countywide fiddlers contest as a climax to a farmers' study course. They're fiddlin' downtown on the Athens Courthouse Square.

Athens Old Fiddlers Association, Mary Ensign, Secretary, 3041 FM 2495, Athens, TX 75751, (903) 675-1859, (903) 675-2325, Fax: (903) 675-6292, mensign@tvcc.cc.tx.us

Dallas: North Central   Artfest
Late May

Artfest includes more than 300 selected artists, continuous live music, and a children's area. Artfest is a Memorial Day weekend tradition, drawing more than 80,000 each year. Events are held at Fair Park.

The 500, Inc., Brent Brown, 11300 North Central Expwy. Suite 415, Dallas, TX 75243, (214) 361-2036, (214) 361-2011, Fax: (214) 361-4703, 500inc@air-mail.net

Killeen: North Central   Festival of Flags and Rodeo
May 26-27, 2001   Memorial Day weekend

Festival of Flags is a festival of fun that brings many worlds together as Killeen celebrates its multinational heritage. Cultural entertainment, wood-carvers, and cowboys fill the weekend with events. Delight yourself with international food, arts & crafts, antique cars, PRCA rodeo, 10K run, military static displays, and much more.

Killeen Special Events Center, Killeen Community Center, W.S. Young Drive, Killeen Festival of Flags, Glenn Morrison, P.O. Box 11159, Killeen, TX 76547-1159, (254) 526-0550, (254) 286-4626, Fax: (254) 526-6090

Lubbock: Panhandle   West Texas "Roots" Music Festival

May 26-27, 2001

Johnny Travis, 3108 Vicksburg, No. 2102, Lubbock, TX 79410, (806) 797-7138, (806) 797-7138

Round Rock: Hill Country   Fiesta Amistad

May 26-27, 2001   Memorial Day weekend

Fiesta Amistad features arts, crafts, and food booths, contests for tortilla spreading, tamale eating, and a menudo cookoff. It's all happening in downtown Round Rock, at the intersection of Main and Lampasas Streets.

El Amistad Club, Andy Martinez, P.O. Box 853, Round Rock, TX 75680-0853, (512) 246-0924, (512) 246-0924, Fax: (512) 246-2708

Houston: Gulf   Houston Downtown Street Festival

May 26-28, 2001

The Houston Downtown Street Festival features live entertainment on six stages including a family stage. This festival salutes the roots of music including blues, rock & roll, jazz, and country from the many cultures and races that make up Houston. Held in the Roots Memorial Square Park, Bell and Clay between Austin and Crawford and on LaBranch between Leeland and Polk, in the area of the park.

Earth Works Productions, Don Schwarzkopf, P.O. Box 8305, Houston, TX 77288, (713) 688-3773, (713) 688-3773, Fax: (713) 688-9617, earthday-texas@juno.com, www.houstondowntownstreetfestival.com

Round Top: North Central   Early Music at Round Top

May 26-29, 2001

Early Music at Round Top features early music groups from Texas that play music written before 1800 on instruments of the period. The festival includes five concerts as well as a guest lecturer. It all happens at Festival Hill at Round Top.

Susan Ferre, 2221 Royal Crest Drive, Garland, TX 75043, (972) 278-2458, Fax: (972) 278-2458, 104247.3404 @compuserve.com

Kingsland: Hill Country — Memorialfest

May 27, 2001

Memorialfest moved in 2000 from Marble Falls to Kingsland, Gary Delz's hometown. We have jet ski races as well as food and art vendors and special events. We welcome all corporate sponsors to support this event. Held in scenic downtown Kingsland, 1 block south of RRs 1431 and 290, on Kingsland Chamber of Commerce grounds.

Gary and Tamara Delz, P.O. Box 1083, Marble Falls, TX 78654, (830) 693-8459, (888) 505-3350, Fax: (830) 693-1821, delzhaus@tstar.net

Houston: Gulf — Robert Earl Keen's Texas Uprising

May 27, 2001

Robert Earl Keen's Texas Uprising is held Memorial Day weekend at the Cynthia Woods Mitchell Pavilion, Pace Concerts, 2000 West Loop South, Suite 1300, Houston, TX 77027, (713) 693-8600, Fax: (713) 693-8649

Somerville: North Central — Stampede Rodeo

May 27-28, 2001

Something for everyone! A rodeo during the day and a dance at night. There is also a small carnival for the kids. There is always plenty of country and rock music. Events take place at Ray Maass' Snook Arena, located on Highway 60.

St. Ann's Catholic Church, Frank Maldonado Jr., P.O. Box 99, Somerville, TX 77879, (979) 596-1966, (979) 596-2697, Fax: (979) 596-2857 www.rtis.com/reg/somerville

Eldorado: Hill Country — World Championship Cowboy Campfire Cooking & Pasture Roping

May 27-28, 2002 — Memorial Day weekend

This festival celebrating the origin of the cowboy features a unique dog barking contest. Attractions include the campfire cookoff, pasture and other roping competition, a fiddler's contest, an art show, and a cocktail party.

Schleicher County Chamber of Commerce, P.O. Box 1155, Eldorado, TX 76936, (915) 853-3109

Camp Cook

My "Cooken" is Like Whiskey,
The Older It Gets, The Tastier It Gets!

Port Arthur: Gulf   **S.A.L.T. Fishing Rodeo**

May 27-29, 2001

The S.A.L.T. Fishing Rodeo features three full days of fishing with huge fish weighed in, inshore and offshore diving, street dancing, arts and crafts, and food. Held at the Sabine Neches Club House on Pleasure Island.

Saltwater Anglers League of Texas, Jean Jourgensen, 3015 Avenue L, Nederland, TX 77627, (409) 722-0865, (409) 722-8784, Fax: (409) 722-1299

Kountze: East   **Southern Gospel & Bluegrass Gospel Singing**

May 28, 2002   **Memorial Day**

Join the fun of singing the old southern gospel songs as you remember your parents and grandparents singing. We will start at 4 P.M. and end much later. Spend Memorial Day weekend with us and let's have a great time. For more information, call (409) 246-2508.

Nacogdoches: East   Nacogdoches Heritage Festival

May 31 - June 3, 2001

The Nacogdoches Heritage Festival is a weeklong event celebrating the city's heritage with a charity ball, golf tournament, tour of homes, arts and crafts, food, and a Taste of Nacogdoches. Held at the Fredonia Convention Center.

Nacogdoches Historical Trust Foundation, Betty Shinn, 3101 Chalon Road, Nacogdoches, TX 75961, (936) 564-7351, (936) 569-9481, Fax: (936) 560-9402, chamber@nactx.com, www.visitnacogdoches.org

June

You ain't herred the Weather "Fer Cast"?

Could this have been the birth of Tuubin' in Texas?

June is here and the sun is ridin' high across the sky during these long hot days. You've probably noticed that more and more of the events have some part of it that is held in or near water: creeks, rivers, streams, bayous, ponds, and of course along the beautiful Gulf Coast.

So now it's time to introduce you non-Texans to something called tubing, or tubin', or toobin', or tuubin'. However you choose to spell it, tubin' is pure Texas fun, and it's cool.

Most of Texas is crisscrossed with waterways of some type. What could be better than combining a good time with staying cool? So Texans started using truck tire inner tubes to float down the river. No big deal, it's been done before. But these folks didn't just want to float; they wanted to take the whole party with them. Soon there were specially designed tubes that accommodated your cold drinks, snacks, and even some to carry your waterproof sound system!

Tubers getting' "saddled up" for a leisurely ride downstream.

Next you string a series of tubes together with a rope, and you just lean back and relax while you drift along in the cool, clear, water.

Soon businesses popped up that would rent you the tubes, send you off down the river, then pick you up several miles downstream and bring you and the tubes back to where you started. Now that's a pretty darn fine way to spend a day.

Tubers enjoy a summer day on the Guadalupe River.

In June Texas history again plays a significant part in the festivals. On June 19, 1865, Union general Gordon Granger read the Emancipation Proclamation in Galveston that belatedly freed the slaves in Texas. The celebration that followed was the first Juneteenth and the birth of what has become a national holiday.

Always double check the dates of the events.

Mesquite: North Central Mesquite Championship Rodeo
April through September, every Friday and Saturday night

From home-cooked barbecue to live Texas music to pro-cowboy competition, the Mesquite Championship Rodeo gives you a full night of real Texas fun—affordably and just 15 minutes from downtown Dallas. Any Friday or Saturday night April through September. Events include bull riding, bronc riding, calf roping, and more.

118 Rodeo Drive, off the Military Parkway exit from I-635. (214) 285-8777, www.mesquitetexas.com

Mesquite Chamber of Commerce, 617 N. Ebrite, Mesquite, TX 75149, (972) 285-0211, www.mesquitechamber.com

Rodeos are a year round Texas tradition. You don't have to look far to find one, like this one in Mesquite. Photo courtesy of the Dallas Convention & Visitors Bureau.

Kerrville: Hill Country Kerrville Folk Festival
May 24 - June 10, 2001 **Last week in May till nearly mid-June**

Allen Damron and Rod Kennedy founded the Kerrville Folk Festival in 1972, and a legend was born. It is the best known of all Texas music festivals. Stretching over 18 days, the festival features more than 120 accomplished international, national, and regional musicians. Held at the Quiet Valley Ranch, 9 miles south on Highway 16.

Kerrville Festivals, Rod Kennedy, P.O. Box 1466, Kerrville, TX 78029, (830) 257-3600, (800) 435-8429, Fax: (830) 257-8680, staff@kerrville-music.com, www.kerville-music.com

Iraan: West — Alley Oop Day

May or June of odd-numbered years

V.T. Hamlin, the creator of the Alley Oop cartoon strip, lived in Iraan, Texas. Enjoy the parade, dance, golf cart races, pet shows, and even a chili cookoff. There's also an arts and crafts fair and live entertainment provided by musicians and dancers.

Iraan Chamber of Commerce, P.O. Box 153, Iraan, TX 79744, (915) 639-2528

Lufkin: East — Neches River Rendezvous

June 1, 2002   **1st Saturday in June**

A 15-mile family canoe trip down the Neches River includes a special spaghetti supper after the event. Starts at the Highway 7 bridge where it crosses the Neches.

Contact Lufkin Convention and Visitors Bureau, 1615 S. Chestnut, Lufkin, TX 75901, (800) 409-5659, lufkintx@lcc.net

El Paso: West — VIVA! El Paso!

From 1st weekend in June through August

Experience four centuries of history in this outdoor musical at the picturesque McKelligan Canyon Amphitheater, El Paso. For more information, call (915) 565-6900. www.viva-ep.org

Itasca: North Central — Annual Itasca Chamber of Commerce BBQ

June 1-2, 2002

Contact: Bob Wilson, (254) 687-2331, www.ribman.com, www.itascatx.com

Teague: North Central — Freestone County Benefit BBQ Cookoff

June 1-2, 2002

Contact: Tom Hanrahan, (254) 379-3116. www.ribman.com

Haskell: Panhandle — Annual Wild Horse Prairie Days Barbecue Cookoff

June 1-2, 2002

Held at City Park, on West U.S. 380. Scott Bingham, (940) 864-3523. www.ribman.com

Buckholts: North Central   Cotton Festival Cookoff
June 1-2, 2002

Jay Beckhusen, (254) 593-4175 (after 8 P.M.). www.ribman.com

Arlington: North Central   Texas Scottish Festival & Highland Games
Early June

This is one of the largest ethnic festivals in North America. Featured are bagpipe bands, dining, storytelling, athletics, children's events, food and drink, vendors and crafts. The all-weather festival site will once again be Maverick Stadium on the University of Texas at Arlington campus.

For more information or for tickets, write to: Texas Scottish Festival & Highland Games: P.O. Box 151943, Arlington, TX 76015, TxScotFest@aol.com.

Littlefield: Panhandle   Summer Festival
June 1-3, 2001

There are arts and crafts, a chili cookoff, a concert on Saturday night by Ricky Lynn Gregg, a midway featuring live music, and a gospel concert on Sunday. Events are held at Lamb County Fairgrounds, on East 17th Street and Highway 385.

For information call Emil Macha, 720 East 14th, Littlefield, TX 79339, (806) 385-3870, Fax: (806) 385-6229

Bryan: North Central   Bryan Bluegrass Music Festival
June 1-2, 2002   1st Saturday and Sunday in June

Bryan Bluegrass Festival is a family event with great music and special events including canoe and sailboat races, horseshoe pitching contest, quilting competition, cowboy poetry, and juried arts competition.

Linda Giffen, Special Events Programmer, 201 East 29th Street, Bryan, TX 77803, (979) 361-3656, (979) 779-5207, Fax: (979) 361-3766, lgiffen@ci.bry-an.tx.us. For more information contact the reservations line at (409) 361-3656, visit the website at www.ci.bryan.tx.us/city, or contact Rodney: rplos@myr-aid.net

Easton: East   Heritage Turnip Greens Festival
June 1-2, 2001

There's a cookoff in Texas for nearly everything. Come on down and help Easton celebrate its favorite vegetable. There's a cookoff, a street dance, a car and truck show, a hoop-it-up contest, carriage rides, a dunking booth, and even a softball tournament. For information call (903) 643-7819

Dallas: North Central   Festival of Arts & Jazz

June 1-3, 2001

Dallas Festival of Arts & Jazz is to become the premiere evening jazz and visual arts festival in downtown Dallas. This festival formerly known as Mandalay, will now present Dallas with jazz in June. Events are held in downtown Dallas and uptown on McKinney Avenue.

Stephen Millard, 2200 North Lamar, Suite 104, Dallas, TX 75202, (214) 855-1881, Fax: (214) 855-1882, mei@meifestivals.com, www.meifestivals.com

Nocona: North Central   Western Swing Weekend

June 1-3, 2001   First weekend in June

The Western Swing Festival is an event celebrating the western swing movement in Texas. The event is held during the 1st weekend of June (Thursday, Friday, and Saturday). This festival takes place at the Benton Amphitheater; food booths are open during the shows.

W.R. Tucker, Route 3, Box 550, Nocona, TX 76255, (940) 825-4425, (940) 825-4425, Fax: (940) 825-4650, wrt@tenet.edu

Yoakum: South   Tom Tom Festival

June 1-4, 2001

The Tom Tom Festival is one of the oldest festivals in the region and features three dances, PRCA Rodeo, barbecue cookoff, old fiddlers contest, carnival, arts and crafts, food booths, and a parade. Yoakum Community Center, 105 Huck Street.

Yoakum Area Chamber of Commerce, Debbie Condel, P.O. Box 591, Yoakum, TX 77995, (361) 293-2309, Fax: (361) 741-6739, infor@yoakumarea-chamber.com

Haskell: Panhandle   Wild Horse Prairie Days

June 1-4, 2001

Wild Horse Prairie Days features cowboy poetry and music, ranch rodeo, calf roping, Queen contest, chuck wagon cookoff, kids rodeo, Sunday church service, and two dances each night (Friday and Saturday). Held at the Haskell County Fair Grounds and Haskell Civic Center.

Abe Turner, 307 North First Street, Haskell, TX 79521, (940) 864-2477, Fax: (940) 864-5617, rturner@westex.net

Levelland: Panhandle   True Value/Jimmy Dean Country Showdown

June 2, 2001

Take the family and cheer the Texas talent. The True Value/Jimmy Dean Country Showdown is part of a national talent search for up-and-coming country performers. Held in the Levelland town square.

Levelland Chamber, Sandy Parker, 1101 Ave. H, Levelland, TX 79336, (806) 894-3157, Fax: (806) 894-4284, levellandcoc@door.net, www.levelland.com/levhome.html

Gatesville: North Central   Shivaree
June 2, 2001

This old-time tradition is a combination of old and new. Shivaree includes an arts and crafts show, antique tractor and engine show, military exhibits, and live bands all day. Local bands provide entertainment. Events are held at the town square and Raby Park, on Highway 84 East.

Gatesville Chamber of Commerce, Kay Smart, Executive Director, P.O. Box 206, Gatesville, TX 76528, (254) 865-2617, Fax: (254) 865-5581, www.ci.gatesville.tx.us

Port Arthur: Gulf   Gulf Coast Jam
June 2, 2001

Great rock music in an outdoor live music concert, which also features R&B, blues, swamp pop music from the '60s and '70s, and the popular sounds of the Gulf Coast regions of Southeast Texas and Southwest Louisiana. Bring your lawn chairs and dancing shoes. Arts and crafts booths and children's activities are also available. Events are held at Pleasure Island Music Park. (409) 722-3699, (800) 235-7822, Fax: (409) 722-2255, triangleconcert@webtv.net, www.portarthurtexas.com

Pasadena: Gulf   Family Festival in the Park
June 2, 2001

Great family fun. This neat festival is held in Strawberry Park. The fun includes pony rides, a petting zoo, amusement activities, crafts, and lots of good food. For information call (713) 948-0322

Livingston: East   Alabama-Coushatta Indian Powwow
June 2-3, 2001

The Alabama-Coushatta Indian Powwow is a two-day festival featuring colorful Indian dancing, arts and crafts show, food booths, and cultural tours providing rare photo opportunities. A gourd dance will precede the grand entry of more than 200 colorfully dressed dancers. Events are held at the Alabama-Coushatta Indian Reservation, which is located 17 miles east of Livingston.

Alabama-Coushatta Powwow Association, Sharon Miller, Route 3, Box 640, Livingston, TX 77351, (936) 563-4391, (800) 444-3507, Fax: (936) 563-4397

Longview: East   AlleyFest

June 2-3, 2001

AlleyFest presents a fes-
tival of music featuring the
best and brightest new stars
performing simultaneously
on two live stages. A wide
variety of sounds include
Cajun, blues, R&B, rock, and
pop. Held in downtown
Longview.

There's plenty to do at the AlleyFest in Longview. Photo courtesy of the Longview Convention & Visitors Bureau. Taken by
Paul Anderson.

One Hundred Acres of
Heritage, Pam Kilfoyle, P.O.
Box 3721, Longview, TX 75606, (903) 237-4000, (903) 237-4040, Fax: (903)
237-4049, lcvb@longviewtx.com, www.longviewtx.com

Lewisville: North Central   SummerBlast

June 2-3, 2001

Something for everyone. Try these on for size, the Old Town Hot Rod
Reunion, the wacky Weenie Dog Races, swap meet, live entertainment, and
Arts & Crafts Festival. Held on Mill Street in Old Town Lewisville.

Fred Herring, (972) 219-3551, fherring@cityoflewisville.com, www.cityof-
lewisville.com

Oakland: North Central   Oakland Fireman's Festival

June 2-3, 2001

Oakland Fireman's Festival includes a 5K fun run, barbecue cookoff, fireworks display, helicopter rides, car show, a parade on Sunday, live music,
dancing, a carnival, games, booths, arts and crafts, food, and a Sunday auction
with a variety of items including collectibles. Held in the town square, on Main
Street and FM 532.

Oakland Volunteer Fire Dept., Susie Jahn, P.O. Box 59, Oakland, TX 78951,
(979) 263-5959, (979) 263-5575

San Antonio: South   Tejano Fest

June 2-3, 2001

Each year Tejano Fest brings true tejano music to town, when the downtown
YMCA sponsors this festival and fajita cookoff. Held at Market Square, at 514
West Commerce.

YMCA San Antonio, Blanche Mendoza, 1123 Navarro Street, San Antonio,
TX 78205, (210) 246-9622, (210) 246-9626, Fax: (210) 246-9638,
http://netscape.digitalcity.com/ sanantonio/music/

Round Rock: Hill Country   Williamson County Old Settlers Celebration
June 2-10, 2001

Get your feet to tappin' at the Williamson County Old Settler's Celebration. Each year this special event includes a bluegrass festival, gospel, country and western music, and a very popular fiddlers contest all over a PA system. Events take place at Old Settlers Park, on Highway 79, east of Round Rock.

Old Settlers Association, Irene K. Michna, P.O. Box 678, Round Rock, TX 78680, (512) 388-1733, www.ci.round-rock.tx.us

Dallas: North Central   Double Extravaganza
June 3, 2001

A great opportunity to hear Texas musicians entertain and to network with other musicians. The talent showcase will include styles ranging from rock/alternative, hip-hop/rap, jazz, Latino, and country. Events are held at Fair Park in Dallas.

Jean Mays, Event Coordinator, P.O. Box 170881, Arlington, TX 76003, (817) 277-7440, (817) 277-7440

Austin: Hill Country   The Texas Toot (was Texas Early Music Festival)
June 3-9, 2001   1st or 2nd week in June

Held twice a year. Also held on the weekend before Thanksgiving.

The Texas Toot is a friendly, student-centered workshop. The setting is Concordia University, a small Lutheran college in the heart of Austin, just north of the University of Texas campus. Instruction will be offered in lute, early harp, viola da gamba, violin band, renaissance double reeds, percussion, and, of course, recorder. For information, contact, info@toot.org

Waco: North Central   Brazos Nights
June 3, 10, 17, 24, July 4, 2001

A whole month of great musical events. Brazos Nights is a musical entertainment series and street dance the whole family will enjoy. Kids will never want to leave the exciting children's area. Events are held at Indian Spring Park, in downtown Waco.

Heather Ray, P.O. Box 2570, Waco, TX 76702, (254) 750-5875, Fax: (254) 750-5782, HeatherR@ci.waco.tx.us, www.brazosnights.com

Fort Worth: North Central   The International Piano Competition for Outstanding Amateurs

June 5-10, 2001   1st week in June

The International Piano Competition for Outstanding Amateurs is open to anyone for whom making music is more than an avocation but less than an occupation.

The International Piano Competition for Outstanding Amateurs., Todd Holmberg, 2525 Ridgmar Blvd., Suite 307, Fort Worth, TX 76116, (817) 738-6536, Fax: (817) 738-6534, clistaff@cliburn.org, www.cliburn.org

Dallas: North Central   Noches Norteñas

June 6, 13, 20, 27, 2002   Thursdays in June and July

Noches Norteñas concert series will feature regional Mexican artists to appeal directly to first generation Hispanics of Mexican and Central American origin. Events are held on Artist Square.

Marcos Rincon, 6060 North Central Expwy., Suite 670, Dallas, TX 75206, (214) 750-0670, Fax: (214) 750-1038, mary@rinconcommunication.com

Levelland: Panhandle   South Plains Opry Celebration

June 6, 13, 20, 27, 2002   Every Thursday in June

SPC's South Plains Opry features an entertainment "best" for an old-timey celebration of July 4th. Activities for the family are provided by the Levelland Main Street program and local nonprofit organizations. Held in downtown Levelland, on the square.

Levelland Chamber of Commerce, Sandy Parker, 1101 Avenue H, Levelland, TX 79336, (806) 894-3157, Fax: (806) 894-4284, levellandcoc@door.net

Grand Saline: North Central   Salt Festival and Rodeo

June 6-10, 2001

The 25th annual Salt Festival and Rodeo begins at the pavilion with breakfast Tuesday morning. Lunch is served Wednesday-Friday with live entertainment. Other activities include Queen's Pageant, talent show, gospel show, arts and crafts show, dances, and games. Held in downtown Grand Saline, which is located on Highway 80.

Folks find a shady spot to watch the beauty pageant. Photo by Sally Gramon.

Grand Saline Chamber of Commerce, Don Latham, P.O. Box 125, Grand Saline, TX 75140, (903) 962-7147

Lewisville: North Central   Sounds of Summer Music Series
June 6 - August 1, 2001

The Sounds of Summer Music Series spotlights local bands from the Dallas and Fort Worth area with a different musical style featured at each concert. Events are held at the Vista Ridge Amphitheater, located at 3049 Lake Vista Drive.

Lewisville Parks Service, Sarah Connell, P.O. Box 299002, Lewisville, TX 75029, (972) 219-3550, Fax: (972) 219-3741, sconnell@cityoflewisville.com, www.cityoflewisville.com

San Antonio: South   Texas Folklife Festival
June 7-10, 2001

The Texas Folklife Festival is put on by the Institute of Texan Cultures. It features the music, food, dancing, crafts, and stories of more than 40 ethnic and cultural groups from around the state.

Institute of Texan Cultures, 801 S. Bowie St., San Antonio, TX 78205-3296, (210) 458-2300, www.texancultures.utsa.edu

Corpus Christi: Gulf   Bay Jammin' Summer Concert Series
June 7 - August 9, 2001   Thursday evenings from early June through early August

The Bay Jammin' Summer Concert Series features concerts (blues, country, jazz, R&B, reggae, rock, and rockabilly) on Thursday evenings from June 7th through August 9th. Held in the Cole Park Anderson Amphitheater, on Ocean Drive.

Chris Barnes, P.O. Box 9277, Corpus Christi, TX 78469-9277, (361) 880-3474, Fax: (361) 880-3864, www.governor.state.tx.us/MUSIC/tmec_june.htm

Andrews: Panhandle   Bluegrass Summerfest
June 7-9, 2002   1st Friday, Saturday, and Sunday in June

The Bluegrass Summerfest will be held at Florey Park, 8 miles north and 2 miles east of Andrews, Texas.

For information contact the West Texas Bluegrass Association, Jim Brown, 8622 Lamar, Odessa, TX 79765, (915) 367-3438, jbrown@caprok.net

Wichita Falls: Panhandle   Red River Rodeo

June 7-10, 2001

Nights of rodeoin' and dancin', queen's contest, bullfights, specially sponsored rodeo nights, wrangler bullfights, and the world's largest calf scramble with over 3,500 prizes given away throughout the nights, and professional acts.

Wichita County Mounted Patrol, Cletus Schenk, 719 Scott Avenue, Suite 1100, Wichita Falls, TX 76301-2616, (940) 322-4411, Fax: (940) 322-5411

Gladewater: East   Roundup Rodeo

June 7-10, 2001

Four great days of rodeo and street dancing. Lots of live music throughout the event. Events are held in downtown Gladewater, at the Rodeo Grounds.

Gladewater Roundup Rodeo Association, Jackie Wood, President, P.O. Box 1409, Gladewater, TX 75647, (903) 845-5501, (903) 845-5586, Fax: (903) 845-6326

Dallas: North Central   Tejano Wednesdays Concert Series in Dallas

June 7, 14, 21, 28, July 5, 12, 19, 26, 2001

The Annual Tejano Wednesdays will provide fun and entertainment for the entire family. Events are held on Artist Square in Dallas, TX.

Marcos Rincon, 6060 North Central Expwy., Suite 670, Dallas, TX 75206, (214) 750-0670, Fax: (214) 750-1038, mary@rinconcommunication.com

Palo Duro Canyon State Park: Panhandle   Texas - A Musical Romance of Panhandle History

June 7 - August 19, 2001

A great musical drama presented in Palo Duro Canyon State Park near Amarillo. Beneath the stars in the Pioneer Amphitheater, Texas unfolds an 1800s tale of the settling of the Texas Panhandle through song, dance, and drama. The professional cast performs in front of a 600-foot cliff while special effects such as a simulated thunderstorm bring life to the scenic canyon surrounding the amphitheater.

The musical drama "Texas" in the natural amphitheater below the 600-foot cliffs in Palo Duro Canyon. Photo courtesy of the Amarillo Convention & Visitor Council.

Texas Musical Drama, Blaine Bertrand, P.O. Box 268, Canyon, TX 79015, (806) 655-2181, (806) 488-2227 (park), Fax: (806) 655-4730, bbertrand@texas-musicaldrama.com

East Bernard: Gulf   Kolache-Klobase Festival
June 8, 2002   2nd Saturday in June

Talk about good eats! This is the place! There are seven polka bands, Czech singers, cloggers, a barbecue chicken and sausage/sauerkraut lunch, hamburgers, a kolache baking contest, arts and crafts, kiddie rides, and much more. Held at the Riverside Hall, on Highway 90-A.

Jason Hlavinka, P.O. Box 452, East Bernard, TX 77435, (979) 335-7907, (979) 335-7318, Fax: (979) 335-4327, http://members.tripod.com/sbcserv/kkfest/

Irving: North Central   Annual Old-Time Fiddlers Contest
June 8, 2001

Whistle Stop Plaza at Rock Island & Main Street, Irving, Texas. Come enjoy an evening of live music and square dance demonstrations at the 6th Annual Old-Time Fiddlers Contest. Contest open to all ages. kdowns@ci.irving.tx.us, (972) 253-9700 or (972) 259-1249

Crosby: Gulf   Annual Fair and Rodeo
June 8-10, 2001

This is an official PRCA sanctioned rodeo, featuring top Nashville entertainers. The fair features many activities for children. Held at the Crosby Fairground, located at FM 2100 in Northeast Harris County.

Wayne Elliott/Bill Busby, 2003 Krenek Road, Crosby, TX 77532, (281) 328-7113, Fax: (281) 328-7113, billbuzzz@earthlink.net

San Antonio: South   Tejano Thursdays Concert Series in
                                     San Antonio
June 8, 15, 22, 29, July 6, 13, 20, 27, 2001

The 5th Annual Tejano Thursdays provide fun and entertainment for the entire family.

Marcos Rincon, 6060 North Central Expwy., Suite 670, Dallas, TX 75206, (214) 750-0670, Fax: (214) 750-1038, mary@rinconcommunication.com, www.rinconcommunications.com

Denton: North Central   The Dog Days of Summer Celebration
June 8, 2002   2nd Saturday in June

Bring your hound to the courthouse lawn for a pooch-filled day of fun. There is a parade for the dogs, stupid pet tricks, and even paw readers, to tell your pet's future. Courthouse-on-the-Square, downtown Denton, 110 W. Hickory. (940) 349-8529

Rogers: North Central — Annual Rogers Roundup Barbecue Cookoff
June 8-9, 2001

Judy Gross, (254) 642-3884. Wayne or Dorothy Glider (254) 642-3399. www.ribman.com

Bandera: Hill Country — Annual Riverfest
June 8-9, 2002 — 2nd weekend in June

Texas fun for the whole family, including the Everything That Floats But A Boat Regatta, "tube roping," kayaking, arts and crafts, and much more.

Bandera City Park, downtown Bandera. (800) 364-3833. www.bandera-cowboycapital.com

Galveston: Gulf — Galveston Caribbean Carnival Festival
June 8-9, 2002 — 2nd full weekend in June

The Annual Caribbean Carnival Festival is a unique celebration of Caribbean culture, food, music, and dance. Also appearing is the three-time limbo champion from Trinidad and Tobago. Held at Harbor House Park, at 21st and Harborside Drive in the Strand-Seaport District.

African American Chamber of Commerce-Galveston County, Recy Dunn, Mary Phillips, P.O. Box 116, Galveston, TX 77553-0116, (409) 763-5700, Fax: (713) 944-1708, caribfest@africanamericanchamber.org, www.galveston-tourism.com

Wink: West — Roy Orbison Festival
June 8-9, 2002 — 2nd weekend in June

This festival is a great tribute to a great musician and musical innovator. Listen to "Pretty Woman" and "In Dreams" under a starlight sky. Held in scenic downtown Wink, on Highway 115.

Wink Chamber of Commerce, Gary Hawkins, P.O. Box 397, Wink, TX 79789, (915) 527-3441, (915) 527-3035, Fax: (915) 527-3303, garylh2@excite.com, www.sunsetpass.com/royorbison-wink/html/festival.htm

Nacogdoches: East — Texas Blueberry Festival
June 8-9, 2002 — 2nd weekend in June

The Texas Blueberry Festival activities include fresh blueberry sales, street entertainers, arts and crafts, petting zoo, pet and doll parades, pageant, and fish fry. Held in historic downtown Nacogdoches, located on Highway 21 East.

Linda Flores, 513 North Street, Nacogdoches, TX 75961, (936) 560-5533, Fax: (936) 560-3920, lflores@nactx.com, www.nacogdoches.org

Montgomery: East — Montgomery Old West Festival

June 8-10, 2001

Nothing like a cattle drive of Texas longhorns through downtown Montgomery. On Sunday there is an authentic cowboy church service. See how cowboys lived in Texas's third oldest town, which includes an Indian village, saloon, gaming parlor, livery stable, and general store. Held in downtown Montgomery, on Highway 105 West and FM 149.

For information call Sue Warman, P.O. Box 55, Montgomery, TX 77356, (936) 449-5604, Fax: (936) 448-6693, brouse0122@aol.com

Greenville: North Central — Hunt County Fair

June 8-16, 2001

The fair includes carnival rides, creative arts competition, cooking demonstrations, craft demonstrations, livestock shows, and two exhibit buildings for commercial displays and sales. Hunt County Fairgrounds, FM 1570 across from E-Systems.

For information call the Greenville Chamber of Commerce, P.O. Box 1055, Greenville, TX 75403-1055, (903) 527-3105, chamber@greenville-chamber.org, www.greenville-chamber.org

Amarillo: Panhandle — Cowboy Roundup USA

2nd week in June

12th annual celebration of cowboy and western heritage featuring the World Championship Chuck Wagon Roundup and the Coors Ranch Rodeo. Kicks off with a cattle drive up downtown Amarillo's main street. Held at the Tri-State Fairgrounds.

For more information, call the Amarillo Convention & Visitor Council at (806) 374-1497. www.amarillo-cvb.org

Houston: Gulf — Texas Music Awards

June 9, 2001

The 2001 Texas Music Awards (TMA) was held Monday, June 5, from 7:30-9:30 P.M. at Texas Southern University's Charles P. Rhinehart School of Music, at 3100 Cleburne Street.

Robert J. Sye, P.O. Box 88106, Houston, TX 77288-0106, (713) 741-6463, (713) 528-1806, tmlrc@aol.com

Irving: North Central — Annual Irving Heritage Festival

June 9, 2001

Irving's Heritage Park will come alive with entertainment on Saturday, with live entertainment, arts & crafts booths, food, children activities, the Lord's Supper Quilt display, an antique car display, and much more! Held at Heritage

Park, which is located at 217 S. Main Street. (972) 253-9700 (972) 259-1249, kdowns@ci.irving.tx.us, www.ci.irving.tx.us

Columbus: North Central　　　　Texas Swing Evening

June 9, 2001

Enjoy the best in Texas swing. Held at the Stafford Opera House Theatre, at 425 Spring Street.

Stafford Opera House, Buddy Rau, P.O. Box 817, Columbus, TX 78934, (979) 732-5135, (877) 444-7339, Fax: (979) 732-5881, ccvb@intertex.net, www.columbustexas.org

Hereford: Panhandle　　　　Town and Country Jubilee

June 9, 2001

The Town and Country Jubilee includes live entertainment, fiddling contests, rodeo, street dance, food, games, jubilee of arts and crafts, quilt show, a softball tournament, beef fajita cookoff, and jubilee 10K, 5K, and fun run. Held at Dameron Park, located on Main Street.

Deaf Smith County Chamber of Commerce, Mike Carr, P.O. Box 192, Hereford, TX 79045, (806) 364-3333, Fax: (806) 364-3342

Lockhart: Hill Country　　　　Chisholm Trail Roundup "Old-Time Fiddlers" Contest

June 9, 2001

The Chisholm Trail Roundup Fiddling Contest features artists from across the state. Events are held in the Main Pavilion at Lockhart City Park.

Lockhart Chamber of Commerce, Don George, P.O. Drawer 840, Lockhart, TX 78644, (512) 398-2818, Fax: (512) 376-2632, lockhartcc@lockhart-tx.org

The music is non-stop at the Chisholm Trail Roundup. Photo by Mike Annas.

They also do a lot of dancin' at the Chisholm Trail Roundup.
Photo by Mike Annas.

Jacksonville: East   Tomato Fest

June 9-10, 2001

The annual Tomato Fest offers loads of great live music and many other festivities. There are sports events and arts & crafts. Held at the Showbarn, on
Loop 456.

Jacksonville Chamber of Commerce, P.O. Box 1231, Jacksonville, TX 75766,
(903) 586-2217, (800) 376-2217, Fax: (903) 586-6944, chamber@jacksonville-
texas.com, www.jacksonville.com

Waller: North Central   Kickback Country Weekend

June 10, 2001

Short and sweet! This is a one-night music festival, held at Yogi Bear's
Jellystone Park in Waller, located off Hwy. 290.

Yogi Bear's Jellystone Park Camp Resort, Virginia Martinez, Route 3, Box
83-A, Hempstead, TX 77445, (979) 826-4111, Fax: (979) 826-4114

Plano: North Central   Picnic in the Park

June 10, 2001

The Plano Picnic in the Park is an admission-free picnic day on an open field
and features a live stage presenting music of various types (blues, country, etc.).
Events are held in Bob Woodruff Park, on the corner of Park and Shiloh.

Dana Conklin, P.O. Box 860358, Plano, TX 75086-0358, (972) 941-7250, Fax:
(972) 941-7182, www.planotx.org/current/event.html

Bremond: North Central   Polski Dzien - Polish Day

June 10, 2001

Polish Day events include a beauty pageant, 5K run, volleyball, arts and crafts booths, parade, Polish food, and music. Held in downtown Bremond, Main Street.

Bremond Chamber of Commerce, Jeanne Wierzicki, P.O. Box 487, Bremond, TX 76629, (254) 746-7636, jaw7252@aol.com

Round Top: North Central   Round Top Festival

June 10 - July 15, 2001

Round Top offers talented young instrumentalists, singers, and conductors an intensive summer program of individual lessons, master classes, and regular performances of the chamber, vocal, and orchestral repertoire. Held at Festival Hill at Round Top, located on Highway 237 at Jaster Road.

Alain G. Declert, Information Director, P.O. Box 89, Round Top, TX 78954-0089, (979) 249-3129, (979) 249-3086, Fax: (979) 249-3100, festinst@fais.net, www.festivalhill.org

Victoria: South   Victoria Bach Festival

June 13-19, 2001

NPR calls this 25-year-old festival "A Texas Treasure." The Victoria Bach Festival commemorates the death of Bach. Held at the Victoria College Fine Arts Auditorium, at 2200 East Red River.

Dorothy L. Welton, Concert Chairman, P.O. Box 3522, Victoria, TX 77903, (361) 575-1375, (361) 572-2787, Fax: (361) 575-5246, info@victoriabach-festival.org, www.victoriabachfestival.org

Holland: North Central   Corn Festival

June 15, 2002   3rd Saturday in June

The Corn Festival in downtown Holland is a full day of fun, games, music, dancing, good eating, and fellowship. The festival includes corncob relays, corn-eating contests, corncob throwing contests, and corn seed spitting contests for all ages. Live country music is provided throughout the day under a large, cool tent. At night a street dance is featured. Held in downtown Holland.

Holland Corn Festival Committee, Betty Hill, P.O. Box 244, Holland, TX 76534, (254) 657-2368, hometown.aol.com/RPERSKY848

Ft. Worth: North Central   Chisholm Trail Blazer

June 15-16, 2001

Held at the Ft. Worth Stockyards. For information call Karen Wayne, (817) 625-7005 or Laura Blount, (817) 485-8785. www.ribman.com

Stonewall: Hill Country

June 15-16, 2002

Nothing sweeter than Hill Country peaches, and there is a rodeo, parade, dance, bareback riding, calf roping, ladies jackpot barrel racing, team roping, kids calf scramble, clowns, peach pie and cobbler baking contests, barbecue, children's entertainment, peach show and auction, and live music. Held at the Stonewall Chamber of Commerce grounds, located on Highway 290 in Stonewall, at 250 Peach Street.

Mary Lou Klein, P.O. Box 1, Stonewall, TX 78671, (830) 644-2735, www.fredericksburg-texas.com/events.htm

Stonewall Peach Jamboree

3rd weekend in June

In downtown Stonewall a banner announces the Peach Jamboree & Rodeo. Photo by Sally Gramon.

Bowie: North Central

June 15-16, 2002

Jim Bowie Days

3rd weekend in June

The Jim Bowie Days has family activities, a terrapin race, frog jumping contest, quilt show, dance, and a rodeo. Events are held in Pelham Park, at FM 3043 and Pelham Street.

Nan Park, P.O. Box 84, Bowie, TX 76230, (940) 872-2822, www.menard-texas.com/mentxcal.html

Fort Worth: North Central

June 15-17, 2001

Chisholm Trail Roundup

This festival includes the Tarrant County Fair, chuck wagon cooking contest, live pig and armadillo races, gunfights, arts and crafts, a trail ride, Comanche Honor Dance, fiddlers contest, grand parade, barbecue cookoffs, street dances, and continuous musical entertainment. Held at the Fort Worth Stockyards, at 131 East Exchange Avenue.

Chris Farkas, President, P.O. Box 4815, Fort Worth, TX 76164-0815, (817) 625-7005, Fax: (817) 625-4036, ctru@chisholmtrail.org, www.chisholmtrail.org

Houston: Gulf

June 16, 2001

June Bug Jamboree

More fun for the whole family, but with a special emphasis on the little friskers. There is a Bugs of June costume contest, BBQ dinner, and live music to dance to. Held at the Knights of Columbus Hall, at 607 E. Whitney. Information: (713) 694-2341

San Antonio: South   Father's Day Celebration
June 16, 2002

The Father's Day Celebration features live entertainment, food, drink, and plenty of other activities. Held at Rosedale Park, located at 340 Dartmouth.

YMCA San Antonio, Blanche Mendoza, 1123 Navarro Street, San Antonio, TX 78205, (210) 246-9622, Fax: (210) 246-9638, www.governor.state.tx.us/MUSIC

Dallas: North Central   Dallas International Festival
June 16-17, 2001

Over 120 communities come together on July 14 at the Morton H. Meyerson Symphony Center and Artist Square in the Dallas Arts District through world music performances, ethnic food, dance, and crafts. Held in downtown Dallas, the Morton H. Meyerson Symphony Hall and Annette Strauss Artist Square in the Arts District.

Dallas International, Anne Weiss-Armush, 16114 Red Cedar Trail, Dallas, TX 75248, (972) 458-7007, (972) 701-0548, Fax: (972) 458-1974, aweiss@airmail.net, www.dallasinternational.com

Ingram: Hill Country   Texas Heritage Music Jazz Festival
June 17, 2001

Cool summertime jazz at the Point Theater Outdoor Pavilion.

Texas Heritage Music Foundation, Kathleen Hudson, P.O. Box 1945, Kerrville, TX 78029-1945, (830) 367-3750, Fax: (830) 367-4888, khudson@schreiner.edu, www.texasheritagemusic.org

Different location each year   Texas State Bluegrass Festival
June 18-22, 2002   **3rd week in June (Tuesday through Saturday)**

Love that bluegrass. This year held at the Trades Day Park.

Pat Conrad, 1004 Bonham Street, Paris, TX 75460, (903) 785-5394, Fax: (903) 739-2000, patc@neto.com

Fort Worth: North Central   Juneteenth Celebration
June 19, 2002

This annual festival kicks off with a parade in downtown Fort Worth and daylong activities downtown, near the Fort Worth/Tarrant County Convention Center. For more information call: 1-800-433-5747. www.eventguide.com/dfw

Waco: North Central   Juneteenth Celebration

June 19, 2002

Juneteenth Celebration events include a parade, arts and crafts, talent show, live entertainment, gospel show, baby contest, trade show, style show, Mrs. Juneteenth Contest, Miss Jr. Juneteenth Contest, booths, and fundraisers. Held at the East Waco Community Center, at 409 Turner Street.

Heart of Texas Black Chamber, Ida N. Pinkard, P.O. Box 1485, Waco, TX 76703, (254) 756-0933, Fax: (254) 756-3733

Corsicana: North Central   Music in the Park at Fullerton-Garrity
                                  Amphitheater

June 20, 27, 2002   Thursdays in late June and early July

Great music for the family on Thursday evenings at Fullerton-Garrity Park Amphitheater, at 3201 McKnight Lane.

Navarro Council of the Arts, Sylvia Rodriguez Bonin, Director, P.O. Box 2224, Corsicana, TX 75151-2224, (903) 872-5411, Fax: (903) 872-2100, www.ci.corsicana.tx.us

Kilgore: East   Texas Shakespeare Festival

June 21 - July 22, 2001

For fifteen years the students and faculty at Kilgore College have put on Shakespeare's plays every summer. Don't miss some fine performances.

Raymond Caldwell, Artistic Director. Texas Shakespeare Festival, 1100 Broadway, Kilgore, TX 75662-3299, (903) 983-8117, (903) 983-8601, Fax: (903) 983-8124, info@texasshakespeare.com, www.texasshakespeare.com

Luling: Hill Country   Luling Watermelon Thump

June 21-24, 2001

A classic Texas festival that's been getting better for 48 years! The Luling Watermelon Thump features the World Championship Seed-Spitting contests with cash prizes. Street dances with live entertainment as well as contests, arts and crafts, carnival, kiddie rides, and more. Events are held in downtown Luling, at 421 East Davis Street.

Sundown at the Luling Watermelon Thump. Photo by Sally Gramon.

Luling Watermelon Thump Association, Trey Bailey, P.O. Box 710, Luling, TX 78648, (830) 875-3214, Fax: (830) 875-2082, thump@bcsnet.net, www.bcsnet.net/lulingcc/chamber.html

Watermelons were the theme of the day at the Thump. Photo by Sally Gramon.

Temple: North Central   World of Texas Championship BBQ
June 22-23, 2001
Michelle Hunt, (254) 298-5415. www.ribman.com

Fort Griffin: Panhandle   Fort Griffin Fandangle
June 22-23, 29-30, 2002   Last 2 weekends in June
The *Fort Griffin Fandangle* is an outdoor musical based on the pioneer chronicles of West Texas. Tom Perini, renowned cowboy cook from the Perini Ranch, will be preparing chuck wagon dinners on the courthouse lawn. Events are held at the Prairie Theatre.

Fort Griffin Fandangle, Debbe Hudman, P.O. Box 155, Albany, TX 76430, (915) 762-3838, Fax: (915) 762-3125, www.albanytexas.com

Navasota: North Central   Navasota Blues Festival
June 22-23, 2001
Come enjoy the musical heritage of the Navasota area. The event is held Friday and Saturday with blues bands and dances in the evenings. Held at the VFW Hall, located at West Highway 105.

Navasota Blues Festival, Mary K. Crawford, P.O. Box 1633, Navasota, TX 77868, (936) 825-6600, (800) 252-6642, Fax: (936) 825-8013, www.rtis.com/reg/navasota

Temple: North Central   Pioneer Day

June 23, 2001

Pioneer Day is a daylong program of live entertainment honoring the people who have lived in Central Texas for more than 50 years. Pioneer Day has been celebrated since 1932. Held at the Mayborn Civic Center, located at 3303 North Third.

Temple Daily Telegram, Steve Walters, P.O. Box 6114, Temple, TX 76503, (254) 778-4444, tdt@vvm.com, www.ci.temple.tx.us

Whitehouse: East   Yesteryear Festival & Celebration

June 23, 2001

Honoring the community's rich history, this small town near Lake Tyler has a parade, lots of good food, and other neat events.

Dale Moran, (903) 839-6785, sitemaster@thatcompany.com, www.white-housetx.com

Sealy: North Central   Summer Polka Festival

June 23-24, 2001

The Summer Polka Festival features a polka mass, held 3:30 Saturday afternoon at the Knights of Columbus Hall, 1310 Highway 90 West.

Knights of Columbus Council #3313, B.J. Stolarski, P.O. Box 1133, Sealy, TX 77474-1133, (979) 885-6370, (979) 885-6786, kofc3313@usa.net

Lubbock: Panhandle   Lubbock Summer Jazz Festival

June 26, 2001

This wonderful festival spotlights Texas jazz artists. Events are held in Hemmle Recital Hall, at 18th Street and Boston Avenue.

Texas Tech Jazz Department, Alan Shinn, P.O. Box 42033, Lubbock, TX 79409-2033, (806) 742-2270 ext. 256, Fax: (806) 742-2294, nzads@ttacs.ttu.edu, www.texastech.edu

Rowlett: North Central   Festival of Freedom

June 28-30, 2001

A great salute to freedom in this great land. The festival features live music (classical, country, and rock), arts and crafts, games, carnival, petting zoo, fireworks displays, skydivers, hot-air balloons, 5K run, military flyovers, and street dances. Held at the Pecan Grove Park and Rowlett Community Centre at 5300 Main Street.

City of Rowlett, John Godwin, P.O. Box 99, Rowlett, TX 75030-0099, (972) 412-6140, (972) 412-6293, Fax: (972) 412-6118, www.ci.rowlett.tx.us/events/events.htm

Pecos: West   Night In Old Pecos/Cantaloupe Festival

June 29, 2002   Last Saturday in June

A one-day event that takes place in the evening hours from 6 P.M. till midnight. The streets are blocked off and there is wide range of activities, which include a street dance with live music and a variety of vendors. Held in downtown Pecos.

For more information, call (915) 445-2406. Held annually the last Saturday of June, www.pecostx.com/annualevents.htm or www.pecos.net/news/pages/rodeowk.htm

San Antonio: South   Freedom Fest

June 29 - July 1, 2001

This is an annual family-style celebration, featuring a mariachi music festival, street dancing, children's activities, and a traditional Fourth of July Parade on Commerce Street with marching bands. Held at El Mercado on Market Square, at 500 West Commerce.

La Villita Tortillas, Inc., Sylvia Larios, 4706 Paradise Woods Street, San Antonio, TX 78249-1821, (210) 207-8600, (210) 227-9189, www.governor.state.tx.us/MUSIC/tmec_june.htm

Austin: Hill Country   Austin Summer Chamber Music Festival

June 30 - July 21, 2001

Held in conjunction with the Chamber Music Workshop, this festival features such activities as all-day chamber music coaching, piano ensembles, lecture presentations, sessions on jazz composition and improvisation, and special sessions for adult groups. Evening performances are held at venues all over Austin.

Austin Chamber Music Center, Felicity Coltman, 4930 Burnet Road, Austin, TX 78756, (512) 454-7562, (512) 454-7562, Fax: (512) 454-0029, felicity@austinchambermusic.org, www.austinchambermusic.org

July

We pick these
"hybrid 'maters"
while they are small!!

S ince the time of the Alamo, patriotism has always been a Texas tradition. We are proud of our state, our country, and our country-state. As a group we are fierce defenders of the Constitution, despite our feelings about the skills of our elected officials.

In Texas it is unlawful for any jurisdiction to keep an elected official from attending a legislative session. So more than once we've had an official in jail somewhere who had to be let out to attend the legislative session. Then they return to jail to resume serving their sentence. Why we've even had a couple of these rascals that were re-elected for another term, while they were sitting in jail! What a state!

Every town in Texas with more than two dogs in it puts on a 4th of July celebration of some sort. Wherever you hang your hat, you aren't far from a parade, barbecue or chili cookoff, horseshoe toss, washer toss, and some sort of fireworks show. They put balloons on the tractors and a bandana on Rover, and things just start to happen. All over these small towns you can smell the cooks preparing their entries for the cookoff competition. Meanwhile old iceboxes or watering troughs are filled with iced down watermelons.

And in the bigger towns you will find that the events also include rodeos, livestock shows, and carnivals. Don't miss the chance to have a bunch of fun while celebrating this nation's birth.

SPECIAL NOTE: Have a great time but do be careful with the fireworks. They can be dangerous to handle. Also keep in mind that this is the dry season, and it doesn't take much to start a grass fire. So be extra careful while you're having fun.

Always double check the dates of the events.

Mesquite: North Central   Mesquite Championship Rodeo

April through September, every Friday and Saturday night

From home-cooked barbecue to live Texas music to pro-cowboy competition, the Mesquite Championship Rodeo gives you a full night of real Texas fun. Any Friday or Saturday night April through September. Events include bull riding, bronc riding, calf roping, and more.

118 Rodeo Drive, off the Military Parkway exit from I-635. (214) 285-8777, www.mesquitetexas.com

Seguin: South   Freedom Fiesta

Celebrated in early July

This fiesta features two dances each night for the three-day event. Country and western, tejano, and blues bands will by playing. There will be food booths, family entertainment, and arts and crafts with a large carnival on the grounds. The event is held at Max Starcke Park East under the large pecan trees next to the Guadalupe River in downtown Seguin.

Seguin Area Chamber of Commerce, Carol Artz, 427 North Austin, Seguin, TX 78155, (830) 379-6382, www.seguintx.org

Corpus Christi: Gulf   Bay Jammin' Summer Concert Series

June 7 - August 9, 2001   **Thursday evenings from early June through early August**

The Bay Jammin' Summer Concert Series features concerts (blues, country, jazz, R&B, reggae, rock, and rockabilly) on Thursday evenings from June 7th through August 9th. Held in the Cole Park Anderson Amphitheater, on Ocean Drive.

Chris Barnes, P.O. Box 9277, Corpus Christi, TX 78469-9277, (361) 880-3474, Fax: (361) 880-3864, www.governor.state.tx.us/MUSIC/tmec_june.htm

El Paso: West   VIVA! El Paso!

From 1st weekend in June through August

Experience four centuries of history in this outdoor musical at the picturesque McKelligan Canyon Amphitheater, El Paso. For more informat, call (915) 565-6900. www.viva-ep.org

Dallas: North Central   Tejas Storytellers Summer Conference

Early July

www.tejasstorytelling.com

BBQ, barbeque, or barbecue, however you spell it, the fajitas, brisket, and ribs are great! Photo courtesy of the Dallas Convention & Visitors Bureau.

Sulphur Springs: North Central   Independence Day Symphony on the Square

July 1, 2001   Weekend of or just prior to Independence Day

Join us on the square in downtown Sulphur Springs for a celebration in old-fashioned style, a program of marches and patriotic favorites by the North East Texas Symphony Orchestra. When darkness falls the sky erupts in a blaze of colors as fireworks light up the sky over the historic Hopkins County Courthouse. Admission: free, bring your lawn chair! For more information: (888) 300-6623

Houston: Gulf   Celtic Midsummer Festival

July 1, 2001

Garden in the Heights will host the Celtic Harvest Festival, featuring lively Celtic music and dance with performances. The event will also feature traditional Highland games, Celtic food, drink, and crafts. Garden in the Heights, one block north of Memorial and two blocks west of Waugh.

Michael Martin, 3926 Feagan, Houston, TX 77007, (713) 880-1065, (713) 908-2536, Fax: (713) 880-1586, www.underwayproductions.com/Celtic/CMS

Woodville: East   Bluegrass and Gospel

July 1, 2001

Don't miss the jammin' bluegrass and gospel music. There will also be the world famous Pickett House Restaurant on the grounds, 1840-1920 early East Texas farming village with railroad museum, wagon museum, 1860 country store, and more. Held at the Woodville Heritage Village Museum, on Highway 190 West.

Ofeira A. Gazzaway, P.O. Box 888, Woodville, TX 75979, (409) 283-2272, (800) 323-0389, Fax: (409) 283-2194

Rockport: Gulf   Arts Festival

July 1-2, 2001

This fun festival features fine arts, plenty of food, and a variety of music, including jazz, blues, folk, classical, country, and pop. Held at the waterfront in the Ski Basin Area, located at 902 Navigation.

Mary Lucille Jackson, 902 Navigation Circle, Rockport, TX 78382-2780, (361) 729-5519, Fax: (361) 729-3551

Clarendon: Panhandle   Saints Roost Celebration

July 1, 3-4

Saints Roost Celebration includes a guitar pickers contest, western dances, rodeos, arts and crafts fair, parade, and reunions. Held at the Clarendon Outdoor Entertainment Arena.

Ken Shelton, President, Route 1 Box 47, Clarendon, TX 79226, (806) 874-3837, (806) 874-3709

Kingsland: Hill Country   Aqua-boom Celebration

July 1-4, 2001

Aqua-boom Celebration is an annual Fourth of July celebration including arts and crafts booths, land and water parades and activities, personal watercraft timed events, ski show, fireworks, puppet shows, and various types of live music all day. Held at the Kingsland Chamber Grounds, on Highway 1431.

Kingsland/Lake LBJ Chamber of Commerce, Sharon Bowen, P.O. Box 465, Kingsland, TX 78639, (915) 388-6211, Fax: (915) 388-0615, kchamber@ptstar.net

Belton: North Central   God and Country Concert

July 2

The God and Country Concert begins at 3 P.M. The First Baptist Sanctuary Choir and Fort Hood bands feature a musical celebration of God's blessing on our nation. Held at the Bell County Expo Center, on Loop 121 and IH 35.

First Baptist Church, Larry Putman, 506 North Main Street, Belton, TX 76513, (254) 939-0705, Fax: (254) 939-2141

Austin: Hill Country   Cactus Pear Music Festival

July 2-16

Summer chamber music is one of the best ways to relax and beat the heat, and Austinites can do just that when artists from the Cactus Pear Music Festival return for two cooling evenings. Jessen Auditorium in Rainey Hall, UT Campus across from Dobie Mall.

Stephanie Sant'Ambrogio, 403 Stone Wood, San Antonio, TX 78216, (210) 824-5377, (512) 477-6060

Bedford: North Central   City of Bedford 4thFest

July 3-4, 2001

On July 3rd the city of Bedford hosts two concerts, followed by the first of two firework shows. An annual parade, carnival, roving entertainment, and another live concert, followed by the largest fireworks show in North Texas. It all takes place at 2801 Forest Ridge Drive. Call (817) 952-2222 ext. 514, or visit www.ci.bedford.tx.us.

Canyon Lake: Hill Country   4th of July Festival

July 3-4, 2001

Family games and fun, including a kid wash, dunking booth, kiddy games, horseshoes, bingo, and more. Held at the Startzville Field of Dreams Ball Park. For information call (830) 899-7500.

Snyder: Panhandle   Fourth of July Celebration

July 3-4, 2001

Fourth of July Celebration includes an early morning prayer breakfast with gospel music. Other activities include local quartets or groups, patriotic music, a parade, food booths, craft show, sports contests, carnival, fireworks, and a street dance featuring country music. Held at Towle Memorial Park on South College Avenue.

Snyder Chamber of Commerce, Donna Fowler, P.O. Box 840, Snyder, TX 79550, (915) 573-3558, Fax: (915) 573-9721, alvincvb@alvintexas.com, or www.alvintexas.com

Brookshire: Gulf   Fourth of July Freedom Celebration

July 3-4, 2001

Fourth of July Freedom Celebration features live music, arts, crafts, barbecue cookoff, and games, including a volleyball tournament.

Brookshire Convention Center, Fourth of July Freedom Celebration, P.O. Box 459, Brookshire, TX 77423, (281) 934-2465, (281) 375-5298

Lubbock: Panhandle   4th on Broadway Celebration

July 3-4, 2001

4th on Broadway Celebration is a daylong event that includes seven sound stages showcasing West Texas talent and an evening performance by the Lubbock Youth Symphony Orchestra and a choreographed fireworks show. Broadway Avenue is transformed into a festival atmosphere that includes live music, cowboy poetry, a parade, exhibitions, games, and a variety of foods.

Broadway Festivals, Inc., Stephanie Allison, P.O. Box 1643, Lubbock, TX 79408, (806) 749-2929, Fax: (806) 749-3237, sallison@hub.ofthe.net, www.hub.ofthe.net

Grand Prairie: North Central   July Fourth Celebration

July 3-4

The July Fourth Celebration features arts and crafts, exhibits, bounce houses, food, and live music (country, R&B, jazz, rock) prior to the fireworks display at dusk. Held at Lone Star Park, at 1000 Lone Star Parkway.

Grand Prairie Convention and Visitors Bureau, 2170 North Beltline Road, Grand Prairie, TX 75050, (972) 263-9588, Fax: (972) 642-4350

Lampasas: Hill Country   Spring Ho Festival

July 3-9, 2001

A great festival includes two street dances with live country bands at the courthouse square, Gospel Night, and a talent show at W.M. Brook Park, 200 arts and crafts vendors at the park, grand parade, kid's day, barbecue cookoff, carnival, county fair, 10K and 1-mile run. Held on the courtyard square and W.M. Brook Park.

Lampasas Spring Ho Festival, Connie Cummings, P.O. Box 985, Lampasas, TX 76550, (512) 556-5301, (512) 556-5301, Fax: (512) 556-5301

Village of San Leanna: Annual 4th of July Parade and Picnic
Hill Country

July 4, 2002

A beautiful little Texas village salutes its veterans and our nation. This happens to be where Rancho Gramon is located. Come on by, I'll see you there. Held in the Village Park.

Dan LaFleur (512) 282-2126

Glen Rose: North Central   Independence Day Parade / Tractor Pull

4th of July weekend

A tractor parade and a tractor pull, welcome to Texas. Crafts, booths, artists, and musicians bring the town square in Glen Rose to life. Call (254) 897-3081. www.texasoutside.com/glenrose/calendar.html

Sulphur Springs: North Central   Hopkins County Independence Day and
Fireworks Show

4th of July weekend

The Independence Day Concert and Fireworks Show features a rousing patriotic concert presented by the Northeast Texas Symphonic Orchestra, followed by an inspiring fireworks display.

Bill Elliott, P.O. Box 347, Sulphur Springs, TX 75483, (903) 885-6515, (888) 300-6623, Fax: (903) 885-6516, chamber@sulphurspringstx.com

Sanderson: West   July Fourth Old-timers Reunion
4th of July weekend

Old-fashioned, small town, West Texas Fourth of July celebration on the courthouse square. A barbecue, dance, live music (tejano & country), rodeo roping, softball tournament, arts and crafts booths, and fireworks create an all-American feeling.

Terrell County, Terry Tex Toler, P.O. Drawer 4890, Sanderson, TX 79848, (915) 345-2275, (915) 345-2275, Fax: (915) 345-2653, cactuscapital@sandersontx.net, www.sandersontx.net

Leakey: Hill Country   July Jubilee
4th of July weekend

The July Jubilee features a parade, fiddling contest, a rodeo, a street dance, mariachi bands, square dancers, and arts and crafts on the courthouse square.

Frio Canyon Chamber of Commerce, Linda Hassell, P.O. Box 743, Leakey, TX 78873, (830) 232-5222

Freeport: Gulf   Annual Fishing Fiesta
4th of July weekend

Fishing and fun on the Texas coast. Fisherman are drawn to this tournament from all over the Southwest in the hopes of catching the biggest snapper, amberjack, or any other fish. Activities center around the Freeport Municipal Park, Brazosport Blvd. Call (409) 233-3306 or (409) 235-3356.

Brady: Hill Country   July Jubilee Celebration
4th of July weekend

The July Jubilee Celebration features a carnival at Richards Park, downtown parade, and a street dance on Saturday night. The street dance is usually held around the east side of the courthouse square at Richards Park, located at Memory Lane.

Brady/McCulloch County Chamber of Commerce, 101 East First Street, Brady, TX 76825, (915) 597-3491, Fax: (915) 597-2420

Garland: North Central   Star-Spangled Fourth
4th of July weekend

This festival was the 1999 winner of the Bronze Grand Pinnacle award for Event Of The Year from the International Festivals and Events Association. Each year Garland salutes the Fourth with a star-spangled party and street festival. Held in Historic Downtown Garland, Fifth Street and Main.

Star-Spangled Fourth, Donna Basham, P.O. Box 469002, Garland, TX 75046, (972) 205-2632, (972) 205-2807, Fax: (972) 205-2504, dbasham@ci.gar-land.tx.us

Stamford: Panhandle   Texas Cowboy Reunion

4th of July weekend

The classic events of the rodeo, including some unique to the TCR (wild cow milking, wild mare race), get underway nightly at the beautiful SMS ranch. Ranchers, cowboys, and those interested in western preservation return each year to the TCR Poetry Gathering to celebrate the history of the American cowboy. Events are held at the Texas Cowboy Reunion Grounds on Business Loop 277.

Texas Cowboy Reunion, Gary Mathis, P.O. Box 928, Stamford, TX 79553, (915) 773-3614, Fax: (915) 773-3278, www.tcrrodeo.com/index.htm

Whooooops!

Some cowhands have a
coupla' more thing to learn!

Wharton: Gulf   Wharton County Freedom Festival

4th of July weekend

Wharton County Freedom Festival, Wharton County's first official Independence Day celebration, features antique, food, and craft booths. Live entertainment pauses only for a fireworks spectacular around 9:15 P.M. Music is as rich and diverse as the country's heritage: country, rock, blues, tejano, patriotic, gospel, and soul. Held on Monterrey Square in downtown Wharton.

Wharton Chamber of Commerce, Monica Fraker, P.O. Box 866 ~ 225 North Richmond, Wharton, TX 77400, (979) 532-1862, (979) 532-1862, Fax: (979) 532-0102, wchamber@whartontexas.com

Grand Prairie: North Central   Lone Stars and Stripes

4th of July weekend

The Lone Stars and Stripes Festival features music, arts and crafts, children's activities, games and contests, a gigantic fireworks show, and thoroughbred horse racing. Held at Lone Star Park at Grand Prairie, 1000 Lone Star Parkway.

City of Grand Prairie - Parks and Recreation - Lone Star Park. Doug Beich, Special Events Supervisor, 326 West Main Street, Grand Prairie, TX 75053, (972) 237-8112, (972) 237-8112, Fax: (972) 237-8267, dbeich@ci.grand-prairie.tx.us

The Woodlands: Gulf   Red HOT & Blue Festival

July 4, 2002

Come enjoy the parade and fireworks. 1-800-207-9463

The beautiful Cynthia Woods Mitchell Pavilion hosts many great events in The Woodlands. Photo courtesy of the Greater Montgomery County Convention & Visitors Bureau.

Stephenville: North Central   Family Fun Fair
July 4, 2002

Family Fun Fair is an old-time Independence Day celebration, held in City Park, with all-day activities for all age groups. The day ends with a gigantic fireworks display.

Stephenville Chamber of Commerce, 298 West Washington, Stephenville, TX 76401, (254) 965-3864, Fax: (254) 965-3814

Belton: North Central   Festival on Nolan Creek
July 4, 2002

The Festival on Nolan Creek features arts and crafts, food, fiddlers contest, carnival, and local musical entertainment. PRCA Rodeo in the air-conditioned Bell County Expo Center at 8 P.M. Events held at Confederate Park and Yettie Polk Park, IH 35 exit 294A.

Belton Chamber of Commerce, Linda Hatcher, P.O. Box 659, Belton, TX 76513, (254) 939-3551, Fax: (254) 939-1061, beltoncoc@vvm.com, www.beltontxchamber.com

Deer Park: Gulf   Fourth Fest
July 4, 2002

Fourth Fest will features great live music (rock and oldies), then a super fireworks display. Events held at Deer Park Activity Center, 500 West 13th Street.

Deer Park Parks and Recreation Department, Charlie Sandberg, P.O. Box 700, Deer Park, TX 77536, (281) 478-2050, Fax: (281) 479-8091, csandberg@deerparktx.org, www.deerparktexas.com

Mesquite: North Central   Fourth Fest and Fireworks
July 4, 2002

The Fourth Fest and Fireworks begins at 4 P.M. Country, rock, and Christian concerts are at 6 P.M. and 8 P.M. and fireworks beginning at 9:15 P.M. Events are held at Paschall Park.

Mesquite Chamber of Commerce, Terry McCullar, P.O. Box 850115, Mesquite, TX 75185-0115, (972) 285-0211, Fax: (972) 285-3535

Alvin: Gulf   Fourth of July Celebration
July 4, 2002

The celebration begins at 5 P.M. with live patriotic music and fireworks at 9:15 P.M. Held at the Alvin Community College at 3110 Mustang Road.

City of Alvin, Don Cramer, 216 West Sealy, Alvin, TX 77511, (281) 388-4299

Brownfield: Panhandle   **Fourth of July Celebration**

July 4, 2002

The Fourth of July Celebration features food booths and live country entertainment at Terry County Park with fireworks.

Brownfield Chamber of Commerce, Jamie Greenfield, P.O. Box 152, Brownfield, TX 79316, (806) 637-2564, Fax: (806) 637-2565

Del Rio: West   **Fourth of July Celebration**

July 4, 2002

The Fourth of July Celebration in Del Rio is held on the banks of the San Felipe Creek at the county fairgrounds. The beautiful amphitheater is cut into the side of a hill and surrounded by musicians, food, and game booths. In the evening the stage is lit up by performances of the community jazz band and local entertainers, and closes with a fireworks display. Held at the San Felipe Creek Amphitheater/Fairgrounds, City of Del Rio Parks Dept.

Rafael Castillo, Jr., P.O. Box 4239, Del Rio, TX 78841-4239, (830) 774-8558, Fax: (830) 774-8542

Wheeler: Panhandle   **Fourth of July Celebration**

July 4, 2002

Wheeler's 4th of July Celebration is reminiscent of old-fashioned celebrations like our grandparents enjoyed. The entire town joins in on the fun. The celebration features all-day entertainment, food booths, activity booths, punt, pass and kick, fun run, tug of war, and a first-class fireworks display. Held at the City Park, at 7th and Grove.

Wheeler Chamber of Commerce, Kathy Hill, P.O. Box 221, Wheeler, TX 79096, (806) 826-3408, Fax: (806) 826-3219

Beaumont: Gulf   **Fourth of July Celebration on the Neches River**

July 4, 2002

Fourth of July Celebration on the Neches River offers local musical groups performing and a concert by the Beaumont Symphony Orchestra. The orchestra will perform aboard a barge anchored in the Neches River as the audience savors the music from the park's grassy knoll. At 9 P.M. fireworks explode in the sky in conjunction with the Symphony's "1812 Overture." Held at Riverfront Park, at 701 Main Street (at the rear).

Beaumont Civic Center, Claudie Hawkins, P.O. Box 3827, Beaumont, TX 77704, (409) 838-3435, (800) 782-3081 ext. 204, Fax: (409) 838-3715, bookings@beaumont-tx-complex.com, www.beaumont-tx-complex.com

Dalhart: Panhandle   Fourth of July Fireworks Display

July 4, 2002

The Fourth of July Fireworks Display features food and game booths and music beginning at 6 P.M. with fireworks at dusk. Held at Lake Rita Blanca on FM 281.

Dalhart Chamber of Commerce, P.J. Pronger, P.O. Box 967, Dalhart, TX 79022, (806) 249-5646, Fax: (806) 249-4945, chamber@dalhart.org, www.dalhart.org

Denton: North Central   Fourth of July Jubilee

July 4, 2002

The Fourth of July Jubilee features the Yankee Doodle Parade at Carroll Courts building at 10 A.M. Other events include live entertainment, horseshoe tournament, craft show and sale, and free carnival games for the kids. Events take place at the Civic Center Park at 321 East McKinney.

Denton Parks and Recreation Department, Teresa Salazar, 321 East McKinney, Denton, TX 76201, (940) 349-8289, Fax: (940) 349-8384, tmmilan@cityofdenton.com

Arlington: North Central   Fourth of July Parade and Celebration

July 4, 2002

This cool 4th celebration features five Arlington high school bands, several choirs, and floats that include live or recorded music. The parade has 150 entries and begins at 9 A.M. The Arlington Civic Band plays at the main review stand located at City Hall. Held in downtown Arlington.

Arlington Fourth of July Association, Frances Foster, P.O. Box 1776, Arlington, TX 76004-1776, (817) 469-9447, (817) 460-7532, Fax: (817) 654-1888, jstiebin@dhc.net

Orange: East   Freedom Festival

July 4, 2002

The Annual Freedom Festival features the Orange Community Band performing before the fireworks. Cajun band Creole Cooking performs at the street dance after the fireworks display. Held in downtown Orange, at 300 Front Avenue.

The Orange Leader, Ray Trahan, P.O. Box 1028, Orange, TX 77631-1028, (409) 883-3571, Fax: (409) 883-6342, www.pnx.com/Orange/events.htm

Friendswood: Gulf   Fourth of July Celebration

July 4, 2002

The 103rd Friendswood Fourth of July Celebration (nation's longest) includes a parade, games, concerts, fireworks, food, and games. Held at Mustang Stadium, at 701 Greenbriar Stadium. ·

Jon Branson, 910 South Friendswood Drive, Friendswood, TX 77546-4856, (281) 996-3220, fwdcs@iwl.net, www.friendswood-chamber.com

Jefferson: East   Jefferson Salutes America Fourth of July Celebration

July 4, 2002

A great 4th of July celebration that begins at 4 P.M. with fireworks at 9:30 P.M. Activities include live music, cake and pie auction, horseshoe tournament and games, local music acts, and the Shreveport Municipal Concert Band. Held at Otstott Park and Riverfront.

Jefferson Salutes America, George Otstott, P.O. Box 665, Jefferson, TX 75657, (903) 665-7777, Fax: (903) 665-3300, www.jeffersontx.com

Lamesa: Panhandle   July Fourth Celebration

July 4, 2002

July 4th Celebration in Lamesa is a daylong event with arts and crafts, food, clothing sales, book sale, jewelry sales, basketball and volleyball tournaments, and live entertainment. Music includes country, square dancing, Christian, banjo pickin', and more. A large fireworks display at dusk rounds off the activities. Held at Forest Park, which is located at Highway 137 and South Ninth Street.

Lamesa Chamber of Commerce, P.O. Box 880, Lamesa, TX 79331, (806) 872-2181, http://www.pics.net/~lamesaedc/communit.html

Lufkin: East   July Fourth Celebration

July 4, 2002

This July Fourth Celebration includes a volleyball tournament, concert, fireworks, arts and crafts, and concessions. Held at Ellen Trout Park, located at 402 Zoo Circle.

Civic Center, Trevor North, P.O. Drawer 190, Lufkin, TX 75902, (936) 633-0250, Fax: (936) 634-8024

Comfort: Hill Country   July Homecoming

July 4, 2002

The Fourth of July Homecoming celebration features a parade, and barbecue will be served at the City Park. Games for the children, food, and arts and crafts booths will be located throughout the park. To round out a full day of activities, an Independence Day dance, with live country music, will be held at the Comfort City Park Pavilion, located on Highway 27.

Comfort Chamber of Commerce, Melinda McCurly, P.O. Box 777, Comfort, TX 78013, (830) 995-3131, (830) 995-3141, Fax: (830) 995-5055

Denton: North Central   Kiwanis Fireworks Show

July 4, 2002

The Kiwanis Fireworks Show features live tejano and kids' music, fireworks, door prizes, car shows, and a ballet folklorico. Held at Fouts Stadium, at the University of North Texas.

Denton Kiwanis, Bill Drybread, 1701-A North Elm, Denton, TX 76201, (940) 387-6323, dfw.citysearch.com/E/E/DALTX/0215/40/24/cs1.html

Luckenbach: Hill Country   Willie Nelson's Fourth of July Picnic

July 4, 2002

Willie Nelson's Fourth of July Picnic features performances by Willie and friends and family, with over 25 bands. Held in scenic downtown Luckenbach.

VelAnne Howle, 412 Luckenbach Town Loop, Luckenbach, TX 78624, (830) 997-3224, Fax: (830) 997-1024, somebody@luckenbachtexas.com, www.luckenbachtexas.com

Dallas: North Central   Old-Fashioned Fourth of July

July 4, 2002

Another old-fashioned 4th celebrates our national independence with an all-join-in-parade and patriotic rally. Live entertainment will be supplied by volunteer groups playing patriotic music and performing traditional folk dances. Games and races fill out this family day. Held at the Old City Park, located at 1717 Gano.

Dallas County Heritage Society, Nancy Farina, 1717 Gano, Dallas, TX 75215, (214) 421-5141 ext. 128, Fax: (214) 428-5361, jbransom@airmail.net

San Marcos: Hill Country   Summerfest

July 4, 2002

Summerfest is an old-fashioned celebration that takes place at Sewell Park featuring fun for families with live music, food booths, and activities as well as fireworks in the evening. Held at Sewell Park, at University Drive.

Summerfest Committee, Cliff Caskey, 630 East Hopkins, San Marcos, TX 78666, (512) 393-8430, Fax: (512) 353-7273

Port Aransas: Gulf   Larry Joe Taylor's 4th of July
                            Island Time Festival

July 4, 2002

Larry Joe Taylor's 3rd Annual 4th of July Island Time Festival in Port Aransas, Texas. Roberts Point Park, Port Aransas, TX.

Larry Joe Taylor, Route 4, Box 212-AA, Stephenville, TX 76401, (254) 968-8505, (254) 968-8505, ljt@2-cool.com, www.larryjoetaylor.com

Waco: North Central   4th On The Brazos

July 4, 2002

Fireworks and festivities celebrate the 4th. This is the grand finale to the month-long Brazos Nights festival. Events are held at 100 S. University Parks.

Dr. Heather Ray, P.O. Box 2570, Waco, TX 76702, (254) 750-5980. Fax: (254) 750-5782, HeatherR@ci.waco.tx.us, www.ci.waco.tx.us

Ladonia: North Central   Frontier Days

July 5-8, 2001

Frontier Days events include a rodeo, square dance, and gospel singing.

Ladonia Chamber of Commerce, P.O. Box 44, Ladonia, TX 75449, (903) 367-7216

Levelland: Panhandle   Early Settlers Festival

July 6, 2002   Held annually the Saturday after July 4th

Celebrating nearly 40 years, the Early Settlers Festival draws some 15,000 people to enjoy country, bluegrass, and tejano music performances, old settler activities, more than 50 food booths, games, horseshoes, activities for kids, and a parade that lasts an hour or more. Sponsored by the Levelland Area Chamber of Commerce. Held downtown on the square, Avenue H. For information call (806) 894-3157.

Austin: Hill Country   Zilker Summer Musical

July 6 - August 12, 2001

A wonderful Austin tradition, the annual Zilker Summer Musical is a live Broadway-caliber musical performed under the stars in historic Zilker Park. The musical is the longest running event of its type in the United States today. Held in the lovely Zilker Park Hillside Theater, on Barton Springs Road.

Zilker Theatre Productions, Randall J. Storm, P.O. Box 180222, Austin, TX 78718-0222, (512) 479-9491, rstorm@zilker.org, www.ci.austin.tx.us/dougherty/hillside.htm

Levelland: Panhandle   Hockley County Early Settlers Reunion

July 7, 2001

Hockley County Early Settlers Reunion is a full day of entertainment, food, games, exhibitors of arts and crafts and all kinds of items, horseshoe and washer pitch tournament, quilt show and raffle, dog show, stick horse races, parade, and a street dance. Events are held at the Levelland City Park.

Levelland Chamber of Commerce, Roy Alexander, 1101 Avenue H, Levelland, TX 79336, (806) 894-3157, (806) 894-2228, Fax: (806) 894-2220, levellandcoc@door.net, www.levelland.com

Mason: Hill Country   Jaycee Roundup Weekend

July 7-8, 2001

The Roundup Weekend features a parade on Saturday, arts and crafts fair on the courthouse lawn, rodeo both nights at Fort Mason Park, a dance both nights at the dance slab in the park, queen contest, storytelling, fiddlers contest. Held at Fort Mason Park Arena and Dance Slab, which is 1 mile south of Mason on Highway 87.

Mason Jaycees, Gloria Nebgen, P.O. Box 211, Mason, TX 76856, (915) 347-6759, (915) 347-5927, Fax: (915) 347-6607

Overton: East   Overton Bluegrass Music Festival

July 7-8, 2001

The festival features the finest in bluegrass and gospel music in a beautiful outdoor setting. Events are held at Overton City Park, on Highway 850 at Lakeshore Drive.

Charles Gardner, Drawer D, Overton, TX 75684, (903) 834-3171, (903) 834-3171, Fax: (903) 834-3174, gsmith@ci.overton.tx.us, www.ci.overton.tx.us

Dallas: North Central   The West End's Taste of Dallas

July 7-8, 2001

A fun and FREE outdoor festival featuring three stages of music, cultural performances, and children's performers. Fun for the whole family. Held in the West End Historic District, at 301 North Market.

Alliance for the West End, Dianne Vaughn, 2200 North Lamar, Dallas, TX 75202, (214) 741-7180, (214) 741-7185, Fax: (214) 741-7184, dv@dallas-westend.org, www.dallaswestend.org

Bridgeport: North Central　　　Butterfield Stage Days

July 8, 2001

Butterfield Stage Days features a variety of activities, including 75 arts and crafts booths, games, contests, carnival rides, stagecoach rides, swimming contests, vintage car display, dance, Old West shootouts, horseshoe pitching, domino tournament, bingo, dunkin' booth, and much more. Held at the Harwood City Park, at the Highway 114 bypass.

Bridgeport Chamber of Commerce, Ann Scott, P.O. Box 1104, Bridgeport, TX 76426, (940) 683-2076, Fax: (940) 683-3969, codec@wf.net, www.bridgeport-tx.com

Tulia: Panhandle　　　　　　Swisher County Picnic Celebration

July 9-14, 2001

The Swisher County Picnic Celebration features a carnival lasting the entire week at downtown square, a junior rodeo, professional rodeo, dances featuring live music, and a kiddie parade followed by a larger parade Saturday morning. Held at Connor Park, Swisher County Showbarns, Downtown Area, Highway 86.

Swisher County Activities Association, Rhoda Rogers, Treasurer, P.O. Box 603, Tulia, TX 79088, (806) 995-3726, (806) 995-2296

Jacksonville: East　　　　　　Tops in Texas Rodeo

July 12-15, 2001

Tip-top Texas rodeo action. The Tops in Texas Rodeo is a PRCA Rodeo and features top country entertainment. Held at Jacksonville Rodeo Arena on College Avenue.

Jacksonville Rodeo Assoc., Bob Campbell, P.O. Box 1856, Jacksonville, TX 75766, (903) 586-5451, (903) 586-7164, Fax: (903) 586-7266

Round Rock: Hill Country　　　Frontier Days

July 13-14, 2002　　　　　　　　2nd weekend in July

Down home partying takes place at the site of the famous shootout between outlaw Sam Bass and the law. The event is complete with a reenactment of the shootout, a frog-jumping contest, hands-on demonstrations of butter-churning, whittling, soap making, and other pioneer skills. Great fun for the kids. There is plenty of food, live music, and fun for the whole family.

Old Settlers Park, Round Rock, Texas, (512) 255-5805

Hare: Hill Country　　　　　　Annual Hare BBQ

July 13-14, 2001

Call Fernando for the information, (512) 862-3270, www.ribman.com

Longview: East   Great Texas Balloon Race

July 13-15, 2001

This is a sporting and music event. Eighty of the best balloon pilots in the country compete for $30,000 prize purse and $50,000 Key Grab. Events are held at Gregg County Airport.

Great Texas Balloon Race, John Green, 1618 Judson Road, Longview, TX 75601, (903) 757-2468, Fax: (903) 758-2965, greenad@iamerica.net, www. greattexasballoonrace.com

Balloons light up night sky during the Great Texas Balloon Race in Longview. Photo courtesy of the Longview Convention & Visitors Bureau. Taken by Paul Anderson.

Glen Rose: North Central   Mays' Bluegrass

July 13-15, 2001

Mays' Bluegrass Festival features pickin' under the stars at Oakdale Park with bluegrass fiddlers, carousel, and open stage. Held at the Oakdale Park, Highway 144 South.

Scott May, P.O. Box 548, Glen Rose, TX 76043, (254) 897-2321, www.texasoutside.com/glenrose/calendar.html

San Antonio: South   Conjunto Shootout

July 13-15, 2001

The San Antonio Conjunto Shootout features more than 25 bands going head to head in a competition to benefit the Southwestern Bell YMCA's youth programs. Events are held at Market Square, on West Commerce Street.

YMCA San Antonio, Blanche Mendoza, 1123 Navarro Street, San Antonio, TX 78205, (210) 246-9626, Fax: (210) 246-9638, sanantonio.citysearch.com

Weatherford: North Central   Parker County Peach Festival

July 14, 2001

The Parker County Peach Festival features a country fair atmosphere with continuous live entertainment. Events are held on the courthouse square.

Weatherford Chamber of Commerce, Adrienne Taylor, P.O. Box 310, Weatherford, TX 76086, (817) 594-3801, (888) 594-3801, Fax: (817) 594-1623, info@weatherford-chamber.com, www.weatherford-chamber.com

Addison: North Central   Spikefest

July 14-15, 2001

This is the largest amateur grass volleyball tournament in the country. There are men's, women's, and co-ed teams competing in skill levels ranging from beginners to the "Take No Prisoners" division. Call 1-888-3VOLLEY. www.spikefest.com

Elgin: North Central   Western Days

July 19-21, 2001

Elgin Western Days features a parade, rodeo, cooking fair, fiddling contest, needlework contest, Miss Western Days contest, carnivals, golf tournaments, a rodeo, street dancing, kiddie parade, arts and crafts, live entertainment, and much more for five full days of fun. Events are held in Elgin Memorial Park.

Elgin Chamber of Commerce, Patricia Parkhill, P.O. Box 408, Elgin, TX 78621, (512) 285-4515, www.elgintx.com

Fredericksburg: Hill Country   A Night in Old Fredericksburg

July 20-21, 2001

A Night in Old Fredericksburg features German music, horseshoe and washer pitching, cloggers, folk dancers, and the best food in the Hill Country, including our famous Opa's sausage. Oompah bands perform Saturday afternoon and night. The event also offers an arts and crafts show, children's entertainment, and the Polka Capital of Texas Polkafest. Held in the downtown Market Square.

Fredericksburg Chamber of Commerce, Peggy Crenwelge, 106 North Adams Street, Fredericksburg, TX 78624-4204, (830) 997-6523, Fax: (830) 997-8588, pegcoc@ktc.com, www.fredericksburg-texas.com

Garland: North Central   Annual Charity Bar-B-Que Cookoff

July 20-21, 2001

Good food and a good cause. Held at Hella Temple, at 2121 Rowlett Road. The proceeds benefit the Shrine Hospital for Children. For information contact John Lloyd, 1158 Hwy. 78 S., Farmersville, TX 75442, (972) 784-7231, www.ribman.com

Austin: Hill Country   Austin Songwriters Conference

July 21-23, 2001

I've been a member of the Austin Songwriters Group for years. If you like music I guarantee you will have a great time. This is their annual Austin Songwriters Conference and is a great opportunity for songwriters to meet, network, participate in songwriting workshops, song and lyric evaluation, instruction, pitch-a-thons, and to get your songs heard by industry professionals.

Austin Songwriters Group, Reneé French, P.O. Box 2578, Austin, TX 78768, (512) 442-8863, (979) 277-9591, Fax: (512) 347-9044, asginfo@aol.com

Fort Worth: North Central   Gran Fiesta de Fort Worth
July 21-23, 2001

The free-to-attend event is a three-day outdoor celebration of Latin music, art, and cuisine. A major concert stage features continuous musical entertainment and performing arts. Theater, dance, and puppet performances take place under large colorful tents and on outdoor stages. Events are held on Main Street, in downtown Fort Worth.

Stephen Millard, 2200 North Lamar, Suite 104, Dallas, TX 75202, (214) 855-1881, Fax: (214) 855-1882, mei@meifestivals.com

Salado: North Central   Salado Legends-Outdoor Musical Drama
July 21, 28, August 4, 2001

The Tablerock Festival of Salado promotes the arts in Central Texas. *Salado Legends* is an outdoor musical drama portraying the Scottish settling of Salado and Central Texas. The play serves as a record of life in America at the end of the 20th century. Original music by ten Texas award-winning composers and musicians. Features singers from all over Central Texas. Held at Tablerock Amphitheater, on Royal St.

Tablerock Festival of Salado, Jackie Mills, President, P.O. Box 312, Salado, TX 76571, (254) 947-9205, Fax: (254) 947-5269, tablerock1@aol.com

Salado Legends is a wonderful show. Shown here, Mark Gunter, Sheri Price, and Seth Foster, during the show. Photo by Salado.

In another scene from the play, Dave Jackson as Tonweya. Photo by Salado.

Decatur: North Central   Wise County Old Settlers Reunion
July 23-28, 2002

The Wise County Old Settlers Reunion is for those who own camps. The ones who don't own camps are invited to enjoy the music, and the children can enjoy the carnival. The activities are only at night. Held at Joe Wheeler Park, on Highway 511 South.

Wise County Reunion Committee, Cyndi Fernihough, P.O. Box 203, Decatur, TX 76234, (940) 627-7090, Fax: (940) 627-1003, chalet@ntsw.net, www.decaturtx.com

Clute: Gulf   Great Texas Mosquito Festival
July 25-27, 2002   Last Thursday, Friday, and Saturday in July

Things are buzzing at the Great Texas Mosquito Festival. Activities include live entertainment, a mosquito calling contest, 5K fun run, barbecue and fajita cookoffs, horseshoe and volleyball tournaments, a carnival, and a variety of both food and arts and crafts booths. Also featured are fun contests for youth and adults. Variety of entertainment including country, old rock and roll, blues, and tejano. It all happens at the Clute Municipal Park, at 100 Park View Drive.

City of Clute, Dana Pomerenke, P.O. Box 997, Clute, TX 77531, (979) 265-8392, (800) 371-2971, Fax: (979) 265-8767

Bonham: North Central   Kueckelhan Rodeo
July 26-29, 2001   Last week of July

Country stars light up the rodeo on Wednesday and Thursday nights. Approved by CRRA and UPRA. Held on the Kueckelhan Ranch, on Route 3 in Bonham.

Haynes Kueckelhan, Route 3, Box 186, Bonham, TX 75418, (903) 583-5337, (903) 583-5337, Fax: (903) 583-5337

Moulton: South   Moulton Town & Country Jamboree
July 27-28, 2001

Held in downtown Moulton. Gussie Machalec, (361) 596-4034, www.ribman.com

Uvalde: Hill Country   Sahawe Indian Dancer's Summer Ceremonials
July 27-28, 2002   Held for 50 years, the last weekend of July

The Sahawe Indian Dancers, members of Boy Scout Troop and Venture Crew 181 from Uvalde, annually present their summer ceremonials the last part of July. The fast-moving colorful dances of the Plains and Southwest Pueblo Indians are set against a backdrop of tepees to set the mood for the performance. Held at the Sahawe Outdoor Theater, which is 1 block south of U.S. 90. For more information, call (830) 278-2016.

Indian ceremonial dance. Photo by Javier Cortez.   An Indian dancer in full cere-
                                                          monial costume. Photo by
                                                          Javier Cortez.

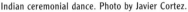

Amarillo: Panhandle   Mobeetie Bluegrass Festival

July 27-29, 2001

This is a great three-day bluegrass music jamboree with stage shows as well as "shade-tree pickin'" around the campsites. Events are held at the Old Mobeetie Jail Museum.

Panhandle Bluegrass & Old Tyme Music Association, Reno DeLeon, P.O. Box 31042, Amarillo, TX 79120, (806) 259-0708, Fax: (806) 622-2808, helion@arn.net

Medina: Hill Country   Texas International Apple Festival

Jul 28, 2001   Last Saturday in July

An annual festival to celebrate wonderful Texas apples. Gallons of ice-cold apple cider, apple pie, and apple pizza will be on hand. Tours of apple orchards. Arts and crafts and live entertainment on six stages. Entertainment includes a children's stage, gospel music stage, fiddling competition, main performance stage, storytelling stage, and special entertainment stage. It all happens down-town on the Medina River, at 113 Broadway.

Genie Strickland, P.O. Box 125, Medina, TX 78055, (830) 589-7224, Fax: (830) 589-2715, mtcd@indian-creek.net

Knox City: Panhandle   Watermelon Festival

July 28, 2001

A great way to beat the Texas heat. It features a golf tournament, horseshoe pitching, sand volleyball tournament, fiddling contest, street dance, radio con-trolled cars, food booths, watermelon slices, music, watermelon sculpting contest, and watermelon-eating contest. Held at City Park on 200 South Third & Fourth Streets.

Knox City Chamber of Commerce, Doris Crownover, P.O. Box 91, Knox City, TX 79529, (940) 658-3442, Fax: (940) 658-3442

Wallis: South   Old-Time Fun Festival

July 28-29, 2001

Come join the fun. Events are held in the American Legion Hall, on Legion Road.

Wallis Chamber of Commerce, Mark Walger, P.O. Box 610, Wallis, TX 77485, (979) 478-6362, (979) 478-6578

Moulton: South   Town and Country Jamboree

July 28-30, 2001

Folks gather from far and wide for the Town and Country Jamboree. The activities include a barbecue, chili and bean cookoffs, dances, carnival, and parade as well as a variety of country, modern, and polka bands. You will also find arts and crafts, food booths, softball, basketball, and volleyball tournaments. Events are held in the City Park, at 102 Veterans Drive.

Moulton Chamber of Commerce, Mark Zimmerman, P.O. Box 482, Moulton, TX 77975, (361) 596-7205, Fax: (361) 596-7075, moultontexas@gvec.net, www.mobeetie.com

August

Folks, It's Hot!!

Don't let it get around, but it gets hot in Texas. Not sultry, toasty, uncomfortable, or unpleasant. HOT!!! We're talking cooking-eggs-on-the-sidewalk hot! In August we have to let up on the outdoor activities a bit, unless they are down by the water. There are a number of arenas that can accommodate rodeos, livestock shows, and concerts indoors and away from the sun. The other way to beat the heat is to hold events in the evening.

Rodeoing is a longstanding tradition in Texas. Originally, the contests were just the everyday skills the cowboys used on the ranch. Riding, roping, and breakin' broncs were part of the average workday of the cowhands. Farm critters are cantankerous and can be dangerous. These skills were necessary to get the job done and survive.

That tradition lives on with today's cowboys, who have a vital role in keeping this nation well fed. Riding and roping are rights-of-passage for youngsters growing up on a ranch. Don't miss the chance to check out a rodeo near you and see some of these skills firsthand.

TIP: Most of these rodeoing folks are good as gold and would be happy to show you a little about what they do. If you get to the arena a couple of hours before the show, the folks are often there and willing to chat. Maybe you can learn the proper technique for tossin' a loop.

And, always double check the dates of the events.

El Paso: West   VIVA! El Paso!

From 1st weekend in June through August

Experience four centuries of history in this outdoor musical at the picturesque McKelligan Canyon Amphitheater, El Paso. For more information, call
(915) 565-6900. www.viva-ep.org

Mesquite: North Central   Mesquite Championship Rodeo

April through September, every Friday and Saturday night

From home-cooked barbecue to live Texas music to pro-cowboy competition, the Mesquite Championship Rodeo gives you a full night of real Texas
fun—affordably and just 15 minutes from downtown Dallas. Any Friday or Saturday night April through September. Events include bull riding, bronc riding,
calf roping, and more. 118 Rodeo Drive, off the Military Parkway exit from
I-635, (214) 285-8777, www.mesquitetexas.com

Corpus Christi: Gulf   Bay Jammin' Summer Concert Series

June 7 - August 9, 2001   **Thursday evenings from early June through
                                       early August**

The Bay Jammin' Summer Concert Series features concerts (blues, country,
jazz, R&B, reggae, rock, and rockabilly) on Thursday evenings from June 7th
through August 9th. Held in the Cole Park Anderson Amphitheater, on Ocean
Drive.

Chris Barnes, P.O. Box 9277, Corpus Christi, TX 78469-9277, (361)
880-3474, Fax: (361) 880-3864, www.governor.state.tx.us/MUSIC/tmec_
june.htm

Quitman: East   Old Settlers Reunion

August 1-5, 2001

The Old Settlers Reunion features bluegrass, country, and gospel music.
Activities include fiddling contests, talent contests, singing contests, a carnival,
bingo, and dunkin' booth during the four-day event. Tuesday night is Kid's
Night at the carnival. Held at Governor Hogg Quitman City Park, at 518 South
Main.

Old Settlers Reunion Association, Clent Tucker, 506 Puckett, Quitman, TX
75783, (903) 763-2971, (903) 763-2971, www.lakeforkresources.com/quit-
man.html

Dalhart: Panhandle   XIT Rodeo and Reunion, Rita Blanca Park

August 2-4, 2001

A PRCA rodeo and a reunion for cowboys, most from the XIT Ranch, which
at one time was the largest ranch in Texas (3 million fenced acres!!). Activities

also include storytelling, dances, pony-express races, and parades. Held at the Rita Blanca Lake.

XIT Rodeo and Reunion, Inc., Seth Ralston, P.O. Box 966, Dalhart, TX 79022, (806) 249-5646, (806) 384-3333, www.dalhart.org/xitrodeo.html

Schulenburg: North Central   Schulenburg Festival
August 3-5, 2001

The Schulenburg Festival includes country, polka, and tejano music, a chili cookoff, 5K fun run, a great parade, volleyball and softball tournaments, and arts and crafts. A sampling of other popular events include horseshoe pitching, egg tossing, cow chip tossing, and homecoming class reunions. Held at Wolter's Park, at South Bohlmann Avenue.

Schulenburg Festival Association, Roger Blaschke, Entertainment Director, P.O. Box 115, Schulenburg, TX 78956, (979) 743-4126, Fax: (979) 743-4760, tblaschke@hotmail.com, ww.schulenburgfestival.org

Plano: North Central   Picnic in the Park
August 4, 2001

Fun for the family. Held at Bob Woodruff Park, on the corner of Park and Shiloh.

City of Plano Parks and Recreation Department, Dana Conklin, P.O. Box 860358, Plano, TX 75086-0358, (972) 941-7250, Fax: (972) 941-7182, www.planotx.org/current/event.html

Houston: Gulf   Celtic Harvest Festival and Highland Games: Lughnassadh
August 5, 2001

The Celtic Harvest Festival features lively Celtic music and dance. Held in the Garden in the Heights, one block north of Memorial and two blocks west of Waugh.

Michael Martin, 3926 Feagan, Houston, TX 77007, (713) 880-1065, (713) 908-2536, Fax: (713) 880-1586, www.underwayproductions.com/Celtic/LUGH

Conroe: East   Montgomery County PRCA Pro Rodeo
August 6-8, 2001

Don't miss the fun of watching the pros in action. (936) 760-1666.

DeLeon: North Central   Peach and Melon Festival
August 7-11, 2001

The Peach and Melon Festival has a carnival, old-time fiddlers contest, a tractor pull, arts and crafts, a 42 tournament, dances, a talent show, and a parade. There is a bike ride known as the Melon Patch Tour, which is held

Saturday every year of the festival (500 attendance). Held downtown and the Festival Grounds, on Highway 6.

De Leon Peach and Melon Festival, Inc., Betty Terrill, P.O. Box 44, DeLeon, TX 76444, (254) 893-6600, Fax: (817) 893-3702, deleontexas.com/festival

Amarillo: Panhandle   August Lights Arts Festival

August 10-11, 2002   2nd weekend in August

More than 30 artists open their studios at the Las Tiendas Art Colony in Amarillo for a weekend festival. Sponsored by the Arts Committee of the Amarillo Chamber of Commerce, this festival includes food, drink, and activities for the kids. Held at Las Tiendas, 6666 W. Amarillo Blvd., Amarillo, TX 79106. For information call (806) 373-7800.

Hitchcock: Gulf   Good Ole Days Barbecue Cookoff and Festival

August 10-11, 17-18, 2001

The Good Ole Days Barbecue Cookoff and Festival features live entertainment, carnival, crafts, beauty pageant, and a streetdance on Friday with barbecue judging on Saturday. The cookoff is August 10-11, the festival 17-18. Don't miss the country, blues, Cajun, polka, and Latin music. Held at the Good Ole Days Park, located at 8300 Highway 6.

Hitchcock Chamber of Commerce, Harry Robinson, P.O. Box 389, Hitchcock, TX 77563, (409) 986-9224, Fax: (409) 986-6317, c.leonard52@aol.com, www.freightlines.com

Fall Creek Vineyards: Hill   Fall Creek Grape Stomp

August 10, 17, 2002   2nd and 3rd Saturdays of August

Stompin' and a squishin'. This Hill Country vineyard opens its doors for two days in August (11 to 5) and allows folks to come in and stomp some grapes just for the fun of it. Don't miss learning how a winery works and this very special between-the-toes experience. Fall Creek Vineyards, two miles north of Tow, on FM 2241 in Llano County, (512) 476-4477, www.fcv.com

Lewisville: North Central   Texas Open Chili Cookoff

August 11, 2001

The Texas Open Chili Cookoff features a chili tasting, entertainment, country music, singing contests, a car show, arts and crafts show, and more than 250 chili cooks plus RV and watercraft show. Held at Lake Park.

City of Lewisville Parks Service, Sarah Connell, P.O. Box 299002, Lewisville, TX 75029, (972) 219-3550, Fax: (972) 219-3741, sconnell@cityoflewisville.com, www.cityoflewisville.com

Henderson: East   Sacred Harp Singing Convention

August 11-12, 2001

Sacred Harp is a historic form of Christian folk music sung in four-part harmony without musical accompaniment. Sitting in a hollow square, facing each other, the singers sing with a power and involvement that is unmatched by any other type of singing. Held at the Henderson Community Center on South High Street.

Emmie and John Morris, 8023 CR 374 South, Henderson, TX 75652, (903) 657-0306, Fax: (903) 657-0329

Fort Stockton: West   Harvest Fest

August 12, 2001

Harvest Fest features fun for the entire family, including live country and tejano music, games, tournaments, arts and crafts, food and more. There is even a street dance. Held at Rooney Park, on South Highway 285.

Harvest Fest Committee, Elsa Sloan, P.O. Box 1357, Fort Stockton, TX 79735, (915) 336-2541, Fax: (915) 336-6107

The partyin' doesn't have to slow down in the summer, you just move it over under the trees. Notice all of the available tables are in the sun.

Alvarado: North Central   Pioneers and Old Settlers Reunion

August 14-19

The Pioneers and Old Settlers Reunion events include the parade and queen contest Monday, the baby contest Tuesday, a musical Wednesday, a country and western band Thursday, a fiddler contest Friday, and a country and western band Saturday. There is a large carnival on the midway all week. Held at the Reunion Pavilion and Grounds, located at 111 Reunion Drive.

Reunion Association, Otis A. Lane, P.O. Box 217, Alvarado, TX 76009, (817) 790-6667

Flatonia: North Central   Prazka Pout and Praha Feast

August 15, 2001

The Prazka Pout welcomes Czechs from Texas and around the U.S. to celebrate with food, games, and live polka music throughout the day. Held at St. Mary's Church in Praha, TX, FM 1295 off U.S. 90, 2 mi. east of Flatonia.

St. Mary's Parish-Praha, Louis Barta, 821 FM 1295, Flatonia, TX 78941-5016, (361) 865-3560, www.schulenburgchamber.org

Johnson City: Hill Country   Blanco County Fair and Rodeo
August 16-18, 2001

Old-fashioned fair and rodeo featuring a livestock show, arts and crafts, food and baked goods booths. Dances on Friday and Saturday night with live country music. Held at the Blanco County Fairgrounds, ½ mi. north on Highway 281.

Blanco County Fair & Rodeo Association, Howard Dufner, P.O. Box 485, Johnson City, TX 78636, (830) 868-7684, (830) 868-4542, www.johnsoncity-texas.com (hyphen is included in website address)

New Boston: East   Pioneer Day
August 16-18, 2001

Pioneer Days includes arts and crafts, live entertainment, fiddling contests, gospel choirs, street dances, and games. There is also a four-wheeler mud race, a petting zoo, carnival, dunking booth, pony rides, gyros, a parade, and much, much more. Held downtown on the square, on Main Street.

New Boston Chamber of Commerce, Max Jones, 220-A West U.S. Highway 82, New Boston, TX 75570-2810, (903) 628-2581, Fax: (903) 628-2581, nbchamb@flash.net

Taylor: Hill Country   Taylor International Barbecue Cookoff and Rodeo
August 17-18, 2002   **3rd weekend of August**

Serious barbecuein' and rodeoin' in a beautiful town. The folks come from all over the countryside and sleep with their rigs on Friday night, as they prepare for the Saturday competition. Magic, mystical recipes are used for cooking all sorts of meats. All this is done to the accompaniment of live music. Meanwhile there are topnotch rodeo cowboys performin' in the nearby arena. Held at Murphy Park, (512) 352-1988, www.taylorchamber.org

Denton: North Central   North Texas State Fair and Rodeo
August 17-25, 2001

Fun for all at the North Texas State Fair includes an old-timers fiddlers contest, rodeo, chili and barbecue cookoffs, games, livestock show, commercial exhibits, carnival, rodeo dances, live entertainment, beauty pageant, pet show, amateur photography contest, children's art contest, and more. Held at North Texas State Fairgrounds, 2217 North Carroll Blvd.

North Texas State Fair Association, Ken Burdick, P.O. Box 1695, Denton, TX 76202, (940) 387-2632, Fax: (940) 382-7763, www.northtexasstatefair.com

Pleasanton: South   Cowboy Homecoming Celebration

August 18-19, 2001

The Cowboy Homecoming Celebration starts on Thursday with county team roping. Friday morning features the Cowboy Breakfast, rodeo, queen's coronation, Working Cowboy of the Year Presentation, and induction into the Cowboy Hall of Fame. Saturday's activities include a parade, chili cookoff/CASI sanctioned, food, arts and crafts, darling contest, children's stick horse rodeo, 3v3 basketball tournament, karaoke contest, open car show, and carnival. Held at the Pleasanton City Park, located on West Adams Street.

Pleasanton Chamber of Commerce, Margie Mendez, P.O. Box 153, Pleasanton, TX 78064, (830) 569-2163, Fax: (830) 569-2164, mmendez115@aol.com, http://atascosa.ebgi.com/pleasant.htm

Crockett: North Central   World Championship Fiddler's Festival

August 18-19, 2001

My Granddaddy would have loved this one. The World Championship Fiddlers' Festival has fiddlers from around the world. Fiddlers and fans of fiddlin' music have been coming to Crockett since 1937 to hear the best in old-time fiddlin music. Enjoy two days of young and old fiddlers competing for the coveted title of World Champion Fiddler. Most events are held at the Crockett Civic Center, located at 1100 Edmiston Drive and Loop 304.

Houston County Chamber of Commerce, Harold Dean, P.O. Box 307, Crockett, TX 75835, (936) 544-2359, (888) 269-2359, Fax: (936) 544-4355

Happy: Panhandle   Happy Days and Rodeo

August 18-19, 2001

Happy Days and Rodeo events include an old-timer's barbecue, contests, games, art and crafts, dances, parades, and rodeo. Held in the Main Street Park.

Happy Days Association, Zeke Frost, Route 2, Box 6-A, Happy, TX 79042, (806) 764-3434, Fax: (806) 558-2068

Sonora: Hill Country   Sutton County Days and PRCA Rodeo

August 19-22, 2001

Sutton County Days includes three nights of PRCA Rodeo performances, rodeo dances, parade on Saturday, barbecue, fiddlers contest, local musical talent, arts and crafts, contests, food booths on Saturday and Sunday. Held at the Sutton County Courthouse lawn, Sutton County Rodeo Arena.

Sonora Chamber of Commerce/Sutton County Days Association, Justin McGeath, P.O. Box 1172, Sonora, TX 76950, (915) 387-2880, Fax: (915) 387-5357, soncoc@sonoratx.net, www.sonoratx-chamber.com

Athens: North Central   MDA Benefit Rodeo
August 23-25, 2001

MDA Benefit Rodeo takes place on the third weekend in August. The events begin at 8 P.M. each night. A terrific event with great music. Events are held at the Henderson County Fairpark Complex, ssamonebyrd@aol.com, www.ssrodeo.com

Fredericksburg: Hill Country   Gillespie County Fair
August 23-26, 2001

This great fair features a parade, horse races (Saturday-Sunday), live entertainment, livestock show, 4-H and FFA exhibits, crafts show and sale, and Fair Queen contest. Held at the Gillespie County Fairgrounds, on Highway 16 South.

Gillespie County Fair and Festivals Association, P.O. Box 526, Fredericksburg, TX 78624, (830) 997-2359, Fax: (830) 997-4923, www.gillespiefair.com

Meridian: North Central   National Championship Barbecue Cook-off
August 24-25, 2001

Here's your chance to taste some great barbecue. You can't enter, that's by invitation only, but you can do some taste testing on your own. For information call or write to (254) 435-6113, P.O. Box 669, Meridian, TX 76665, www.ribman.com

Port Arthur: Gulf   Shrimpfest
August 24-26, 2001

Shrimpfest honors the Port Arthur area shrimpers. All types of music and entertainment are provided, including country and western, mariachi, zydeco, rap, and gospel, with an emphasis on live zydeco and Cajun. Other festivities feature a shrimp calling contest, street dance, a children's pageant, and cooking contests and demonstrations with shrimp. Festivities are at the Logan Music Park on Pleasure Island, off the T.B. Ellison Parkway.

Greater Port Arthur Chamber of Commerce, 4749 Twin City Highway, Third Floor, Port Arthur, TX 77642, (409) 963-1107, Fax: (409) 963-3322, pacc@portarthurtexas.com

Big Spring: West   Howard County Fair
August 24-27, 2001

The Howard County Fair features a carnival, livestock show, live entertainment, art exhibit, pet show, and a petting zoo. Held at the Howard County Fairgrounds at FM 700 and Highway 80.

Tom Koger, P.O. Box 1391, Big Spring, TX 79721, (915) 263-7641, www.bigspringtx.com

Round Rock: Hill Country   Accordion Kings Camp and Festival

August 25, 2001

The Accordion Kings Camp and Festival focuses on accordion-based roots music found in Texas. Come learn from and jam with the masters during this weekend of hands-on workshops, performances, demonstrations, and jams! Events are held at the Rabb House on Brushy Creek and at the Old Settlers Park Lakeview Pavilion in Round Rock.

Texas Folklife Resources, Melanie West, 1317 South Congress Ave., Austin, TX 78704, (512) 441-9255, (512) 441-9255, Fax: (512) 441-9222, tfr@io.com, www.main.org/tfr

Amarillo: Panhandle   Polk Street Block Party

August 25, 2001   Held annually in late August

A bigtime party held in the heart of Amarillo, with food, drink, and games. Downtown Amarillo along Polk Street. (806) 372-6744.

Levelland: Panhandle   American Cancer Society Cowboy Ball

August 25, 2001

Put on your "country best" and two-step on over for an excellent fajita dinner, fabulous silent auction, and dance. One of the best cowboy balls in Texas, this annual event raises much-needed funds for cancer research. Chamber of Commerce, Sandy Parker, 1101 Avenue H, Levelland, TX 79336, (806) 894-3157, (806) 894-2228, Fax: (806) 894-4284, levellandcoc@door.net

Dad-gum-it
You "gotts" to get
in Shape fer the
Rodeo Season!!

Paris: North Central   Red River Valley Fair
August 28, 2001

The fun includes a carnival, livestock show, live entertainment, a chili cookoff, children's barnyard, senior citizens olympics, community contests such as arm wrestling, wheel barrel races, antique show, tractor exhibit, food, clowns, remote control car races, and family entertainment. Held at Paris and Lamar County Fairgrounds, Sixth St. and Center St.

Red River Valley Fair Association, Rita Jane Haynes, Executive Director, 570 East Center Street, Paris, TX 75460, (903) 785-7971, Fax: (903) 784-1969, www.paristexas.com

Belton: North Central   Central Texas State Fair
August 29 - September 2, 2001

Have fun at the horse shows, livestock shows, creative arts, commercial exhibits, educational exhibits, live entertainment, carnival, country music nights, a rock and roll night, and a Hispanic night. There is also a petting zoo and PBR bullriding. Held at the Bell County Expo Center, at 301 West Loop 121.

Bell County Expo Center, Katheryn Boren, P.O. Box 206, Belton, TX 76513, (254) 933-5353, Fax: (254) 933-5354, katb@bellcountyexpo.com, www.central-texasstatefair.com

La Grange: North Central   Fayette County Country Fair
August 30 - September 2, 2001   Labor Day weekend

Four full days of fun during the Labor Day weekend. Events include a livestock and poultry show, agricultural exhibits, culinary exhibits, hay show, talent show, a parade, free dancing every night, and a German-Czech mart with good food, drinks, and live music. Held on the Fairgrounds, at Highway 77 to Giddings North.

Fayette County Country Fair Association, William H. Koehl, P.O. Box 544, La Grange, TX 78945, (979) 968-3781, (979) 968-3911, www.fayettecounty-fair.com

Ben Bolt: Gulf   Fiesta Amistad
August 30 - September 2, 2001   Labor Day weekend

Fiesta Amistad is an annual Labor Day weekend festival in Ben Bolt. Event includes: Miss Fiesta Amistad Pageant, live country and tejano entertainment, midway carnival, annual trail ride from Palito Blanco to Ben Bolt, food booths, and it is the home to the "Texas State Championship Tripa Cookoff." Held at Plaza Garcia, in the Ben Bolt Town Square.

Fiesta Amistad Committee, Michael Garcia, P.O. Box 611, Ben Bolt, TX 78342, (361) 668-1608, (361) 668-9291

Boerne: Hill Country   Kendall County Fair

August 30 - September 2, 2001   Labor Day weekend

The Kendall County Fair invites visitors to kick up their heels during the Labor Day weekend. Activities include parade, carnival, and dances. Held at the Kendall County Fairgrounds, on Highway 46, 1 mi. east of town.

Kendall County Fair Association, Glen Feller, P.O. Box 954, Boerne, TX 78006, (830) 249-2839, (830) 537-4087, www.ci.boerne.tx.us

Country fair musicians have figured out how to stay cool. Photo by Sally Gramon.

Kerrville: Hill Country   Kerrville Wine and Music Festival

August 30 - September 2, 2001

Listen to dozens of songwriters and enjoy the products of a dozen Texas winemakers. Bring your lawn chairs and enjoy the concerts, wine tastings, and seminars at the outdoor theater at Quiet Valley Ranch, 9 miles south of Kerrville on Highway 16. Events are held at the ranch, which is at 5600 Medina Highway 16 South.

Kerrville Festivals, Inc., Rod Kennedy, P.O. Box 291466, Kerrville, TX 78029, (830) 257-3600, (800) 435-8429, Fax: (830) 257-8680, staff@kerrville-music.com, www.kerrville-music.com

Texarkana: East   Strange Family Bluegrass Festival

August 30 - September 2, 2001

A cool music festival offering live music, camping facilities, concessions, and family fun. Plenty of good music on stage with daily jamming under the trees. Includes 10 days of jamming before stage shows. Held at the Strange Family Bluegrass/RV Park. Take Highway 59 South to 3244 and follow signs to park.

Sam and Sharon Strange, Route 2, Box 327 B-2, Texarkana, TX 75501, (903) 791-0342, (903) 792-2481, sfbgtxk@juno.com

September

Some kind of Game wer't it!!!

Finally there are hints that the thermometer is not stuck on a hundred and the long hot summer may be coming to an end. September is a big month on the Texas social calendar. The summer is ending, and folks at the feed store are wonderin' if we will ever see rain again. Meanwhile the young'uns are headin' back to school.

Around the Liars' Tables there's talk of fall crops, including the fall crop of football players at all levels. Football is big in Texas, so we had to get it pretty well organized. Here's how the weekly calendar goes. Thursday is for junior high games. Friday is for high school games. Saturday is for college games. Sunday and Monday are for the pros. Tuesday is for talking about last week's games, and Wednesday is for getting ready for the next round of games. If you think it's important socially, you're getting the picture.

I only mention this because it often has a big influence on the timing and location of events during the fall. You aren't the sharpest tool in the workshop if you plan an event in Austin that competes with a University of Texas home game.

Late in the month the Texas State Fair, the largest state fair in the nation, kicks off its month-long run. This event defies description, because it is everything (including the annual OU-Texas football game) all rolled into a month of fun.

If you don't attend any other event in this book, please go to the State Fair. To me it captures the magnificent diversity of Texas. From the pure fun of the carnival midway to the science exhibits, from the football game to the livestock shows and new car exhibits, it really comes close to giving you a glimpse at what makes Texas strong.

Always double check the dates of the events.

Mesquite: North Central   Mesquite Championship Rodeo
April through September, every Friday and Saturday night

From home-cooked barbecue to live Texas music to pro-cowboy competition, the Mesquite Championship Rodeo gives you a full night of real Texas fun—affordably and just 15 minutes from downtown Dallas. Any Friday or Saturday night April through September. Events include bull riding, bronc riding, calf roping, and more. 118 Rodeo Drive, off the Military Parkway exit from I-635.

For more information, call (214) 285-8777. www.mesquitetexas.com

Grapeland: North Central   Salmon Lake Park Bluegrass Festival
August 31 - September 2, 2001

The Annual Bluegrass Festival includes ten bands performing on an outdoor stage, under beautiful shade trees during a 45-minute set. Bluegrass bands consist of banjo, fiddle, guitar, mandolin, and dobro. Events take place at Salmon Lake Park, just east of Redbud Street.

Fannie Salmon, P.O. Box 483, Grapeland, TX 75844, (936) 687-2594, Fax: (936) 687-2594, www.grapeland.com

Roanoke: North Central   Hawkwood Medieval Fantasy Faire
September 1 - October 14, 2001   Held on weekends between late August and mid October

Re-creation of a fictitious Medieval village based around A.D. 1000 with a hundred shops, ten stages, and hundreds of costumed characters. Stunt show! Storytelling, music, dance, combat, comedy, drama, horse shows, games. They have bawdy shows for adults and play areas for the kids! All in the shade of beautiful, old-growth oaks, with nearly 100 percent coverage. Held on the Southeast corner of I-35W & SH 114, 20 miles north of Ft. Worth.

For more information, call 1-800-782-3629. www.hawkwood.org

Bedford: North Central   Bedford Blues Festival & Arts Fair
August 31 - September 2, 2001   Labor Day weekend

A great outdoor festival located on a 27-acre field in the center of the city, it showcases some of the nation's best blues talent in continuous evening performances over Labor Day weekend. The festival features invited artists whose work relates to this most American of music styles.

Stephen Millard, 2200 North Lamar, Suite 104, Dallas, TX 75202, (214) 855-1881, Fax: (214) 855-1882, mei@meifestivals.com, www.meifestivals.com

Fort Davis: West   Labor Day Square Dance Festival

August 30 - September 3, 2001   Labor Day weekend

Grab your partner and head for the Square Dance Festival that is held each fall and spring. The weekend is filled with square dancing, workshops, clogging, and country music. Saturday night's events conclude with a country western dance. All events are held at the Prude Guest Ranch.

John R. Prude, P.O. Box 1431, Fort Davis, TX 79734, (915) 426-3202, (800) 458-6232, Fax: (915) 426-3502, www.prude-ranch.com

Sugar Land: Gulf   The Sugar Festival

August 31 - September 2, 2001   Labor Day weekend

Talk about having a sweet time walking down memory lane! It will host a variety of music including a top-notch Sensational Sixties Oldies show, hot country, and classic rock. All weekend long you will be hearing the great names in music. Daily tickets for the Sugar Festival include admission to the concerts and many exhibits, staged events, arts and crafts booths, a nightly fireworks display. There is also a full-sized carnival and midway. Events are held at the intersection of U.S. 59 and Highway 6.

After a hot day, the cool breeze and the lights of the carnival bring folks from miles around.

Sugar Festival, Jenny Hrbacek, 123 Brooks Street, P.O. Box 902, Sugar Land, TX 77487-0902, (281) 275-2887, (281) 275-2887, Fax: (281) 275-2891, generalinfo@sugarfestival.com, www.ci.sugar-land.tx.us

West: North Central   Westfest

August 31 - September 2, 2001

One of my favorite towns. Talk about incredible kolaches! I can't drive from Austin to Dallas without stopping. Westfest is a two-day Czechoslovakian festival featuring eight polka and waltz bands from around the state on two stages and dance areas. Westfest promotes Czech music, dancing, and food with more than 25 food booths, cultural area with ethnic dance groups, and 100 arts and crafts booths. The fest also features a large children's area, Kolache baking contest on Sunday, horseshoe pitching contest, volleyball and taroky tournaments, and a 5,000-meter run. Held at the West Fair and Rodeo Grounds, one mile south of West. Czech it out (sorry).

Westfest, Inc., Nina Gerik, P.O. Box 65, West, TX 76691, (254) 826-5058, (254) 826-5058, Fax: (254) 826-3669, info@westfest.com, www.westfest.com

Arlington: North Central   Montalba Outdoor Music Celebration

September 1, 2001

A wonderfully creative merging of several art forms. The Montalba Outdoor Music Celebration is made for friends and family and nature. Entrance contribution includes two-day camping accommodations and live entertainment. Live music is performed in harmony with modern poetry and dance. The musical styles include bluegrass, blues, Christian, country, folk, jazz, polka, R&B, and rap. Events are held at Spirit Valley.

Ryan B. Tinch, 114 West Park Row, Arlington, TX 76010, (817) 291-0114, (940) 483-9288, Fax: (817) 801-9502, montalba@fcmall.com

Woodville: East   Bluegrass and Gospel

September 1, 2001

Take in some of the past while enjoying some incredible music. There is an 1840-1920 early East Texas farming village with railroad museum, wagon museum, 1860 country store, and more. Events take place at the Woodville Heritage Village Museum, on Highway 190 West.

Woodville Heritage Village Museum, Ofeira A. Gazzaway, P.O. Box 888, Woodville, TX 75979, (409) 283-2272, (800) 323-0389, Fax: (409) 283-2194

Littlefield: Panhandle   Waylon's West Texas BBQ

September 1-2, 2001

Held in downtown Littlefield. Ernest Mills, (806) 385-5178, www.rib-man.com

South Padre: Gulf   The South Padre Island Jazz and Latin Music Festival

September 1-2, 2001

Hot sun, cool jazz, and rhythmic Latin music on the sandy beach. Now that's fun. South Padre, on the beach between the Sheraton and Holiday Inn Hotels.

Derrick Woods, 13050 Champions Park Drive, No. 507, Houston, TX 77069, (281) 315-8700, (281) 315-8700, Fax: (281) 894-1102, BossProductions@aol.com, www.sopadre.com

Brady: Hill Country   World Championship Barbecue Goat Cookoff and Arts and Crafts Fair

September 1-2, 2001

Talk about some world class eating! The World Championship Barbecue Goat Cookoff features up to 125 participants along with an arts and crafts fair, live entertainment, sheep dog classic, camping, 5K run, horseshoe pitching, washer pitching, and a fiddling contest. On Sunday we have cowboy church. Events take place at Richards Park, on Memory Lane.

Brady/McCulloch County Chamber of Commerce, 101 East First Street, Brady, TX 76825, (915) 597-3491, Fax: (915) 597-2420, www.bradytx.com

Rockport: Gulf   Fiesta en la Playa

September 1-2, 2001

Fiesta en la Playa is held each year to raise money for scholarships for deserving graduates. A variety of live entertainment including mariachi bands and folklorico dancers is featured all day. Other activities include tamale and jalapeno eating contests, children's events, food, and arts and crafts. A tejano concert is featured in the evening on both nights. Events are held at the Ski Basin Festival Grounds, Southeast corner of Business Highway 35 and Laurel St.

Nelda Covarrubias, P.O. Box 2334, Rockport, TX 78381, (361) 729-6683, (361) 729-6445

Harper: Hill Country   Frontier Days and Rodeo

September 1-2, 2001

A great, old-fashioned, rodeo weekend. Frontier Days and Rodeo features a parade, barbecue, rodeo, horseshoe and washer pitch, and fiddlers contest. Each night there are great musical groups performing at the dances. Events are held at Community Park, which is in downtown Harper, just off 290.

Pam Fogle, P.O. Box 124, Harper, TX 78631, (830) 864-4050

Garland: North Central   Jaycee Jubilee

September 1-3, 2001   Labor Day weekend

The Garland Jaycee Jubilee includes arts, crafts, carnival, live entertainment, food, and the Junior Miss Garland competition. Largest parade west of the Mississippi on Labor Day. More than 150 entries including five marching bands. We also feature an eating contest, BB gun tournament for kids, and prize drawings. Held in Central Park, at 1310 West Avenue F.

Garland Jaycees, Greg Peebles, P.O. Box 460001, Garland, TX 75046, (972) 276-9366, (214) 503-1220 booking, Fax: (972) 371-4388

May: North Central   Andrews Bluegrass Festival

September 1-3, 2001   Labor Day weekend

The Andrews Bluegrass Festival is held Labor Day weekend and features bluegrass bands. Other bands and individuals can bring their non-electric instruments and jam with fellow festival participants. The festival also features homemade craft booths, food and drink concessions. Held at Andrews County Park, 10 miles north of Andrews.

Terry and Patricia Way, 301 Mountain View Drive, May, TX 76857-2018, (915) 366-3994

Hamilton: North Central   Hamilton County Dove Festival
September 1-3, 2001   **Labor Day weekend**

This festival features evening dances, a parade, a rodeo, fiddler's contest, arts and crafts, and quilt show. Events take place at the Hamilton Town Square and at the Fair Park, which is just west of town.

Hamilton Chamber of Commerce, P.O. Box 429, Hamilton, TX 76531, (254) 386-3216, www.ci.hamilton.tx.us

Lubbock: Panhandle   The Music Crossroads of Texas Festival
September 1-3, 2001   **Labor Day weekend**

The Music Crossroads of Texas Festival features a music festival, a street dance, and vendors. Wonderful music acts provide rock, rockabilly, tejano, jazz, R&B, and country music. Featured acts have been legendary groups like The Coasters. The Depot District at 17th-19th Streets between Avenue G and Buddy Holly Avenue.

Carol Moore, 1301 Broadway, Suite 200, Lubbock, TX 79401, (806) 747-5232, (800) 692-4035, Fax: (806)763-3122, cmoore@lubbocklegends.com, www.lubbocklegends.com

Bertram: Hill Country   Oatmeal Festival
September 1-3, 2001   **Labor Day weekend**

Don't miss this one! Watch a small town put on a real shindig. 3 Minute Oats helps sponsor the event, and you will notice that things start 3 minutes after the hour, and the Run for Your Oats is 3.3 miles long. There is a grasshopper parade, live music, barbecue, and an oatmeal cookoff. Festivalgoers can attend the on-stage show barbecue, a flea market, and much more entertainment. Events are held in Bertram/Oatmeal, TX, on FM 243 South at Oatmeal & Rodeo Arena, Bertram.

Oatmeal Festival Association, Carolyn Smith, P.O. Box 70, Bertram, TX 78605, (512) 355-2197, (512) 355-2197, Fax: (512) 355-3182, www.canyonof-theeagles.com

Alpine: West   Balloon Rally of Alpine
September 1-3, 2001   **Labor Day weekend**

Approx. 24 brightly colored hot air balloons ascend each morning of Labor Day weekend (Saturday, Sunday, and Monday) over Alpine, starting at daybreak and lasting till about noon. On Saturday evening the balloonists will light up the night sky with the Balloon Glow Fire Concert.

For information contact the Alpine Chamber of Commerce, chamber@alpinetexas.com, 1-800-561-3735, www.alpinetexas.com

Balloons soar quietly over the countryside in the during the Balloon Rally of Alpine. Photo courtesy of the Alpine Chamber of Commerce.

El Paso: West   Fiesta de las Flores
September 1-4, 2001   Labor Day weekend

Don't miss this colorful music and dancing fest. Fiesta de las Flores is a Mexican-American music festival and carnival each Labor Day weekend. Entertainment includes local mariachi bands, folklorico dancers, and trios. Events take place at the El Paso County Coliseum, at 4100 Paisano.

Fiesta de las Flores, Fermin Dorado, 4110 Alameda, El Paso, TX 79905, (915) 542-3464, (915) 542-3491, Fax: (915) 544-7640, fdlflores@aol.com, ww.fiestadelasflores.org

Austin: Hill Country   Austin Salsa Music Festival
September 2, 2001   Sunday of Labor Day weekend

This super festival features internationally known Latin talent, FREE dance lessons (for those of us with multiple left feet), food, and merchant vendors. To get those novice salsa dancers into the swing, there are also cultural exhibits and foods from around the world. Held at Waterloo Park, located at 403 East 15th Street.

Calliope Promotions, Theresa Muñoz, 7703 Malvern Hill Court, Austin, TX 78745-6009, (512) 899-8585, Fax: (512) 899-8550, calliope@flash.net

Junction: Hill Country   Kimble Kounty Kow Kick
September 4-31, 2001

Katchy name for a festival that features arts, crafts, food booths, fiddlers contest, and rides at City Park along the south Llano River. The United Fiddler's Association competes for $500 in prizes plus trophies. It all happens at the City Park.

Kimble County Chamber of Commerce, H.L. Burk, 402 Main Street, Junction, TX 76849, (915) 446-3190, Fax: (915) 446-2871, www.junctiontexas.net

Bandera: Hill Country   All-American Cowboy Get-Together
September 5-6, 2001   Saturday and Sunday of Labor Day Weekend

Come to Bandera—the Cowboy Capital of the World—and relive the Old West. Cowboy entertainers, poets, storytellers, chuck wagon cooks, and western vendors come together to create a true Old West experience. West Quest millennium trail ride and parade on Saturday morning. Cowboy Holy Eucharist on Sunday. Rodeo on Saturday evening. Held in Mansfield Park, which is 3 miles north of Bandera on Hwy. 16.

For more information call (830) 796-3045 or (800) 364-3833.

San Angelo: Hill Country   Cactus Jazz and Blues Festival
September 6-8, 2001

The name says it all. The Cactus Jazz and Blues Festival is an outdoor/indoor festival featuring a wide variety of regional and national artists. This year an Institute Exhibit on Duke Ellington is featured, along with an orchestral tribute to Duke Ellington. LaVerne Butler is also featured. Held on the Riverstage and at the Cactus Hotel.

San Angelo Cultural Affairs Council, Nancy Loving, P.O. Box 2477, San Angelo, TX 76902, (915) 653-6793, Fax: (915) 658-6036, sacac@wcc.net, www.sanangeloarts.com

Lubbock: Panhandle   The National Cowboy Symposium and Celebration – The National Championship Chuck Wagon Cookoff and The American Cowboy Culture Awards Show

September 6-9, 2001

Take a step back into the past at the National Cowboy Symposium and Celebration. Cowboy poetry, music, dances, and lore of the West take you back to the simpler, yet harsher times of the American West. There are hundreds of booths where you can check out boots, saddles, hats, spurs, and most anything else a cowboy might need. The National Championship Chuck Wagon Cookoff covers cowboy and western food. Events are held at the Lubbock Memorial Civic Center and at the Panhandle South Plains Fairgrounds, at 1501 Sixth Street.

American Cowboy Culture Assoc., Alvin G. Davis, 4124 62nd Drive, Lubbock, TX 79413, (806) 795-2455, Fax: (806) 795-4749, adavis@cowboy.org, www.cowboy.org

Hillsboro: North Central   Go-Texan BBQ

September 7-8, 2001

Held in downtown Hillsboro. Call Ronnie Ewing, (254) 576-2992. www.ribman.com

Montague: North Central   Fire Ant Festival Barbecue Cookoff

September 7-8, 2001

Bring on the FIRE. Held in downtown Montague, Texas. Lynn Gray has the information, P.O. Box 75, Montague, TX 76251, (940) 894-2391, www.ribman.com

Victoria: Gulf   Annual Crossroad Championship BBQ

September 7-8, 2001

Held in downtown Victoria. Russell Schmidt, (361) 572-9454, www.ribman.com

Abilene: Panhandle   West Texas Fair and Rodeo

September 7-15, 2001

Have a great time at the West Texas Fair and Rodeo. Great riders, great food, and great music. It all happens at the Taylor County Expo Center, at 1801 East South 11th Street.

Tony McMillan, 1700 Highway 36, Abilene, TX 79602, (915) 677-4376, Fax: (915) 677-0709

Levelland: Panhandle   Algerita Jam and Arts Festival

September 8, 2001

This family festival offers dunking booths, face painting, baking contests, tractor pulls for children, pony rides, and other activities that make this old-fashioned town festival a pleasure for fall. Musical variety includes country music and mariachis.

Levelland Chamber of Commerce, Sandy Parker, 1101 Avenue H, Levelland, TX 79336, (806) 894-3157, (806) 894-2228, Fax: (806) 894-4284, levellandcoc@door.net, www.levelland.com

Dimmitt: Panhandle   Castro County Harvest Days

September 8, 2001

The Castro County Harvest Days features a fiddle contest, rodeo, parade, street dance, tractor pull, volleyball tournament, horseshoe/washer pitching, and arts. Held at the Castro County Exposition Center, at 403 Southeast Fourth Street.

Castro Country Fair Association, Marilyn Neal, 100 Bedford Street, Dimmitt, TX 79027, (806) 647-2524, (806) 647-4115, Fax: (806) 647-3218

Floresville: South   De Fa Tras Chapter Cajun Music Festival

September 8, 2001

There's a gumbo cookoff, Cajun music by Swamp Angels Band, dancing, Cajun food, beer, soft drinks, Cajun waltz and two-step contests, raffle prizes, craft booths, and horseshoe tossing. Held at the Turner Club, near Floresville (FM 1303 and 2759).

De Fa Tras Chapter - Cajun French Music Association, Sam McNabb, President, P.O. Box 23711, San Antonio, TX 78223, (830) 216-7578, (210) 337-9147, poston@texas.net, http://home.satx.rr.com/cfma/

Quanah: Panhandle   Quanah Falls Festival

September 8, 2001

The Quanah Falls Festival features a car show, antique tractor show, game booths, cow patty bingo, and a brisket and red bean cookoff. Other events include live entertainment, downtown street dance, and tours at the Quanah Museum. There is a quilt show, an art show, autograph sessions with local writers, and an Indian symposium featuring artifacts and speakers.

Quanah Chamber of Commerce, Betha Woods, P.O. Box 158, Quanah, TX 79252, (940) 663-2222, Fax: (940) 663-2172

Caldwell: Panhandle   Kolache Festival

September 8, 2001

This is a daylong family event featuring arts and crafts booths, State of Texas Kolache Championship competition, and live entertainment on five stages with the best Czech musicians in Texas. Festival events include a fine arts show, ethnic foods, quilt shows, antique vendors, antique machinery, and an antique auto show. Held in downtown Caldwell, on the square.

Burleson County Chamber of Commerce, Honey Dowdy, Drawer 87, Caldwell, TX 77836-0087, (979) 567-3218

Forney: North Central   Forney Jackrabbit Stampede and Festival

September 8, 2001

The Forney Jackrabbit Stampede and Festival features arts and crafts, food booths, local dancers, sanctioned bike race, and entertainment by local bands, a carnival, antique tractor and car exhibit, and a salsa tasting contest.

Forney Chamber of Commerce, Dr. Wesley Wilson, P.O. Box 570, Forney, TX 75126, (972) 564-2233, Fax: (972) 564-3677, lenny@net-snake.bke.com

While listening to live music the folks take a leisurely tour of the crafts and food booths.

Kerrville: Hill Country   Living History Day

September 8, 2001

Living History Day depicts lives in the Old West and features cowboy poets, cowboy songs, chuck wagon music, and other stories and songs from our rich musical heritage. The tales of Jimmie Rodgers, the father of country music, are part of the day as a tribute to Jimmie Rodgers. Held at Louise Hayes Park, on the Guadalupe River, near downtown.

Texas Heritage Music Foundation, Kathleen Hudson, P.O. Box 1945, Kerrville, TX 78029-1945, (830) 367-3750, Fax: (830) 367-4888, kat@schreiner.edu, www.texasheritagemusic.org

Midland: West   Septemberfest

September 8-9, 2001

Septemberfest is a two-day event with a preview party on Friday night. Held the 2nd weekend of September, the event features artists, entertainers, and a children's area with games and prizes. Always popular, the entertainment area features local dancers, tumblers, individual musicians, bands, and choirs. Held at the Museum of the Southwest, at 1705 West Missouri.

Museum of the Southwest, Jill Johnson, 705 West Missouri, Midland, TX 79701, (915) 683-2882, Fax: (915) 570-7077, jjohnson@museum.org, www.museumsw.org

Texarkana: East   Quadrangle Craft and Music Festival

September 8-9, 2001

Enjoy three stages filled with jazz, barbershop quartets, country, gospel, and traditional music. Held in downtown Texarkana, at 219 North Stateline Avenue.

Texarkana Museums, Ina McDowell, P.O. Box 2343, Texarkana, TX 75504-2343, (903) 793-4831, Fax: (903) 793-7108, gcvanderpool@cableone.net, www.texarkanamuseums.org

Friona: Panhandle   Maize Days

September 8-15, 2001

Maize Days kicks off with a bonfire. Activities held throughout the week include a beauty pageant, cow patty bingo, parade, barbecue, rodeo, and a variety of booths. Wednesday night features Gospel Gathering, a performance by several gospel groups and individuals. Held at downtown Friona.

Friona Chamber of Commerce. Kathryn Goddard, P.O. Box 905, Friona, TX 79035, (806) 247-3491, Fax: (806) 247-2348, fedc@wtrt.net

Hillsboro: North Central   Go Texan Cotton Pickin' Fair

September 9

The Cotton Pickin' Fair is held to celebrate our agricultural roots in the Hill Country. At one time Hillsboro was considered to be the King of Cotton. They want to keep the importance of the farmer, cotton production, and agriculture alive and well. Enjoy arts and crafts, all-day entertainment, food, and the 5k and one-mile runs. Held in downtown Hillsboro, on the courthouse grounds.

Go Texan Cotton Pickin' Fair Committee, Art Mann, P.O. Box 358, Hillsboro, TX 76645-2357, (254) 582-2481, (254) 582-2481, Fax: (254) 582-0465, Fax: (979) 567-0818, hdowdy@mail.startel.net, rtis.com/reg/caldwell/ent/

Wortham: North Central   The Wortham Blind Lemon Jefferson Blues Festival

September 9, 2001

The Blind Lemon Jefferson Blues Festival is a daylong celebration in honor of local blues legend Blind Lemon Jefferson. The festival, now in its fourth year, focuses on up-and-coming Texas blues talent and is modestly priced to encourage families to come out and experience live music on the same streets that began a career for Jefferson. Held in downtown Wortham.

Wortham Chamber of Commerce, Brent Jones, P.O. Box 185, Wortham, TX 76693, (254) 765-3338, (254) 765-3338, miller@pflash.com

Port Arthur: Gulf   Mexican Fiesta

September 9-10, 2001

This is a classic fiesta, with live music, food, children's area, dances, queen's pageant, folkloric dancers, and scholarship awards. Additional live music includes a mariachi band, which this past year performed with our folklore dancers the last two dances of our program. Events are held at the Port Arthur Civic Center, 3401 Cultural Center Drive.

Mexican Heritage, Tony Ramirez, President, 176 Hilldale, Nederland, TX 77627, (409) 724-6134, (409) 727-0727

Glen Rose: North Central　　Spring Bluegrass

September 11-12, 2001

Two wonderful days of nonstop bluegrass and fiddling contests. Tres Rios RV River Resort and Campground, County Road 312, Tres Rios, 2322 CR 312, Glen Rose, TX 76043, (254) 897-4253, Fax: (254) 897-7396, www.texasoutside.com/glenrose/calendar.html

Longview: East　　Gregg County Fair and Expo

September 12-16

A great county fair and plenty of bluegrass, country, jazz, and classical music.

The Gregg County Fair and Expo has been going on since 1949. Acts have included Borderline Band, Cooke County Line Band, Juke Joint Blues Band, Coyote Moon Band and Martha Welch and Friends, and Trafffic Jam Band. Other events included: Eugene Wilkes Magic Shows, Show-Me Safari Petting Zoo, Miss Gregg Beauty Pageant, and many other super events. Held at the Gregg County Fairgrounds, on Jaycee Drive.

Longview Jaycees, Billy Clay, P.O. Box 1124, Longview, TX 75606, (903) 753-4478, Fax: (903) 753-5452, bgcsr8@aol.com

Columbus: North Central　　Colorado County Fair

September 13-17, 2001

This wonderful, down-home county fair includes a rodeo and bull buck out, junior livestock show and sale. There are live country music concerts each evening. Go Texan events on Sunday include a barbecue cookoff. Parade on Saturday. Also, commercial exhibits and a TCAA heifer show. Highway 90 West in Columbus, TX.

Colorado County Fair Association, Mack Janak, Route 1, Box 164, Weimar, TX 78962, (979) 263-5160, (979) 732-9266, Fax: (979) 263-5030

Lubbock: Panhandle　　Sixteenth of September Celebration

September 13-17, 2001

Leave it to us Texans to celebrate a month...This 5-day event features a carnival, game booths, and lots of good food. Held at the Lubbock Memorial Civic Center.

Fiestas del Llano, Inc., Victor Hernandez, 1114 Tenth Street, Lubbock, TX 79401, (806) 765-5481, Fax: (806) 765-5591, vhernandez@mail.ci.lubbock.tx.us

McGregor: North Central　　Central Texas Barbecue Association Cookoff

September 14-15, 2001

Held in downtown McGregor, Texas. Jim Mugge, (254) 840-2779, www.ribman.com

Ain't this Weather
Wonder-full?
That drought-buster
rain is a welcome sight
on the farm.

Grapevine: North Central

September 14-15, 2002

GrapeFest

2nd full weekend in September

It's time to start wining! GrapeFest is Texas's largest wine festival, a celebration of Texas wines and grape growing, and tribute to the city of Grapevine's namesake. GrapeFest offers a GrapeTime for all ages. Enjoy events such as the Texas Wine Tribute, People's Choice Wine Tasting Classic, GrapeFest tennis classic, GrapeGames for children, a quality arts and crafts fair, vintage and classic car show, two days of nonstop live entertainment, and much more. Events are held on Main Street in the Historic District. Grapevine Heritage Foundation, Rick Lott, One Liberty Park Plaza, Grapevine, TX 76051, (817) 410-3189, (800) 457-6338, Fax: (817) 410-3038, www.tourtexas.com/ grapevine/gpvnevents.html

Folks enjoy GrapeFest in (where else?) Grapevine. Photo courtesy of the Grapevine Convention & Visitors Bureau.

Springtown: North Central   Wild West Festival BBQ Cookoff

September 14-15, 2001

Held in downtown Springtown. Kelly Mayo, (817) 220-6462, www.rib-man.com

Sanger: North Central   Sanger Heritage Celebration

September 14-15, 2002   2nd Saturday in September

The Sanger Heritage Celebration will have a street dance, live entertainment, barbecue cookoff ($5,000 prize), arts and crafts booths, and antique tractors. It all happens in downtown Sanger, on the town square.

Sanger Chamber of Commerce, Vickie Jenkins, P.O. Box 537, Sanger, TX 76266, (940) 458-7702, Fax: (940) 458-7823, www.sangertexas.com

Bartlett: North Central   Central Texas Barbecue Association Cookoff

September 14-15, 2001

Held in downtown Bartlett. For information contact Bryan Roberts at (254) 527-4430 or Duane Kurtin, (254) 527-3898. www.ribman.com

Aransas Pass: Gulf   Shrimporee

September 14-15, 2002   2nd weekend in September

Great food, great music, and the Texas coast. That's a good time! The Shrimporee features continuous live music with bands playing country, gospel, and rock music. There is also continuous entertainment for children, arts and crafts, contests, and food. See you there. Held at Aransas Pass Community Park.

Kay Wolf, 130 West Goodnight Avenue, Aransas Pass, TX 78336-2508, (361) 758-2750, Fax: (361) 758-8320, info@aransaspass.org

Anahuac: Gulf   Texas Gatorfest

September 14-15, 2002   The weekend following the September 10th opening of gator season

Check out those snappers! Anahuac, the Alligator Capital of Texas, hosts Gatorfest, which is a fun time for everyone. The central event is the Great Texas Alligator Roundup, which draws gator hunters from throughout the Southwest, all competing to catch the biggest, feistiest gator. Other events throughout the weekend include: the Gator Bait Ski Team water ski show, airboat rides, carnival rides, children's rides, petting zoo, arts and craft booths, an educational wildlife show, food booths with alligator delicacies, and a scenic beer garden overlooking Trinity Bay. Located at Fort Anahuac Park, 6 miles south of exit 810 off of IH-10.

Anahuac Chamber of Commerce, Kim Turner, P.O. Box R, Anahuac, TX 77514, (409) 267-4190, Fax: (409) 267-3907

Houston: Gulf   Festa Italiana

September 14-16, 2001

Like Italian? Don't miss this special event. Activities include a Tenor Competition, Grape Stomping, Bocce Ball Tournament, Gourmet Chef cooking demonstrations, and wine tasting. Featuring handcrafts, nonstop performances at Houston's top Italian restaurants. All events are held in downtown Houston, at 900 Bagby.

Call the Italian Community and Culture Center hotline for information (713) 524-4222.

Addison: North Central   Oktoberfest

September 14-17, 2001

Roll out the barrel, it's polka time. The Addison Oktoberfest is an authentic re-creation of the Munich Oktoberfest. Filled with four days of family fun. No need to go to Germany. You'll find entertainers in authentic German costumes performing traditional German folk dances, schuhplattling, folk songs, oompah music, sing-a-longs, yodels and more. Lots of great German food. For the kids there are carnival rides, midway games, a petting zoo, and camel rides.

Addison Conference and Theatre Centre, 15650 Addison Road, Town of Addison, Barbara Kovacevich, P.O. Box 9010, Addison, TX 75001-9010, (972) 450-6221, (800) ADDISON, Fax: (972) 450-6225, bkovacevich@ci.addison.tx.us, www.ci.addison.tx.us

Snyder: Panhandle   Scurry County Fair

September 14-16, 2001

Fun at the fair, which includes a carnival, livestock show, arts & crafts, dominoes, horseshoe tossing, washer tossing, flower show, and a variety of historic displays. And of course plenty of good food to go with the wide variety of live music. Held at the Scurry County Coliseum, at 900 East Coliseum Drive.

Scurry County Fair Association, Phil Robinson, P.O. Box 840, Snyder, TX 79550, (915) 573-3558, Fax: (915) 573-7970

Sulphur Springs: North Central   Hopkins County Fall Festival

September 14-21, 2002   2nd thru the 3rd Saturdays in September

The Hopkins County Fall Festival features traditional Hopkins County Fall Festival stew cook-off, games, gospel music, contests, domino tournament, a carnival, street dance, arts and crafts, and a Star Night concert. There are scheduled performances by major entertainers. Hopkins County Regional Civic Center, 1200 Houston Street.

Fall Festival, Inc., Rod Henderson, P.O. Box 177, Sulphur Springs, TX 75483, (903) 885-8071, Fax: (903) 885-2811, hccc@neto.com

The Hopkins County Courthouse is another example of a beautiful Texas downtown courthouse square.

Odessa: Panhandle   Permian Basin Fair and Exposition

September 14-22, 2002   For nine days, starting the 2nd weekend in September

The Permian Basin Fair and Exposition includes a livestock show, sheep dog trials, beauty pageant, creative arts, business and industry exhibits, carnival food booths, and land, air, and water exhibits. Live entertainment includes cowboy poets, country, rock, Christian and Latino bands. Held at the Ector County Coliseum and Exposition Center, at 42nd Street and Andrews Highway.

Permian Basin Fair and Exposition, Don Thorn and Gerri Lu McAdams, P.O. Box 4812, Odessa, TX 79720, (915) 550-3232, Fax: (915) 366-5647, or www.tourtexas.com/odessa

Angleton: Gulf   Brazoria County Fair

September 15 - October 14, 2001

The Brazoria County Fair includes cookoffs, rodeo, live entertainment, and dancing. Brazoria County Fair is the largest county fair in Texas. Events in September include talent show tryouts, a golf tournament, team roping, a rodeo queen contest, and fair entry judging. There is something for everyone during the actual nine-day fair which runs from October 5th to the 13th. Held at the Brazoria County Fairgrounds, at 901 Downing Road.

Brazoria County Fat Stock and Fair Association, P.O. Box 818, Angleton, TX 77516, (979) 849-6416, Fax: (979) 849-6985, bcfa@mastnet.net, www.bcfa.org

Pittsburg: East   Pioneer-Chickfest

September 15, 2001

Pioneer Days Festival in Pittsburg invites visitors to step back into time in a city with rich heritage to experience life as it was around the turn of the century. Pioneer Days has two music areas with local entertainment, fishing, horseshoe pitching, arts and crafts. Local events are early in the week, ending up with the *Spirit of Pittsburg* play and numerous homecomings at the end of the week. Saturday is the big day with downtown streets blocked off for vendor sales, musical entertainment, cornbread 'n beans contest, children's activities, and ending with a street dance. Events are held on the courthouse lawn and downtown.

Dan Blake, Executive VP, 202 Jefferson Street, Pittsburg, TX 75686-1304, (903) 856-3442, (903) 856-3442, Fax: (903) 856-3570, campcocc@tyler.net

Sherman: North Central   Sherman Arts Festival

September 15, 2001

The Sherman Arts Festival is in its 17th year. There are over 75 craft vendors and three stages of live continuous entertainment consisting of dancers, singers, and bands. Much of the entertainment is local. The festival also includes a children's stage, which promotes youth entertainment and goes along with the children's art show held at the festival every year. Held at the Municipal Building grounds, at the corner of Elm and Rusk.

Sherman Council for Arts and Humanities, Claudette S. Peercy, P.O. Box 1029, Sherman, TX 75091-1029, (903) 893-1184, Fax: (903) 893-4266, shermanchamber@texoma.net

Mountain Home: Hill Country   Y.O. Social Club Party

September 15, 2001

The Y.O. Social Club is a nonprofit organization of fun seekers, dedicated solely to commemorating the romantic history of the Y.O. Ranch and the Texas Hill Country and preserving our western heritage by hosting the biggest, best, most talked about party in the great state of Texas. Held at the Y.O. Ranch, on Highway 41.

Y.O. Social Club, Marilyn Leinweber, 509 Junction Highway, Kerrville, TX 78028, (830) 896-8777, Fax: (830) 896-8677

Bartlett: North Central   Friendship Fest and Bartlett VFD
                                    Barbecue Cookoff

September 15, 2002

Friendship and BBQ all over Bartlett. Don't miss the streets lined with cookers, fun booths, and street dance. (254) 527-4623. www.ohwy.com/tx/b/bartlett.htm

Arlington: North Central

September 15-16, 2001

Pecan Street Fall Arts Festival

Held every spring and fall

The fall festival returns to Pecan Street with even more artists, crafts, and music providing fun for the whole family. Held on Pecan Street, between Border and Mitchell. For information, call (817) 275-2613. www.arlington.org

Austin: Hill Country

September 15-16, 2001

Austin Jazz and Arts Festival

The Annual Austin Jazz and Arts Festival (formerly the Clarksville-West End Jazz and Arts Festival) is always a blast. It takes place at East 11th Street at Waller, and across the street, indoors and out, at the Victory Grill and grounds. Local and national talents keep the toes tapping all weekend long.

DiverseArts Production Group, Piper Anderson, 1705 Guadalupe Street, Artplex Suite 234, Austin, TX 78701, (512) 477-9438, Fax: (512) 477-9344, darts@eden.com

Del Rio: West

September 15-16, 2001

Diez y Seis de Septiembre

Diez y Seis de Septiembre is a celebration of Mexican heritage and history. Talent includes musical performances, folklore dancers, and arts and crafts. Brown Plaza, Jones and Cisneros Streets.

Mary Reyna, P.O. Box 4239, Del Rio, TX 78841-4239, (830) 774-8641

El Paso: West

September 15-16, 2001

El Grito: Celebration of Mexican Independence Day

El Grito is a one-day event to celebrate Mexican Independence Day and honor its history and heroes. Reenactments, mariachis, ballet folklorico, and plenty of great food guarantee a good time. Held at 800 South San Marcial.

Consolado General de Mexico, Mariloli Limongi, 910 East San Antonio, El Paso, TX 79901, (915) 533-6311, (915) 533-3645, Fax: (915) 532-7163

Magnolia: East

September 15-16, 2001

Country Fair and Barbecue Cookoff

The Magnolia Country Fair features craft booths, an old car show, games, a beauty pageant, talent show, carnival rides, food concessions, and a barbecue cookoff. Both silent and live auctions are held. Country Music Jamboree Lease Hall, 377937 FM 1774.

Magnolia Area Chamber of Commerce, Anne Sundquist, P.O. Box 399, Magnolia, TX 75953-0399, (281) 356-1488, Fax: (281) 356-2552, macctx@juno.com

San Marcos: Hill Country Republic of Texas Chilympiad
September 15-16, 2001

Republic of Texas Chilympiad features the Texas Men's State Chili Championship. Activities include arts and crafts, food booths, special exhibits, and a parade. Concerts are provided Friday night, Saturday night, and a matinee. The special events are Harley Davidson exhibit, the Texas State Collegiate Chili Cookoff, a Miss Chilympiad contest, and the Third Annual Chilympiad Hot Sauce Contest. Held at the Hays County Civic Center, on the east access road of IH-35 South.

El Jefe's, Cathy Mayfield and Pat Murdock, 709 Mountain View, San Marcos, TX 78666, (512) 396-5400, (512) 353-4377, chaos@itouch.net

Mineola: East Pickin' in the Pines
September 15-17, 2001

Pickin' in the Pines, plenty of blues, bluegrass, country, cowboy, and folk music. It is held on approximately 15 acres in the beautiful East Texas Piney Woods, in Pine Mills. It is a camping weekend with campfire jams. Plenty of fun for all. Texas Piney Woods in Pine Mills, TX, Interstate of FM 49 and 312.

Tri-M Music, Dick and Geri Miller, Route 1, Box 177-M, Mineola, TX 75773, (903) 857-2253, t-roy@lakecountry.net

San Antonio: South Jazz'SALive
September 15-17, 2001

Jazz'SALive offers a variety of jazz along with arts and crafts, food, and artisans. Entertainment is scheduled from noon until 10 P.M. both weekend days. More than 20 of San Antonio's best restaurants are participating along with artists from all over the U.S. Proceeds benefit the San Antonio Parks Foundation. Events are at Travis Park, at 300 East Travis.

San Antonio Department of Parks, Dora Jordan, P.O. Box 839966, San Antonio, TX 78283-3966, (210) 207-3025, Fax: (210) 207-3045

Amarillo: Panhandle Annual Tri-State Fair
September 15-22, 2001   Held in mid-September each year

The Tri-State Fair features all the activities you'd expect from a top regional fair: food, games, rides, midway, concerts, educational shows, and demonstration. Held at the Tri-State Fairgrounds, on Grand Ave., 1 mile north of Interstate 40. Call (806) 376-7767.

Texarkana: East — Four States Fair and Rodeo

September 15-23, 2001

The Four States Fair and Rodeo features PRCA rodeo, carnival, exhibits, crafts, horse shows, livestock shows, and live entertainment. Held at Four States Fairgrounds, on Loop 245 and East 50th Street.

Four States Fair, Nancy Herron, P.O. Box 1915, Texarkana, AR 75504, (870) 773-2941, (800) 776-1836, Fax: (870) 772-0713, nancyh@fourstatesfair.com

Amarillo: Panhandle — Tri-State Fair

Mid-September annually

The Amarillo Tri-State Fair is the largest annual event in the Panhandle of Texas. This year's fair includes agricultural, home arts, fine arts, and commercial exhibits. What do you like? A carnival midway, regional talent show, and pop, Latino, bluegrass, and country music shows. Held at the Tri-State Fairgrounds, which are located at 3301 East 10th Street.

Amarillo Tri-State Exposition, Cheri Christensen, P.O. Box 31087, Amarillo, TX 79120, (806) 376-7767, Fax: (806) 376-6942, tsfair@tcac.net

Fort Worth: North Central — Czech Heritage Day

September 16, 2001

Check out Czech Heritage Day, and pass the kolaches! Costumed participants, great food, and plenty of live Czech music guarantee a good time. National Hall, 3316 Roberts Cutoff Road, Fort Worth.

Al Kercho, 2444 Stonegate Drive North, Bedford, TX 76021, (817) 282-5065, (817) 624-1361

Denton: North Central — Blues Festival

September 16, 2001

Don't miss the chance to catch some of the great blues bands. Civic Center Park, 502 Oakland Street.

Blues Festival, John Baines, 625 Dallas Drive, Suite 200, Denton, TX 76205, (940) 565-9015, Fax: (940) 382-9695

San Antonio: South — Diez y Seis Guadalupe Street Parade & Festival

September 16

This Mexican independence day celebration has something for everyone, including lots of live music for every taste (tejano, salsa, rock, R&B, pop, and country). This cool parade was even broadcast by Telemundo last year. It takes place at Plaza Guadalupe, at 1327 Guadalupe Street.

Avenida Guadalupe Association, Celia Mendoza, 1327 Guadalupe Street, San Antonio, TX 78207, (210) 223-3151, Fax: (210) 223-4405

San Antonio celebrates El Grito/Diez y Seis. Photo courtesy of the San Antonio Convention & Visitors Bureau. Taken by Al Rendon.

Nacogdoches: East   Do Dat Barbecue
September 16, 2001

A fun time for a great cause. The Do Dat Barbecue holds a dance on Friday night inside the Expo center with a country and western band. Saturday features the barbecue cookoff where nearly a hundred teams will be competing for trophies. Talk about smelling and tasting good! All proceeds benefit local charities. It all happens at the Nacogdoches County Exposition Center.

Nacogdoches Daily Sentinel, Gary Borders, P.O. Box 630068, Nacogdoches, TX 75961, (936) 564-8361, Fax: (936) 560-4267

BARBECUE
In Texas, it's not just for breakfast anymore! Photo by Dyanne Fry-Cortez.

Eastland: Panhandle   Eastland Old Rip Fest & Parade
September 16, 2001

The Old Rip Fest is one of the highlights of the year. Our parade is the largest in the Big Country and features numerous bands and drill teams, antique cars, horse groups, floats, as well as celebrities. Food booths and arts and crafts booths are located around the square, and live entertainment is featured throughout the day. Entertainment from the EHS Band, Siebert Singers,

Ranger College Band, CJC Band, and fiddlers Robert and Randy Weeks. Held on Eastland Square.

Chamber of Commerce, Ann Folsom, 102 S. Seaman St., Eastland, TX 76448, (254) 629-2332, Fax: (254) 629-1629

Tyler: East   Festival on the Square

September 16, 2001

Festival on the Square features great music, food, and fun. There will be children's activities on stage all day as well as regional artists and craft booths. Held on the town square.

Heart of Tyler/Main Street Project, Kathey Comer, P.O. Box 158, Tyler, TX 75710, (903) 593-6905, Fax: (903) 597-0699, kcomer@tylertexas.com

Dallas: North Central   Fiesta Diez y Seis

September 16-17, 2001

Fiesta Diez y Seis features main attractions as live entertainment on 3 stages, family-oriented activities, carnival rides and games, sampling booths, contests and prizes, great Mexican food, and a parade award ceremony in Fiesta Patrias. We are proud to invite you to participate in the best Mexican Independence Day Festival in the Dallas/Fort Worth metroplex. "Diez y Seis de Septiembre" commemorates Mexico's independence from Spain. Held on Artist Square, 1800 Leonard Street.

Marcos Rincon, 6060 North Central Expwy., Suite 670, Dallas, TX 75206, (214) 750-0670, Fax: (214) 750-1038, rincon@syberramp.net

Plano: North Central   Annual Southwestern Bell Plano
                                      Balloon Festival

September 20-22, 2002   3rd weekend of September (Fri, Sat, and Sun)

A spectacularly colorful three-day festival. Balloons will launch at 7 A.M. and 6 P.M. each day. There are also unique arts and crafts to choose from. Don't miss it. Oak Point Park, 2801 E. Spring Creek Parkway.

Plano Convention and Visitors Bureau at (972) 422-0296. www.planotx.org/current/event.html

Brenham: South   Washington County Fair

September 20-23, 2001

A great, down-home county fair, the Washington County Fair has the rodeo, livestock show, country store, junior livestock show, commercial heifer sales, barbecue cookoff, horseshoe and washer pitching contests, and even a volleyball tournament. Held at the Washington County Fairgrounds, at 1305 East Horton.

Washington County Fair, Julie Jaster, P.O. Box 1257, Brenham, TX 77834-1257, (979) 836-4112, Fax: (979) 830-8074

Dallas: North Central   Greek Festival
September 20-23, 2001

Visit the islands without leaving Texas. The Greek Festival includes singers, dancers, authentic Greek food, and live music. All proceeds go to the church and its charities. Held at the Greek Orthodox Church, at 13555 Hillcrest Road, Dallas, TX 75240-5412, (972) 991-1166, (972) 233-4880, Fax: (972) 661-1717, htgoc@tifnet.com

Groves: Gulf   Texas Pecan Festival
September 20-23, 2001

Texas Pecan Festival has three full days of continuous entertainment that includes a wide variety of live music: jazz, rock, country, and Christian. Held at Lion's Park, Lincoln Avenue and Jackson Boulevard.

Groves Chamber of Commerce, George King, 4399 Main Avenue, Groves, TX 77619, (409) 962-3631, (800) 876-3631, Fax: (409) 963-0745

Lubbock: Panhandle   Annual Fiestas del Llano
September 21-22, 2002   3rd weekend in September

Celebrate Mexican Independence Day with great food, dance, and music. Enjoy ethnic foods and entertainment throughout the festival and dance each evening to the sounds of popular Hispanic bands.

Lubbock Memorial Civic Center, 1501 6th St., (806) 762-5059.

Fort Worth: North Central   Fiesta Patrias
September 21-22, 2002   3rd weekend in September

Fiesta Patrias is a downtown party that takes place on Main Street; celebrations begin with a parade on Main Street and continue with a great line-up of tejano, Mexican, salsa, and cultural presentations by ballet folklorico dance groups.

Marcos Rincon, 6060 North Central Expwy., Suite 670, Dallas, TX 75206, (214) 750-0670, Fax: (214) 750-1038, rincon@syberramp.net

Temple: North Central   Texas Train Festival
September 21-22, 2002   3rd weekend in September

Plenty of fun and history, to honor the impact of the train in this community. Enjoy live music, ethnic food, Civil War reenactments, skilled craftsmen, and lots of great food. Also there are hundreds of model trains set up at the Mayborn Convention Center. (254) 298-5172. www.ci.temple.tx.us

Hondo: Hill Country   Medina County Fair
September 21-22, 2002   3rd weekend in September

Medina County Fair has rodeo games, arts and crafts, home arts booths, dancing, music, food booths, a petting zoo, parades, magic shows, and a carnival. We also have family games such as an egg toss, wheelbarrow races, and stick horse races. Live music at several places on the fairgrounds including at the Saturday night dance. Held in the Hondo City Park and Fairgrounds, Highway 462 North.

Medina County Fair Association, Kenneth O. Bendele, Manager, P.O. Box 4, Hondo, TX 78861, (830) 426-5406.

Brownwood: Hill Country   Old Depot Arts Fest
September 21-22, 2002   3rd weekend in September

The Old Depot Arts Fest features arts, crafts, demonstrations, and entertainment including a children's area and commercial food vendors. Live music includes jazz, folk, and swing. Events are held at the Depot Civic and Cultural Center, at 600 Depot Street.

Arts Council of Brownwood, Donna Posey, Executive Secretary, P.O. Box 880, Brownwood, TX 76804, (915) 646-9535, Fax: (915) 643-6686, bwdtexcc@web-access.net

Waco: North Central   McLennan County Go-Texan Cookoff
September 21-22, 2001

Held in Cameron Park, in Waco. For information contact Ginger Tolbert, (254) 859-5064, www.ribman.com

Houston: Gulf   Houston Caribbean Festival
September 21-22, 2002   3rd weekend in September

Visit the Caribbean Y'all! This neat festival includes a walk-a-thon and the festival itself. The Houston Caribbean Festival Parade will start at Travis and Texas and move east to Main Street. The Parade will showcase the talents of Caribbean artisans in costumes portraying themes ranging from indigenous aspects of the Caribbean to fantasy. Parade music will include soca, reggae, and calypso. Held at Herman Square.

Houston Caribbean Festival, Janet Eastmond, P.O. Box 722361, Houston, TX 77272-2361, (713) 434-1931, (713) 774-0802, Fax: (713) 688-9617

Comanche: North Central   Comanche County Powwow & Barnie McBee Memorial Brisket Cookoff
September 21-22, 2001

Events are held at City Park.

Darlene Causey, Comanche Chamber of Commerce, P.O. Box 65, Comanche, TX 76442, (915) 356-3233, www.ribman.com

Another Day, Another Great Festival
Javier Cortez stands in front of his teepee. Photo by Dyanne Fry-Cortez.

Arlington: North Central   Festival of Quilts 2001
September 21-23, 2001

See some great handiwork from the Quilters Guild of Arlington. Held at the Bob Duncan Community Center, at Vandergriff Park, which is at 2800 S. Center Street. Contact: (214) 767-4776, ext. 222 or www.qgoa.org

Mansfield: North Central   Mansfield Hometown Festival
September 22, 2001   Held every September

Old-fashioned fun and plenty of good food. Don't miss it. Downtown Mansfield, mcofc@flash.net

Houston: Gulf   Houston Hot Sauce Festival
September 22, 2001

Take it from me. Get yourself a cold drink FIRST! This really hot festival showcases the HOTTEST hot sauces, salsas, picante sauces, chipotle, jams, spices, BBQ sauces, chips, dips, peppers, fiery food, and nonfood products, entertainment, variety of food & cold beverages. FREE children's activities, and more.

For information call Carol Steffan (281) 558-3518, carolfmhou@houston.rr.com, www.houstonhotsauce.com

La Grange: North Central   Main Street Arts & Crafts Show
September 22-23, 2001   3rd weekend in September

Talented artists from across the country come to La Grange to have fun and show their crafts. Come join in the fun, talent, and cool breezes under the centuries-old gentle oak trees of this grand courthouse square. Held at the Fayette County Courthouse. For information call (979) 968 8701.

Commerce: North Central   Bois D'Arc Bash

September 22-24, 2001

A neat town and a great festival. The Bois D'Arc Bash features live music of every style, all day along with food, demonstrations, arts and crafts. At night there is a street dance. There is also a 5K run/walk, a pet show, a salsa contest, quilt show, and car show. Held on the square downtown.

Commerce Chamber of Commerce, Karen Starks, P.O. Box 290, Commerce, TX 75429, (903) 886-3950, Fax: (903) 886-8012

Lubbock: Panhandle   Panhandle South Plains Fair

September 22-30, 2001

The Panhandle South Plains Fair serves a 22-county area in West Texas and features agriculture and livestock shows, arts and crafts, commercial vendors, homemaking exhibits, and a variety of paid and free entertainment in the coliseum and on the outdoor stage. The coliseum showcases paid entertainment by country music stars or free variety shows. Attractions on the grounds include a fashion/clothing show, carnival rides, and food concessions furnished by local nonprofit groups. Held on the Fairgrounds, located at 105 East Broadway.

Panhandle South Plains Fair Association, Steve L. Lewis, P.O. Box 208, Lubbock, TX 79408, (806) 763-2833, Fax: (806) 744-5903

Longview: East   Dalton Days

September 23, 2001

Longview's colorful past comes to life as the Dalton Gang robbery of First National Bank is reenacted on the streets of downtown. Additional activities focus on the city's history and heritage. There will be cowboy poets and storytellers, cowboy music, trick roping, horseshoe pitching, and a chuck wagon demonstration. Held in downtown Longview, at 214 North Fredonia.

Gregg County Museum, Janet Brown, P.O. Box 3342, Longview, TX 75606, (903) 753-5840, Fax: (903) 753-5854

Midlothian: North Central   Fall Festival

September 23, 2001

The Fall Festival is a fun family event that includes country/western bands, beauty pageant, food booths, arts and crafts, entertainment, Christian music, petting zoo, and children's rides. Held at Civic Center Fairgrounds, at Highway 287 & 11th St.

Midlothian Chamber of Commerce, Iris Stewart, P.O. Box 609, Midlothian, TX 76065, (972) 723-8600, (972) 723-8600, Fax: (972) 723-9300, irisc@fastlane.net

Clarendon: Panhandle Charles Goodnight's Chuck Wagon Cookoff

September 23, 2001

Ruth Robinson, 4 Maple Drive, Clarendon, TX 79226, (806) 874-2057, ruthr@arn.net

Lakehills: Hill Country Medina Lake Cajun Festival

September 23, 2001

Grab yourself some gumbo and mud bugs, and enjoy the sounds from the bayou. Continuous entertainment on two stages with Cajun waltz and freestyle dance contests. Gumbo cookoff contest where you can sample a wide variety of gumbos prepared by both amateur and professional cooks. Cajun food like crawfish pies, crawfish etouffee, boudain, shrimp and ham jambalaya, barbecue shrimp, and bread pudding with whiskey sauce. Held at Medina Lake Civic Center & Pavilion, on Park Road 37, it is 1.7 miles west of FM 1283.

Medina Lake Betterment Association, Bob Caswell, P.O. Box 830, Lakehills, TX 78063, (830) 751-3401, (830) 751-2727, Fax: (830) 751-2601

Sealy: North Central Fall Polka Festival

September 24, 2001

The Fall Polka Festival includes live polka music and dancing on wooden floor, food, and refreshments. Held at the Knights of Columbus Hall, at 1310 Highway 90 West.

Knights of Columbus Council #3313, B.J. Stolarski, P.O. Box 1133, Sealy, TX 77474-1133, (979) 885-6370, (979) 885-6786, kofc3313@usa.net

Victoria: South Victoria County Czech Heritage Festival

September 24, 2001

The Victoria County Czech Heritage Festival features live entertainment throughout the day with two dance bands. Event hours are 10 A.M.-7:30 P.M. There will be booths, displays, children's games, and tarok tournament. Held at the Victoria Community Center, at 2905 East North.

Victoria County Czech Heritage Society, Marjorie Matula, 745 Hosek Road, Victoria, TX 77905-5637, (361) 575-0820

Serbin: North Central Wendish Festival

September 24, 2001

The annual Wendish Fest features the Kovanda Czech Band, as well as a German sing-a-long. The Wendish noon meal centers around sausage. Cook-off and various arts and craft demonstrations such as egg decoration, butter making, and more. Exhibits, games, and contests take place all afternoon. There are three categories in the Coffee Cake Bakeoff and the State of Texas Noodle Cookoff is held in conjunction with the festival. Held at the St. Paul Lutheran

Picnic Grounds and Texas Wendish Heritage Society Museum, 5 miles southwest of Giddings via US 77 & Farm Road 2239.

Texas Wendish Heritage Society, Evelyn Kasper, Route 2, Box 155, Giddings, TX 78942, (979) 366-2441, Fax: (979) 366-2805, wendish@bluebon.net

Fredericksburg: Hill Country   Texas Woodcarver's Guild Fall Roundup

September 24-30, 2001

A great opportunity to see many of the state's top crafters.

Fredericksburg Convention & Visitor Bureau, 106 N. Adams, Fredericksburg, TX 78624, (830) 997-6523, Fax: (830) 997-8588, asstdir@fbg.net, www.fredericksburg-texas.com

Derek Spence does magical things with a chainsaw. He is a true artist. Photo by Sally Gramon.

New Braunfels: Hill Country   Comal County Fair

September 25-30, 2001

The Comal County Fair is celebrating its 105th anniversary with events such as a parade, bands, chili cookoff, and a PRCA rodeo. Area bands for entertainment Wednesday through Sunday. Other events include a best-dressed western contest for children, a baby barnyard, and a carnival. Held on the Comal County Fairgrounds, at 701 Common.

Comal County Fair Association, Jackie Smith, P.O. Box 310223, New Braunfels, TX 78131-1059, (830) 625-1666, (830) 625-1505, Fax: (830) 625-8411

Glen Rose: North Central   Fall Bluegrass

September 26-28, 2001

The Fall Bluegrass Festival at the RV River Resorts and Campground is one of the largest held in the state of Texas. Bluegrass artists from all over America perform old-time favorites, great gospel, and new traditional toe-tapping music. Grassroots music is for all ages so bring the family 'cause it's that kind of festival and that kind of park. Free cornbread and beans on Wednesday and open showcase. Held at RV River Resorts and Campground, at 2322 County Road at Hwy 67.

Machelle Ralls, 2322 County Road 312, Glen Rose, TX 76043, (254) 897-4253, Fax: (254) 897-7613, www.texasoutside.com/glenrose/calendar.html

Caldwell: Panhandle   Burleson County Fair
September 27-30, 2001

This old-fashioned country fair features five days of fun and entertainment with a variety of good food. Activities include a parade, junior livestock show and auction, carnival, commercial livestock exhibition, queen's contest, and a Little Miss award. Other events include a bake sale, creative living exhibits, crafts, and more. Held on the Burleson County Fairgrounds, on Highway 36.

Burleson County Fair Association, Jean Trout, P.O. Box 634, Caldwell, TX 77836, (979) 567-3218, Fax: (979) 596-2024, rtis.com/reg/caldwell/ent/

Titus: Hill Country   Titus County Fair
September 27-30, 2001

The Titus County Fair is a four-day event that features academic, agricultural, and sports events for all ages. A wide range of entertainment attractions are scheduled throughout the fair. The chicken stew challenge and creative arts contest attract adult participants. Different horsemanship events are scheduled nightly along with the traditional junior livestock shows. Nightly entertainment features country, gospel, and Hispanic music. Held at the Titus County Civic Center, on North Jefferson Street.

Titus County Fair, Steve Russell, P.O. Box 1232, Mount Pleasant, TX 75456-1232, (903) 577-8117, (903) 577-8117, Fax: (903) 577-3601, info@tituscountyfair.com

Kyle: Hill Country   Claiborne Kyle Day
September 28-29, 2002   4th weekend in September

A great weekend of festivities in a beautiful small town. A wide variety of events are held, including many booths with a variety of vendors. Saturday is officially Claiborne Kyle Fried Chicken Day, and the Kyle Log House is the center of a bunch of good eatin'. Don't miss it. Events are held in downtown Kyle, on I-35 15 minutes south of Austin.

For information contact City of Kyle, Stephen Harrison, City Administrator, 101 S. Burleson, Kyle, TX 78640, (512) 268-5341, www.kyle-tx.com/kyleweb

Lufkin: East   Texas State Forest Festival
4th week in September

The Texas State Forest Festival was created to recognize the importance of the timber industry to East Texas. Highlights include local entertainment, hushpuppy cookoff, arts and crafts, food, lumberjack show, woodcarving, and much more. Angelina County Exposition Center, Loop 287 at MLK.

Angelina County Chamber of Commerce, Sheila Adams, P.O. Box 1606, Lufkin, TX 75901, (936) 634-6644, Fax: (936) 634-8726, lufkintx@lcc.net

McKinney: North Central   Harvestfest & The Great McKinney Bed Races

September 28-29, 2002   **Last full weekend in September**

This is pure fun. That's right, bed races every hour. Then there is the Old-Time Fiddler's Association contest, two stages with live entertainment, a petting zoo, train rides, "celebrity" scarecrows, and the "maize maze." Located 30 mi. north of Dallas, off Hwy. 75, exit 40A, turn east on Louisiana. For details call (972) 562-6880 or (972) 562-6880.

Old Town Spring: Gulf   Heritage Holiday

September 28-29, 2002   **Last weekend in September**

A fun tribute to the many cultural influences on this town. There will be free street entertainment with singing, dancing, historic reenactments, clowns, and fun for the entire family. All ages will enjoy roaming the town and perusing the many classic automobiles that line the street for the Longhorn Rod Run. Ride the trolley for a view of the entire town, or stroll along; either way it's a step back in time. Don't miss this chance to have a blast and learn more about the town. Call 1-800-OLD-TOWN

San Antonio: South   International Accordion Festival

September 28-29, 2002

This free festival features some of the best accordionists in the world and lots of polka music. Pick a style you like; they play German, Colombian/ Vallenato, Irish, Argentine tango, Cajun/zydeco, Dominican merengue, and conjunto/tejano music. The events are held downtown in historic La Vallita, one of San Antonio's original settlements.

For information contact Juan Tejeda at (210) 207-6967, or e-mail at OCA1@ci.sat.tx.us, or call the San Antonio Convention & Visitors Bureau toll free at 1-800-THE-ALAMO, ext. 10. www.accordionusa.com

Plantersville: North Central   Texas Renaissance Festival

September 28 - November 17, 2002 Last weekend in September through mid-November

Fifty acres of fun, the Texas Renaissance Festival is a re-creation of a 16th-century English village. As you wander back in time you will be able to enjoy the fine arts, food, and frivolity of this significant period in world history. There are numerous musicians, from ancient instrument ensembles to strolling minstrels, plus arts and crafts and food booths to delight the eye and please the palate. Fun for all! Six miles south of Plantersville on FM 1774.

Texas Renaissance Festival, Shown Nichols, 21778 FM 1774, Plantersville, TX 77363, (936) 894-2516, (800) 458-3435, Fax: (936) 894-2391, herald@texrenfest.com

Texas Renaissance Festival
A trip back to the 16th century, without leaving Texas. Photo by Mike Annas.

Amarillo: Panhandle

League of Celtic Nations Festival & Highland Games

September 28-29, 2002   Last weekend in September

A salute to the Irish influence on Amarillo. There are band and dance competitions, Gaelic workshops, Highland athletic competitions, food, and music. Call (806) 374-3414

Trinity: East

Trinity Community Fair

September 28-29, 2002   Last weekend in September

This is a wonderful fair that combines the old and new. The whole community works on this fair, and there is something here for everyone including country western music, square dancers, Cajun music, and Scottish bagpipes complete with Highland dance and games. There are also art, agricultural, and horticultural exhibits, contests, bakeoffs, a parade, midway carnival, puppet shows, arts and crafts, petting zoo, and more. The festivities culminate with the 4-H FFA Youth Livestock Auction. Held on the Fairgrounds at the Community Center on Highway 19.

Trinity Fair Association, Derrell Martin, President, P.O. Box 549, Trinity, TX 75862, (936) 594-3856, (936) 594-4902, Fax: (936) 594-0558, trpcc@lcc.net

Hearne: North Central

Hearne Chamber of Commerce & Robertson County Go-Texan Cookoff & Sunflower Festival

September 28-29, 2002

Three neat events merged into one great weekend. Held at the Robertson County Fairgrounds in Hearne.

Hearne Area Chamber of Commerce 304 S. Market St., Hearne, TX 77859, (979) 279-2351, herncc1@alpha1.net, www.hearnechamber.com, www.ribman.com

Fort Bend: Hill Country

Fort Bend County Fair

Last weekend in September thru the 1st weekend in October
September 28 - October 6, 2002

Nine days of partying. The Fort Bend County Fair is an annual event that includes entertainment for all ages. Food, live music of every type, commercial booths, arts and crafts exhibits, livestock exhibits, petting zoo, pet show, daily rodeos, and, of course, a barbecue cookoff. Fort Bend County Fairgrounds, 4310 Highway 36 South.

Fort Bend County Fair Association, Travis Boeker, P.O. Box 428, Rosenberg, TX 77471, (281) 342-6171, Fax: (281) 342-0808, travis@fbcfa.org

Dallas: North Central

State Fair of Texas

September 28 - October 21, 2001

Four wonderful weekends. Don't you dare miss the opportunity to meet Big Tex! One of the largest and oldest fairs in the world, this event has something for everyone. The Fair is a 24-day entertainment showcase presented each fall in historic Fair Park in Dallas. Millions have enjoyed top country and pop artists, Broadway musicals, performances by the U.S. Marine Drum and Bugle Corps, and daily shows on outdoor stages. Other attractions include parades, laser show, crafts, exhibits, midway rides, livestock, college football, State Fair musical, and a gigantic new car show. Held at Fair Park, on Cullum Blvd. at Parry Avenue.

Big Tex greets visitors to the Texas State Fair in Dallas.

State Fair of Texas, Errol McKoy, President, P.O. Box 150009, Dallas, TX 75315, (214) 565-9931, Fax: (214) 421-8710, emckoy@greatstatefair.com, www.bigtex.com

Glen Rose: North Central   Glen Rose Bluegrass Reunion
September 29 - October 1, 2001

The Glen Rose Bluegrass Reunion is a hillbilly musicians program for non-professional and professional musicians. Bluegrass music and jam sessions go around the clock. There are also arts and crafts booths. Events are held at Oakdale Park, which is South of Hwy 67 on 144 South.

Oakdale Park, Pete May, P.O. Box 548, Glen Rose, TX 76043, (254) 897-2321, www.texasoutside.com/glenrose/calendar.html

Houston: Gulf   3rd Coast Music Conference
September 29-30, 2001

The 3rd Coast Music Conference was held September 30 through October 3 in Houston, Texas. This is a networking and showcasing event for the entertainment industry. The conference features live performances by today's hottest R&B and hip hop artists. We bring aspiring artists and established entertainment companies together for four days of music, fun, fashion, and sports. Held at Club Oasis, located at Westpark and Gessner.

Texas Quizzard Entertainment Quiz, 11000 Kinghurst Drive, Suite 147, Houston, TX 77099, (713) 478-2762

Corpus Christi: Gulf   Bayfest
September 29 - October 1, 2001

Bayfest is a weekend on the waterfront that began as a bicentennial celebration but has mushroomed into an event with regional popularity. Activities include fireworks, arts and crafts, carnival, games, a children's area, plenty of food booths, seven stages of continuous entertainment (bluegrass, blues, children's, Christian, classical, country, cowboy, folk, jazz, polka, R&B, rock, Latin/tejano). Events are held at I-37 and North Shoreline Boulevard.

Bayfest, Inc., Sharon Emerson, P.O. Box 1858, Corpus Christi, TX 78403-1858, (361) 887-0868, Fax: (361) 887-9773, bayfest@interconnect.net

Amarillo: Panhandle   Celtic Festival and Craft Faire
September 29 - October 1, 2001

The League of Celtic Nations presents its annual Celtic festival, Celtic arts, crafts, jewelry, musical instruments, clothing, and ethnic foods. Professional music concerts this year featured Eugene Byrne (Dublin, Ireland), Allen Damron (Austin, Texas), and more. Events are held at the Tri-State Fairgrounds (Rex Baxter Building), 2 miles north of I-40 on Grand Street and 10th Street.

League of Celtic Nations, Taylor Norman, P.O. Box 1397, Amarillo, TX 79105-1397, (806) 374-4243, (806) 374-4243, Fax: (806) 372-4203, lcnamarillo@yahoo.com

Wimberley: Hill Country   Day of the Scots

September 29 - October 1, 2001

The Day of the Scots festival features bagpipe players, Scottish bands, guitarists, accordionists, Highland dancing, sheep dog demonstrations, sportsfield demonstrations, folk songs, food concessions, vendors, and seminars on various Scottish topics. Held at the John Knox Ranch, 10 mi. west of Wimberley off RR 32.

John Knox Ranch, Rob Watson, 1661 John Knox Road, Fischer, TX 78623, (830) 935-4568, Fax: (830) 935-4189, johnknox@gvtc.com, www.texashill-cntry.com/wimberley

Wichita Falls: Panhandle   FallsFest

September 29-30, 2001

The FallsFest includes arts and crafts, fun run, food, games, and great musical fare on the banks of the Wichita River in Wichita Falls' Lucy Park. A festival that joins Wichita Falls and surrounding communities together for an eventful two days, FallsFest features exciting entertainment for the entire family and is now in its 13th year. Held at Lucy Park, on Seymour Highway at Sunset Blvd.

Junior League of Wichita Falls, 2302 Midwestern Parkway, Wichita Falls, TX 76308-2328, (940) 692-9797, Fax: (940) 691-3031

Hallettsville: North Central   Kolache Fest

September 30, 2001

The Kolache Fest is a German-Czech celebration featuring live polka and German music all day at the Knights of Columbus Hall. Other activities include the Kolache Bake Show, Kolache Eating Contest, a kolache demonstration, the downtown kolache parade, arts and crafts, Little Buns Diaper Derby, Country Walk, tug-a-war, volleyball tournament, horseshoes and washers, car show, golf tournament, rides, rodeo, food, biergardens, and a street dance. Held in the City Park.

Hallettsville Chamber of Commerce, Pat Carr, P.O. Box 313, Hallettsville, TX 77964, (361) 798-2662, Fax: (361) 798-2662, visit@hallettsville.com

Austin: Hill Country   Old Pecan Street Fall Arts Festival

September 29-30, 2001

The Old Pecan Street Fall Arts Festival includes arts and crafts, food, beverages, street performers, and more than 70 acts on five outdoor stages. Held on Sixth Street, between Congress Avenue and IH-35.

French Smith, 1710 South Lamar Blvd., No. B-C, Austin, TX 78704-8963, (512) 441-9015, Fax: (512) 441-9016, pop@mail.roadstarproductions.com

October

"Trail Ridin' Time Ain't It???

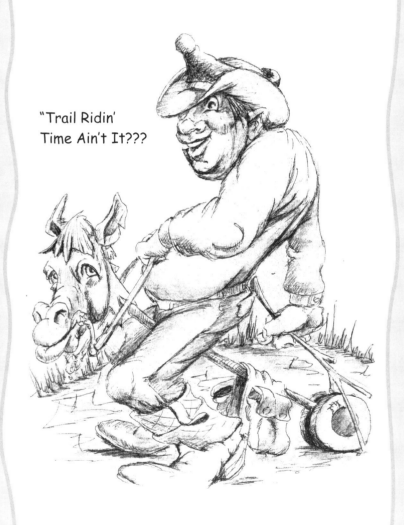

W ell there's a touch of fall in the air, and the festivals and fairs are in full swing. Of course the grandaddy of them all, the Texas State Fair, is in full swing. Don't miss this one.

Many Texans have roots in Germany, and October is a busy time in Texas. We have dozens of German communities in Texas that do a bit of celebratin' at this time of year. Over the years I've particularly enjoyed visiting the events at New Braunfels and Fredericksburg.

It's also pumpkin time, and throughout the state folks gather to have some Halloween fun. Costumes and craziness are always welcome.

And there are more Texas history related celebrations to honor the firing of the first shots in the battle for Texas independence on October 2, 1835.

Meanwhile in Luckenbach there is a ladies-only chili cookoff championship. My friend Hondo put it together years ago because some cookoffs, back then, didn't allow the ladies to enter.

Always double check the dates of the events.

Dallas: North Central   State Fair of Texas
September 28 - October 21, 2001

Four wonderful weekends. Don't you dare miss the opportunity to meet Big Tex!

One of the largest and oldest fairs in the world, this event has something for everyone. The Fair is a 24-day entertainment showcase presented each fall in historic Fair Park in Dallas. Millions have enjoyed top country and pop artists, Broadway musicals, performances by the U.S. Marine Drum and Bugle Corps, and daily shows on outdoor stages. Other attractions include parades, laser show, crafts, exhibits, midway rides, livestock, college football, State Fair musical, and a gigantic new car show. Held at Fair Park, on Cullum Blvd. at Parry Avenue.

State Fair of Texas, Errol McKoy, President, P.O. Box 150009, Dallas, TX 75315, (214) 565-9931, Fax: (214) 421-8710, emckoy@greatstatefair.com, www.bigtex.com

Angleton: Gulf   Brazoria County Fair

September 15 - October 14, 2001

The Brazoria County Fair includes cookoffs, rodeo, live entertainment, and dancing. Brazoria County Fair is the largest county fair in Texas. There is something for everyone during this nine-day fair. Held at the Brazoria County Fairgrounds, at 901 Downing Road. Events begin in September, ending with fair held October 5-13.

Brazoria County Fat Stock and Fair Association, P.O. Box 818, Angleton, TX 77516, (979) 849-6416, Fax: (979) 849-6985, bcfa@mastnet.net, www.bcfa.org

Whitney: North Central   Pioneer Days

Held every October

The town is located on Corps of Engineers' Lake Whitney, which is a nice place to camp in the fall. Festival includes a parade, arts and crafts area, kids' games, horseshoe tournament, live entertainment all day, and a street dance. The local fire department also puts on a dance Saturday night, giving you double opportunity to meet others. Call (254) 694-2540 for more information.

Roanoke: North Central   Hawkwood Medieval Fantasy Faire

September 1 - October 14, 2001   Weekends between late August and mid-October

Re-creation of a fictitious Medieval village based around A.D. 1000 with a hundred shops, ten stages, and hundreds of costumed characters. Stunt show! Storytelling, music, dance, combat, comedy, drama, horse shows, games. They have bawdy shows for adults and play areas for the kids! All in the shade of beautiful, old-growth oaks, with nearly 100% coverage. Held on the southeast corner of I-35W & SH 114, 20 miles north of Ft. Worth. For more information, call 1-800-782-3629. www.hawkwood.org

Conroe: East   Lobsterfest

October 4, 2001

Great fun and, needless to say, some mighty good eatin'. (936) 756-6644. www.conroe.org/

Marietta: East   Fall, Fun, Food, Fest

October 5, 2002   1st Saturday in October

Parades, bake auctions, needlepoint contest, tournaments for dominos, volleyball, horseshoe, washer toss, and tug of war. A wide variety of entertainers keep the music and the party going all day long and a street dance that night. We give away everything from a rifle to quilts, drawings all through the day. Come on down to our hometown and enjoy it all day. Call (903) 835-2060 Cindy Climer or (903) 835-2902 Pat Holmes.

Denton: North Central   Arts, Antiques & Autos Extravaganza
October 5, 2002   1st Saturday in October

More family fun. Juried art show booths, Antique Walk, classic car show, special Kid Zone, and festival foods. Have your family heirloom appraised, enjoy strolling entertainment, or check out the dream machines lining the historic downtown square. Call (940) 349-8529.

Cameron: North Central   Arts & Crafts Fair
October 5, 2002   1st Saturday in October

Fun, food, and loads of crafts in 150 booths, under the shady oaks in City Park, which is located on Highway 36, (254) 697-4979, camerontx@tlab.net

Midland: West   AirSho 2001
October 5-6, 2002   1st weekend in October

The AirSho features the Air Force's World War II Airpower Demonstration and the world-renowned "Tora Tora Tora!" reenactment. Held at the Confederate Air Force/American Airpower Heritage Museum. Call (915) 563-1000.

Gonzales: South   "Come and Take It" Days Celebration
October 5-6, 2002   Weekend nearest October 2

Gonzales' "Come and Take It" Days is a three-day festival that commemorates the firing of the first shot for Texas's Independence on October 2, 1835. Attractions include live music under the beer tent all weekend, as well as street dances. Music includes country, rock, polka, and tejano. It all happens on the square in scenic downtown Gonzales.

The famous "Come and Take It" cannon that fired the first shot for Texas independence on October 2, 1835, in Gonzales, Texas.

Gonzales Chamber of Commerce, Barbara Hand, P.O. Box 134, Gonzales, TX 78629, (830) 672-6532, (830) 672-6532, Fax: (830) 672-6533, info@gonzalestexas.com

Refugio: Gulf   Refugio's Festival of the Flags
October 5-6, 2002   Held the 1st full weekend in October

Join us for a 2-day festival celebrating our Native American culture on the downtown streets of Refugio. Enjoy a Native American powwow, storytelling, demonstrations, art and craft booths, food booths, children's area, musical entertainment, volleyball and horseshoe tournament, and historic homes tour (Sunday only for tour). No carnival or alcohol. Located in the Texas Gulf Coast Region. For more information call (512) 526-2835.

Temple: North Central — Early Day Tractor and Engine Association Annual Show

October 5-6, 2002   1st full weekend in October

The festival takes place on a 48-acre fairground near IH-35 in Temple. Watch as hundreds of antique tractors, engines, and farming implements demonstrate early day farming activities, from grain threshing to corn shelling, rope making, and water pumping. Enjoy delicious homemade ice cream, barbecue, and beans. Become a member and enjoy swapping parts or yarns and restore a piece of your heritage. Bring the whole family! Take Exit 302 west on Nugent, then right on Eberhardt. For more information, call (254) 774-9988 or (254) 298-5720.

Lake Lewisville: North Central — Escape to Chili Island - Chili Cookoff & Junkanoo BBQ

October 5-6, 2001

Sneaky Pete's Restaurant, at Lake Lewisville, is the site for another cool cookoff.

Kim Worley, Lone Star Parrot Head Club, (817) 472-9095, doornbr3@flash.net, www.ribman.com

Fredericksburg: Hill Country — Oktoberfest

October 5-7, 2001   1st weekend in October

The Polka Capital of Texas, Fredericksburg's authentic Oktoberfest combines the traditions of the Old World with the best of Fredericksburg! Polka, waltz, two-step, and line dancing featured. Food concessions, arts, and heirloom displays. German music is the main emphasis with three days and three stages of the best German music around. There are over 20 bands that will perform throughout the weekend. Held at the Market Square, at 100 East Main Street downtown.

Creative Marketing, Debbie Farquhar, P.O. Box 222, Fredericksburg, TX 78624, (830) 997-4810, Fax: (830) 997-9628, creative@ktc.com, www.fredericksburgtexas.net

Winnie: Gulf — Texas Rice Festival

October 5-7, 2001

Texas Rice Festival provides a county fair atmosphere with entertainment for people of all ages. Festivities include, BBQ & fajita cookoff, open horse show, carnival, rice education exhibit, 4-H & FFA livestock show, craft show, photography contest, art contest, antique car show, farm equipment display, Go

Texan activities, old-time fiddlin' contest, street dance, grand parade, and live music daily (country, Cajun, jazz, bluegrass, and Christian). Held at the Winnie-Stowell Park, between LeBlanc and South Park Streets.

Texas Rice Festival, Carol Gentz, P.O. Box 147, Winnie, TX 77665, (409) 296-4404, (409) 296-4404, Fax: (409) 296-9293, trf@IH2000.net

Sanderson: West   Prickly Pear Pachanga

October 5-7, 2001

The cactus capital of Texas celebrates cactus in music, food, costume, art, and products. Costume contest, coronation of Miss Cactus Flower and King Tuna, chili cookoff (CASI), hot sauce contest, cactus cooking contest, cactus-theme arts and crafts booths, parade, live music and dance, ranchero music festival. Held on the courthouse square.

Prickly Pear Pachanga, Sally Rawlins, P.O. Drawer 640, Sanderson, TX 79848, (915) 345-2275, Fax: (915) 345-2653, cactuscapital@sandersontx.net, www.sandersontx.org

Center: East   East Texas Poultry Festival

October 5-7, 2001

East Texas Poultry Festival is a three-day event that includes a broiler show and auction, carnival, art show, street dance, arts and crafts, food booths, queen's contest, and live entertainment and other local talent. Held on the town square.

Shelby County Chamber of Commerce, Pam Phelps, Executive Director, 100 Courthouse Square, No. A-101, Center, TX 75935, (936) 598-3682, Fax: (936) 598-8163, shelby@qzip.net

Waco: North Central   Heart O' Texas Fair and Rodeo

October 5-13, 2002   **1st two full weekends in October**

The Heart O' Texas Fair and Rodeo will feature country music favorites such as Jerry Jeff Walker and other Nashville stars. 40,000 attend the PRCA rodeo, carnival midway, food vendors, exhibits, and horse and livestock shows. Held at the Heart O' Texas Fair Complex, at 4601 Bosque Boulevard.

Heart O' Texas Fair Complex, Mark Miller, P.O. Box 7581, Waco, TX 76714, (254) 776-1660, Fax: (254) 776-1667, fairstaff@hot1.net, www.wacocvb.com

Trailridin' Coffee is Somethin' "Special"
"What's Left in This Pot is Fer Road Repair!"

Brownwood: Hill Country   Depot Jazz and Blues Series

October 6, 2001

The Depot Jazz and Blues Series features contemporary jazz and blues by various artists. Multiple artists are scheduled. Reserved and general seating tickets are available. Held at the Depot Civic and Cultural Center, at 600 Depot Street.

Brownwood Chamber of Commerce - Arts Council of Brownwood, Donna Posey, Executive Secretary, P.O. Box 880, Brownwood, TX 76804, (915) 646-9535, Fax: (915) 643-6686, bwdtexcc@web-access.net

Nacogdoches: East   East Texas Pinetop Blues Festival

October 6, 2001

Footprints Foundation invites you to attend the East Texas Pinetop Blues Festival as it features local, regional, and nationally accomplished blues and gospel artists and celebrities. Starting at noon to evening twilight, Saturday, October 6, at the Longview Convention Center, the various flavors of the blues and its influences resound from the main stage at the festival grounds. Also featured will be many kinds of regional and ethnic foods, crafts, and event paraphernalia. Everything combined, this historic East Texas picnic comes alive as blues enthusiasts everywhere make their way to Nacogdoches. Ticket information is available through Longview Convention Center Office at (903) 237-1230. Held at the Longview Convention Center.

Nacogdoches Chamber of Commerce. Kelly McVay, P.O. Box 632125, Nacogdoches, TX 75963, (936) 568-0188, (877) 521-6428, hdinc@flash.net

Jasper: East   Jasper Fall Fest
October 6, 2001

Jasper Fall Fest is a festival filled with special events and live musical performances. Cajun night on Friday includes Cajun music and a gumbo cookoff. Thursday is country & western night. On Saturday, activities include arts, crafts, and antiques show, business expo, antique car show, contests, games, great food, and much more. Held on the courthouse square.

Jasper Chamber of Commerce, Wynn Dee Baker, 246 East Milam, Jasper, TX 75951, (409) 384-2762, Fax: (409) 384-4733, jaspercc@inu.net, www.jaspercoc.org

Luckenbach: Hill Country   Ladies State Chili Bust
October 6, 2001

The Ladies State Chili Bust features music by Gary P. Nunn. Over 100 ladies complete for the state title. Legend has it that Hondo started the Ladies State Chili Bust to give womenfolk a place to cook chili and show off where nobody'll see 'em because Chilympiad in San Marcos did not allow women to cook. This is one of the few weekends that camping is allowed in Luckenbach, and campfire revelry extends into the wee hours. Held in scenic downtown Luckenbach.

VelAnne Howle, 412 Luckenbach Town Loop, Fredericksburg, TX 78624, (830) 997-3224, Fax: (830) 997-1024, somebody@luckenbachtexas.com, www.luckenbachtexas.com

San Marcos: Hill Country   Tejano Fest
October 6, 2001

The San Marcos Hispanic Chamber of Commerce Tejano Fest features live music all day and night, food, arts and crafts, and children's activities. Lots of fun for the entire family! Featured top tejano recording artists. Held at the Hays County Civic Center, at 100 Civic Center Loop.

San Marcos Hispanic Chamber of Commerce. Ray Hernandez, Director, P.O. Box 1051, San Marcos, TX 78667, (512) 353-1103, Fax: (512) 353-2175

Crosby: Gulf   Czechfest
October 6, 2001

The Czechfest features barbecue, games, bingo, arts and crafts, children's area, Czech and western music, auction, cake booth, and plants. Area is under cover and protected from heat and rain. Held on the Crosby Fairgrounds, on FM 2100.

Sacred Heart Church, John Swinney, 915 Runneburg Street, Crosby, TX 77532, (281) 328-4871, (281) 328-1075, Fax: (281) 328-1075

Olmito: Gulf   John Lennon Birthday Jam
October 6-7, 2001

A great event to honor a great songwriter. To celebrate John Lennon's birthday, there are loads of live music, songwriting contests, a street dance, cowboy poetry readings, and a rodeo. Held at the John Lennon Memorial Park.

The John Lennon Society, Bruce Qualley, P.O. Box 366, Olmito, TX 78575, (956) 350-9714, (512) 448-2168

Seabrook: Gulf   Seabrook Music Festival
October 6-7, 2001

The Seabrook Music Festival offers many attractions, including a carnival, food concessions, chili, brisket and gumbo cookoffs, and arts and crafts vendors. There is an area designed for young children with a variety of entertainment options (clowns, jugglers, etc.). There will be two stages of live music and roaming musicians. Held at Seabrook Festival Park, on Highway 146 at Red Bluff.

A typical outdoor music festival in Texas. Bring your chair and cooler. Pull up and sit a spell.

Seabrook Association, Jesse W. Jones, P.O. Box 1107, Seabrook, TX 77586, (281) 474-3838, Fax: (281) 474-3838, akruch@aol.com

Harker Heights: North Central   Annual Star Fest
October 6-7, 2001

The stars are out, and so are the arts, crafts, and food booths. Held at the Carl Levin Park, which is located off FM 2410 and Highway 190 at Miller's Crossing, (254) 699-4999, www.harkerheights.com

Round Rock: Hill Country   Frontier Days
October 6-7, 2001

Frontier Days is a celebration commemorating the early history of the old cattle drive days on the Chisholm Trail. Don't miss the fiddling contests, street dance, and even cowboy poetry readings. Food and arts and crafts booths offer a variety of items to the attendees. Numerous events for children and adults including the reenactment of the shooting of Sam Bass. Dances are scheduled for the evening. Held in downtown Round Rock.

Keith Hickman, P.O. Box 5216, Round Rock, TX 78683-5216, (512) 255-9690, (800) 747-3479

Austin: Hill Country   Austin Record Convention

October 6-7, 2001

The Austin Record Convention is a 250-booth trade fair held twice a year for music enthusiasts interested in albums and CDs. It is the largest record convention in the U.S.—a must for dedicated record collectors or just casual music fans. From old 78s to new CDs and everything in between. Held at the Palmer Auditorium, located at 400 South First Street.

ARC, Doug Hanners, P.O. Box 90806, Austin, TX 78709-0806, (512) 288-7288, Fax: (512) 288-7227, ausrecs@inetport.com, www.austinrecords.com

Snyder: Panhandle   White Buffalo Festival

October 6-7, 2001

The White Buffalo Festival features a chuck wagon dinner at the Hays Ranch with live entertainment and a dance. Others who entertain at the festival include the Hays County Gals and Pals, "Texas Stand," and "Cow Jazz" along with cowboy poets and Indian tribes. Other activities during the festival include a parade, buggy rides, art shows, crafts and food booths, auction, "shootouts," street dance, and a melodrama. Held at the County Courthouse Square.

Snyder Chamber of Commerce, Eddie Williams, P.O. Box 840, Snyder, TX 79550, (915) 573-3558, Fax: (915) 573-9721, SnyChCom@SnyderTex.com, www.SnyderTex.com

Austin: Hill Country   Austin Bob Marley Festival

October 6-7, 2001

The annual Bob Marley Festival Tour includes many Texas dates. The annual festival features live concert entertainment, jugglers, dance troupes, poetry readings, Jamaican, African, Caribbean, reggae, and world beat music provided by bands from all over the world. In addition to the entertainment, the celebration features a special kid's playscape area and at some shows, Caribbean, African, American, and Third World countries arts and crafts along with some of the best Caribbean, African, American, and Third World countries foods anywhere. All proceeds benefit the Capital Area Food Bank. Held on Auditorium Shores, on Town Lake.

Capital Area Food Bank, Pat Costiga, 2200 FM 2001, Buda, TX 78610, (512) 791-6188, (512) 312-0435, Fax: (512) 312-0435, bobmarleyfest@hotmail.com

Rockport: Gulf   Seafair

October 6-7, 2001

The Rockport Seafair is two days of fun, feast, and frolic on festival grounds at the Rockport Ski Basin. Events include a gumbo cookoff, live music, parade, arts and crafts fair, crab races, Gator Bait Ski Team, kids fishing tournament, carnival, and much more. Fun for all ages. Held on the Rockport Festival Grounds in downtown Rockport at Harbor and Ski Basin roads.

Rockport Seafair Inc., Mindy Dieter, P.O. Box 2256, Rockport, TX 78381, (361) 729-3312, (361) 729-1708, www.1rockport.org

Winedale: North Central   Oktoberfest

October 6-7, 2001

Winedale Oktoberfest includes bluegrass and German music, along with a barbershop quartet, tours of restored 19th-century buildings, pioneer demonstrations such as fireplace cooking, spinning, soap making, horsehair braiding, hooked rug making, and one-act German comedies will be performed. Continuous live entertainment along with food and drink. Held at the Winedale Historical Center, on FM 2714 at Round Top.

Winedale History Center, Gloria Jaster, P.O. Box 11, Round Top, TX 78954, (979) 278-3530, Fax: (979) 278-3531, g.jaster@mail.utexas.edu, www.cah.u-texas.edu/divisions/Winedale.html

Think I'm in Bad Shape?
My horse is Passed Out
in the Street!

Lubbock: Panhandle   Farmer Stockman Show

October 9-11, 2001   3 days during the 2nd week in October

The Farmer Stockman Show demonstrates what makes today's farms work. This 3-day agricultural trade show has over 300 exhibitors. Want to try something out? Well you can, because the show is held on 500 acres of land, where there are demonstrations. Outdoor displays take place at the Lubbock City Farm on east 50th. For information call (806) 747-5232.

Houston: Gulf   Harris County Fair

October 10-14, 2001

The Houston-Harris County Fair has a carnival, arts and crafts, food booths, livestock, live music, barbecue cookoff the week before, rodeo on Friday and Saturday nights, competitions, and it ends on Sunday with a junior auction.

Houston Dick Atkins, One Abercrombie Drive, Houston, TX 77084, (281) 463-6650, Fax: (281) 463-4165, www.co.harris.tx.us

Dallas: North Central   North Texas New Music Festival

October 10-14, 2001

This great festival features over 100 acts from the Southwest, from every type of music. The festival includes two days of showcases, a noisy auction benefitting Sweet Relief, and other fun music-related events. Held in the Deep Ellum section of Dallas.

North Texas New Music Festival, Sam Paulos/Jeffrey Yarbrough, 10486 Brockwood Road, Dallas, TX 75238, (214) 349-5057, (972) 994-1053, Fax: (214) 349-3819, musicfest@crystalclearsound.com, www.newmusicfestival.com

Deep Ellum Association, 2932 Main Street, Suite 101, Dallas, TX 75226, (214) 748-4332, info@deepellumtx.com, www.deepellumtx.com

Nacogdoches: East   Piney Woods Fair

October 10-14, 2001

The Piney Woods Fair is an old-fashioned county fair. Shows include home canning, crafts, arts, photography, quilts, and agriculture include dairy, beef, Brangus, lamb, poultry, hog, and agricultural mechanics. We have a variety of music and free entertainment. Held at the Nacogdoches County Exposition Center, located at 3805 Northwest Stallings.

Nacogdoches County Exposition Center, Inc., Kent Crank, 3805 Northwest Stallings Drive, Nacogdoches, TX 75961, (936) 564-0849, Fax: (936) 564-9228, www.nacogdoches.org

Falfurrias: South   Fiesta del Campo
October 11-14, 2001

Fiesta del Campo features live tejano and country music. Fiesta attractions include food, family entertainment, trail ride, pan de campo, arts and crafts, horseshoe tournament, fajita cooking contest, dancing, and a softball and golf tournament. Mary and Ed Lasater Park, Highway 281 North and Forest Street.

Falfurrias Chamber of Commerce, Gus Barrera, P.O. Box 476, Falfurrias, TX 78355, (361) 325-3333, (361) 325-3333, Fax: (361) 325-3887

Beaumont: Gulf   Best of Texas International Music Awards
October 11-14, 2001

The International Music Awards always has a great list of talent lined up. Special guests have included Texas legendary artists/songwriter Floyd Tillman, Grand Ole Opry stars Ernie Ashworth and Claude Gray, Lief Kerstein and the Winchester band. Held at the Hilton Hotel, at 2355 I-10 & Washington Boulevard.

For information call (409) 842-3600. Colonel Billy D. Foster, Executive Director, 7845 Fox Cove, Beaumont, TX 77713, (409) 892-5118, (936) 856-5547, nansaw@gtis.net, ssrecords.techplanet.net/NEWSLETTER.htm

Seguin: South   Guadalupe County Fair
October 11-14, 2001

The Guadalupe County Fair emphasizing agricultural and livestock activities also provides entertainment through carnival, rodeo, live music and dance bands. Held at the Guadalupe County Fairgrounds, on Business Highway 123 South.

Guadalupe County Agricultural and Livestock Fair, P.O. Box 334, Seguin, TX 78155, (830) 379-6477, Fax: (830) 379-6477, www.seguintx.org www.ci.seguin.tx.us

Bellville: North Central   Austin County Fair
October 11-15, 2001

Austin County Fair features Nashville entertainment, carnival, parades, PRCA rodeo, barbecue, live entertainment, hypnotist, clowns, and stilt walkers on the fairgrounds. Activities include horseshoe pitching, team penning, domino tournament, and washer pitch. Held at the Austin County Fairgrounds, on Highway 159 East.

Austin County Fair, Susan Rathbone, P.O. Box 141, Bellville, TX 77418, (979) 865-5995, Fax: (979) 865-5216, acfair@industryinet.com

Austin: Hill Country   Austin Film Festival & Heart of Film Screenwriters Conference

October 11-18, 2001

This wonderful event is the first dedicated to celebrating the art, craft, and business of screenwriters. The festival features a 4-day screenwriters conference and an 8-night film program. The events take place at a number of theaters around town. (512) 478-4795, austinfilm@aol.com, www.austinfilmfest.com

Lufkin: East   Pineywoods Purgatory

October 12, 2002   2nd Saturday in October

Riders to your bikes! Pick your poison and endurance level from the 25-mile, 52-mile, 68-mile, or 102-mile bike rides through the rolling hills of East Texas. Events start at the Angelina County Exposition Center.

For information contact the Lufkin Convention & Visitors Bureau, 1615 S. Chestnut, Lufkin, TX 75901, (800) 409-5659, lufkintx@lcc.net

Tynan: Gulf   Tynan Rec. Club Festival & BBQ

October 12-13, 2001

Held in downtown Tynan. Ed Wilson, (361) 547-8061, www.ribman.com

Kerrville: Hill Country   Kerr County Fair

October 12-13, 2002   2nd weekend in October

Activities include chili and barbecue cookoff teams, stage entertainment featuring storytellers, bands, and performers, various contests including ugly hat and lovely legs, shoe box parade, pig scramble and goat milking, bull and barrel fest, team roping, petting zoo, carnival and midway, cowboy church, 5-K run, talent contest, judged exhibits of crafts and skills, classic car show, and a country auction. Located at the Hill Country Youth Exhibit Center on Hwy. 27 East adjoining the Guadalupe River, 60 miles northwest of San Antonio on IH-10. For more information, call (830) 257-6833.

Rising Star: Panhandle   Annual Octoberfest & Barbecue Cookoff

October 12-13, 2001

Held at the City Park in Rising Star.

For information contact Coan Heath, Chamber of Commerce, P.O. Box 189, Rising Star, TX 76471, (254) 643-2811, www.ribman.com.

New Braunfels: Hill Country   Gruene Musicfest

October 12-14, 2001   2nd weekend in October

Music flows at nearly flood levels on the banks of the Guadalupe River in beautiful historic Gruene (pronounced green) just outside New Braunfels, as the Annual Gruene Musicfest raises money for charity. Held at Gruene Hall, located at 1281 Gruene Road.

New Braunfels Chamber of Commerce, Corbie Jones, 390 South Seguin, New Braunfels, TX 78130, (915) 392-3302, (830) 625-2385, Fax: (915) 392-5467, CactusOz@aol.com, www.gruenehall.com www.gruene.net

Cuero: South   Turkeyfest Parade and Festival
October 12-14, 2001

The Turkeyfest Parade begins in downtown Cuero and proceeds to Cuero City Park. The festival features continuous music (outdoor stage), street dances, cookoffs, art show, cantina, arts and crafts, food, rides, and a Great Gobbler Gallop. The music covers the range from country, rock, polka, and tejano. Held at the Cuero City Park, located in the 1000 Block of East Broadway.

Turkeyfest Association, Brett Duckett, 124 East Church Street, Cuero, TX 77954, (361) 275-6351, (361) 275-2112, www.cuero.org

Wimberley: Hill Country   Gospel Music Festival
October 12-14, 2001   2nd weekend in October

Praise the Lord and sing the music. This wonderful festival features local, regional, national, and international talent. The outdoor, family-style event includes a wide range of music: traditional to contemporary, black to bluegrass, vocal and instrumental gospel at its very best. Festival favorites include Clifton Jansky, The Bells of Joy, Crimson River, The Hillsiders, Step of Faith, John Page's Sax, Bebbie Hernandez, and many more. With an outdoor pavilion, we can play rain or shine! Held at Lion's Field, which is located on FM 2325.

Wimberley Gospel Music Assoc, Kent Singleton, P.O. Box 1825, Wimberley, TX 78676, (512) 847-9357, wimberleychurch@juno.com, www.texashill-cntry.com/wimberley www.wimberley.org

Austin: Hill Country   Mediterranean Festival
October 12-14, 2001

The Mediterranean Festival features live music, ethnic food, and dancing from 6 P.M. on Friday and 5 P.M. on Saturday. Held at 408 East 11th Street.

Louis Mecey, 408 East 11th Street, Austin, TX 78701-2617, (512) 345-9514, (512) 476-2314, webmaster@st-elias.org

Houston: Gulf   Festival Chicano
October 12-14, 2001

Festival Chicano is a celebration of Chicano culture featuring music (from popular tejano to mariachi—all ranges), dance, and drama. Held at the Miller Outdoor Theatre.

Daniel Bustamante, P.O. Box 3493, Houston, TX 77253, (713) 222-2783, (713) 284-8350, Fax: (713) 524-7547

Grand Prairie: North Central   Trader's Village BBQ

October 12-14, 2001

Held in downtown Grand Prairie. Allan Hughes, (972) 647-2331, www.rib-man.com

Conroe: East   Conroe Cajun Catfish Festival

October 12-14, 2001   2nd weekend in October

The Conroe Cajun Catfish Festival offers three days of Cajun music, food, arts and crafts, a parade, kids' village, beer garden, kids' activities, gumbo cookoff, carnival, and Texas Village. It's Conroe's biggest "party on the square" with Cajun catfish, boudain, etouffee, and gumbo. There are also six continuous live music stages, featuring a wide variety of musical styles (Cajun, country, folk, tejano). Events are held downtown, at the Courthouse Square.

Friends of Conroe, Barbara Metyko, P.O. Box 541992, Houston, TX 77254, (713) 863-9994, (800) 324-2604, Fax: (936) 539-6010, bmetyko@gte.net, http://mcia.com/cajun.htm

Pasadena: Gulf   Pasadena Livestock Show, Rodeo and Fair

October 12-20, 2001

The Pasadena Livestock Show, Rodeo and Fair features a barbecue cookoff September 10-13 and rodeo September 18-26. Held on the Pasadena Fairgrounds, located at 7601 Red Bluff.

Sherri Harnar, 7601 Red Bluff Road, Pasadena, TX 77507-1003, (281) 487-0240, Fax: (281) 487-7067, rodeo@pasadenaradio.com, www.pasadena-rodeo.com

Johnson City: Hill Country   Cowboy Songs and Poetry

October 13, 2001

I always enjoy going to this gathering of cowboys at the Johnson National Historic Park as they present some of the lighter moments of the Old West. At the cabin where President Johnson's grandparents lived and ran a cattle business, modern cowboys meet to sing traditional songs, talk about the old days in poetry, and spin tales the equal of any that were told when the west was really wild. This is 1860s entertainment you can't afford to miss. Events are held at the Lyndon B. Johnson National Historical Park, Johnson Settlement, Johnson City, Texas.

Write Park Headquarters, Lyndon B. Johnson National Historical Park, P.O. Box 329, Johnson City, TX 78636-0329, or call (830) 868-7128 ext. 244, www.nps.gov/lyjo/visit.htm

Medina: Hill Country

Bluegrass Festival, Antique Tractor, and Gas Engine Show

October 13, 2001   2nd Saturday in October

A neat festival in a beautiful setting. Listen to the bluegrass whilst sitting in a 100-year-old pecan orchard, on the banks of the Medina River. There is live music, gun shows, and a tractor parade at 2 P.M. This is an alcohol-free event. There are food and drinks available. Bring your lawn chair and enjoy the music all day 10 A.M.-7 P.M., Held on Highway 16 in scenic downtown Medina, on the Apple Festival grounds. Call (830) 589-7224. www.medinatexas.com

Johnson City: Hill Country   Heritage Crafts Day

October 13-14, 2002   2nd weekend in October

Frontier living comes alive as expert artisans demonstrate time-honored skills that went west with the pioneers. Enjoy authentic crafts such as spinning, weaving, lace and basket making, and quilting. Fun for the kids with puppet shows, storytelling, and a chuck wagon camp. Cooking demonstrations by the "cabin lady" and blacksmithing arts complete the day. Free shuttle via electric bus from the park Visitor Center or stroll down the nature trail. Held at the Lyndon B. Johnson National Historical Park, Johnson Settlement.

Marshall: East   Fire Ant Festival

October 13-14, 2001   2nd weekend in October

How do you call fire ants? What is the best technique for tossing a rubber chicken? These and other questions I'm sure you have worried about are answered at the Fire Ant Festival. There's also a fire ant roundup, beverage coaster throw, street dances, chili cook-off, fire ant fun run, clogging exhibition, barbershop quartets, food, and arts and crafts. Round-the-clock entertainment on the center stage featuring variety acts, live bands (gospel, country, rock, and children's music), karate exhibitions, jump rope teams, clowns, gymnastics demonstrations, and magicians. Street dance with a live band on Saturday night. Held in the downtown square.

A family of fire ants at the Marshall Fire Ant Festival. They even have a fire ant calling contest! Photo courtesy of the Greater Marshall Chamber of Commerce.

Greater Marshall Chamber of Commerce, Pam Whisenant, P.O. Box 520, Marshall, TX 75670, (903) 935-7868, Fax: (903) 935-9982, http://www.tourtexas.com/marshall/marshall_events.html

Amarillo: Panhandle — Big Boo Halloween Festival

October 14-31, 2001 — **2 weeks preceding Halloween**

Great Halloween fun for all ages. The grounds of the Big Texan Steak Ranch become a large Halloween festival with haunted houses, mazes, pumpkins, and scarecrows. Weekday evenings and all day on weekends. Held at the Big Texan Steak Ranch on Interstate 40 east in Amarillo. Call (806) 372-6000.

Houston: Gulf — Bayou City Art Festival - Downtown

October 13-14, 2001 — **2nd weekend in October**

The Bayou City Art Festival features over 300 artists displaying their work. There is live music and lots of food. This festival occurs twice a year, in October and March. Hermann Square, 900 Smith, Houston 77002.

Art Colony Association, Lynette Wallace, P.O. Box 66650, Houston, TX 77266-6650, (713) 521-0133, Fax: (713) 521-0013, artfest@swbell.net, http://www.gomainst.com/houston/houevents.htm

Athens: North Central — Black-Eyed Pea Fall Harvest

October 13-14, 2001 — **2nd full weekend in October**

More peas please! It was so good in the spring we decided to have another one in the fall. Events include the cookoff, the Miss Black-Eyed Pea Pageant, Miss Athens Pageant, and Little Miss Black-Eyed Pea Pageant. Gospel music, arts and crafts, square dancing, games for young and old, horseshoe tournament, a carnival, lots of food everywhere, participation sports including a jaunt, bass tournament, terrapin races, pea eatin' pea shellin', watermelon eatin' contests, a pet show, and entertainment at the bandstand. For information, contact the Athens Chamber of Commerce, (903) 675-5181, 1-800-755-7878. Events are held at Central Park. Athens Chamber of Commerce, Stephanie, 1206 South Palestine, Athens, TX 75751, (903) 675-5181, ssamonebyrd@aol.com, www.athensvip.org www.athenscc.org

Shiner: South — Bocktoberfest

October 13, 2001 — **2nd Saturday in October**

Enjoy a full day of great music and fresh beer alongside the Spoetzl Brewery, Texas oldest independent brewery. Gate opens at noon, and it ends with fireworks at 10 P.M. Events take place at the Spoetzl Brewery, at 603 East Brewery.

Bill Lee, P.O. Box 368, Shiner, TX 77984-0368, (361) 594-3383, (800) 574-4637, Fax: (361) 594-4334, shiner@shiner.com, www.shiner.com

All the Cooks
is Redy Fer da
Cookin off!

Mount Vernon: North Central   Countryfest

October 13, 2001   2nd Saturday in October

Always start your partying with a good breakfast! The Countryfest includes a pancake breakfast, stew cookoff, art show, train rides, dunking booth, live entertainment, rod run, and a variety of contests. Events are held downtown.

Mount Vernon Key Club, Vickie Blevins, P.O. Box 879, Mount Vernon, TX 75457, (903) 537-7101, www.mt-vernon.com

Mineral Wells: North Central   Crazy Water Festival

October 13, 2001

The Crazy Water Festival includes a salute to "Crazy Water," live continuous entertainment, arts and crafts, games, contests, 10K run, "42" tournament, softball tournament, and children's game area. Held in downtown Mineral Wells.

Crazy Water Festival, Mark Witschorke, P.O. Box 393, Mineral Wells, TX 76068, (940) 325-2121, (800) 252-6989, Fax: (940) 328-0850

Sherman: North Central   Grayson County Fire Fiddlers Contest

October 13, 2001   2nd Saturday in October

The Grayson County Fire Fiddlers Contest is open to all ages.

Texoma Exposition and Livestock Show Association, Stanley Oakley, 1706 FM 697, Sherman, TX 75090, (903) 892-8816

Rusk: East   Indian Summer Festival

October 13, 2001   2nd Saturday in October

The Indian Summer Festival features arts and crafts, fair, live entertainment, delicious variety of food, daily runs of the Texas State Railroad, and a street dance Saturday night. Held in downtown Rusk.

Rusk Chamber of Commerce, Larry Clark, P.O. Box 67, Rusk, TX 75785, (903) 683-4242, (800) 933-2381, Fax: (903) 683-1054

Mineola: East   Iron Horse Heritage Days Festival

October 13, 2001   2nd Saturday in October

The Iron Horse Heritage Days Festival activities include an Amtrak equipment display and tour, antique and classic car show, parade, arts and crafts, children's arts area, carnival, petting zoo, live tigers, railroad memorabilia display, model trains, pie bakeoff, horseshoe tournament, 3 on 3 basketball and volleyball tournaments, horse show, pony rides, live entertainment on stage daily, and a vocalist showdown with cash prizes. Held in Downtown Mineola.

Main Street Board of Directors, Mercy Rushing, P.O. Box 179, Mineola, TX 75773, (903) 569-6944, (800) MINEOLA, Fax: (903) 569-0856, cityofmineola@juno.com

Katy: Gulf   Rice Harvest Festival

October 13-14, 2001   2nd weekend in October

The Katy Rice Harvest Festival has over 300 food and craft booths. We have a full scale carnival beginning the Wednesday before the festival each year. We have entertainment on two stages: The Katy Talent Showcase Stage features local Katy talents. The Katy Stage is a larger stage that features paid entertainment such as zydeco bands, country and western bands, barbershop quartets, cloggers, square dancers, and much more. We have a dunking booth, cakewalk, and paint ball games for the kids. Held in Olde Towne Katy.

Katy Area Chamber of Commerce. Ann F. Hodge, 6001 Highway Blvd., Suite 6, Katy, TX 77494, (281) 391-RICE, (281) 391-2422, Fax: (281) 391-3297, katycofc@fbtc.net

Liberty: East   Trinity Valley Expo

October 13-21, 2001

Trinity Valley Expo features a county fair and rodeo. Other festivities include a fiddling contest, gospel music, live country music, a concert/dance held in the arena, and a nightly dance with country or Cajun music in an open-air pavilion. October 14th there is a concert/dance in the arena. A rodeo dance is held Tuesday through Saturday, October 17th-21st. Held at the Trinity Valley Exposition Fairgrounds, on FM 53.

Trinity Valley Exposition, James Bricker, Facility Manager, P.O. Box 9047, Liberty, TX 77575, (936) 336-8168, (936) 336-9658, Fax: (936) 336-4063

Port Lavaca: Gulf   Calhoun County Fair
October 16-21, 2001

The Calhoun County Fair features a Queen's contest held on Tuesday night. Held at the Calhoun County Fairgrounds, located on County Road 101.

Joel Gonzales, P.O. Box 42, Port Lavaca, TX 77979, (361) 987-6292, (361) 552-3382, Fax: (361) 552-5424, jaydee@tisd.net

San Antonio: South   Southwest Guitar Festival & Guitar
Foundation of America Convention
October 16-21, 2001

University of Texas at San Antonio Division of Music, Matthew Dunn, 6900 North Loop 1604 West, San Antonio, TX 78249, (210) 458-5682

Gilmer: East   East Texas Yamboree
October 17-20, 2001

The East Texas Yamboree features a pageant and coronation, All Service Club luncheon, barn dance, street dance, home canning and pie contests, art show, photography show, Tater Trot 5K and 2-mile Fun Run, Tour de Yam Bicycle Tour, livestock show and sale, carnival, parades, fiddlers contest, arts and crafts, exhibits, golf tournament, and much more. Events are held at the Upshur County Courthouse and Yamboree Park.

East Texas Yamboree Association, Joan Small, P.O. Box 854, Gilmer, TX 75644, (903) 843-2413, (903) 843-3981, Fax: (903) 843-3759, upchamber@aol.com, www.upshurcounty.com

Gilmer: East   Yamboree Fiddlers Contest
October 17-20, 2001

The Yamboree has a fiddling contest that has been held for more than 65 years. The age division for contestants are 0-12, 13-35, 36-59, 60 and older. Accompanist contest takes two top fiddlers, who then compete for the grand championship prize. Held at the courthouse square.

East Texas Yamboree, Joan Small, P.O. Box 854, Gilmer, TX 75644, (903) 843-2413, (903) 843-3981, Fax: (903) 843-3759, upchamber@aol.com, www.upshurcounty.com/Yamboree/2001_yamboree.htm

Tyler: East   Texas Rose Festival

October 18-21, 2001   3rd week in October

Fun in the flowers. The Texas Rose Festival is a joyous celebration of "Games We Love to Play." Join us for a nostalgic journey through the games of life. Events include Queen's Tea, Queen's Coronation, Rose Show, Rose Museum, Arts & Crafts Fair, Rose Festival Parade, seminars and nursery tours. Held at 1900 W. Front, Tyler.

Call 1-800-235-5712. www.tylertexas.com

Things are bloomin' in Tyler! One of the beautiful gardens you'll get to see. Photo courtesy of the Tyler Chamber of Commerce.

Austin: Hill Country   Texas Interactive Music Conference and Bar-B-Que

October 18-21, 2001

The Texas Interactive Music Conference and Bar-B-Que brings together the brightest minds in the computer industry to discuss, argue, debate, brainstorm, and possibly alter the course of history for music on computers. We are gearing up to answer some of the toughest questions facing our industry today on the topic: "Influencing hardware and software for music over the next five years." Events are held on the secluded grounds of the Guadalupe River Ranch.

For information call The Fat Man, Spanki Avallone, P.O. Box 9726, Austin, TX 78766, (512) 473-3878, Fax: (512) 454-8999, spanki@outer.net, www.projectbarbq.com

Mission: South   Texas Butterfly Festival

October 18-21, 2001

You will be astounded at the quantity and beauty of these butterflies. Located in the southernmost tip known as the Lower Rio Grande Valley, this region is the most biodiverse in the United States. Four ecosystems converge in this four-county region, with its semitropical climate and abundant native growth, the Mission area is a Mecca for butterflying year round. Highlight butterflies include: Guava Skipper, Malachite, Mexican Bluewing, Red Rim, Silver Emperor, Crimson Patch, Clytie Ministreak, Tulcis Crescent, Boisduval's Yellow, Soldier, Violet-banded Skipper, Turk's Cap White Skipper, Silver-banded Hairstreak. www.texasbutterfly.com

Dallas: North Central   New Dimensions Festival

October 18-21

Hear bands and solo songwriters in live venues in Deep Ellum that include all types of music; each style of music is performed in the appropriate setting. Performance times are decided on a first-come, first-serve basis at the time each artist or band registers. Held in the Deep Ellum section of Dallas.

New Dimensions Festival, Barbara McMillen, 2932 Dyer Street, Dallas, TX 75205, (214) 691-5318, Fax: (214) 692-1392, barbe@texasmusicgroup.com

Deep Ellum Association, 2932 Main Street, Suite 101, Dallas, TX 75226, (214) 748-4332, info@deepellumtx.com, www.deepellumtx.com

Beaumont: Gulf   South Texas State Fair

October 18-28, 2001

The South Texas State Fair is a regional fair with livestock and poultry shows, arts and crafts, an auto show, and amateur live entertainment. Also the Bill Hames Shows provides a 50-ride carnival midway. Held at Fair Park, at 2600 Gulf Street.

Young Men's Business League, Chris Colletti, P.O. Box 3207, Beaumont, TX 77704, (409) 832-9991, Fax: (409) 838-0402, www.ymbl.org/fair.htm

Copperas Cove: North Central   Ogletree Gap Folklife Festival
& Barbecue Cookoff

October 19-20, 2001

Held in downtown Copperas Cove. Missy Bowen, (254) 547-6968, www.rib-man.com

Fort Worth: North Central   Fort Worth Music Festival

October 19-21, 2001

This great music festival is held at General Worth Square, in downtown Fort Worth. This music festival showcases top talent from rock-n-roll to country. Dance in the streets while enjoying great musical entertainment. Held on Main Street, in downtown.

Stephen Millard, 2200 North Lamar, Suite 10, Dallas, TX 75202, (214) 855-1881, Fax: (214) 855-1882, mei@meifestivals.com, www.meifestivals.com

Yorktown: South   Western Days

October 19-21, 2001

Western Days is a three-day festival that includes arts and crafts booths, a carnival, a variety of food booths, CASI chili cookoff, Go Texan horseshoe and washer throw, and much more entertainment. The festivities also feature continuous music and five free street dances playing country and tejano music.

There is a children's parade on Friday, and a larger parade Saturday morning. Events are held at the City Park.

Yorktown Chamber of Commerce, Mari Gohlke, P.O. Box 488, Yorktown, TX 78164, (361) 564-2661, www.yorktowntx.com

Austin: Hill Country   Austin Blues Festival

October 19-21, 2001

The Austin Blues Festival books regional and national blues talent to perform at 15-20 Austin venues including Antone's, Babe's, Caucus Club, Club DeVille, Continental Club, Earl Campbell's, Lucy's, Spiros, Emos, Fat Tuesday's, Iron Cactus, Joe's Generic Bar, La Zona Rosa, Maggie Mae's, Red-Eyed Fly, Soho Lounge, and Stubb's. The festival attracts attention of blues record labels, agents, and industry professionals while also providing media and corporate sponsors recognition.

Collin Barnes, 701 S. Capital of Texas Highway, No. C-1263, Austin, TX 78746, (512) 327-9243, Fax: (512) 328-7886, pubserv@swbell.net

San Antonio: South   Greek Funstival

October 19-21, 2001

The Greek Funstival features traditional Greek food and wine, dancing, church tours, a Greek market, live music, and the Founder's Hall Display Room of Greeks in Texas. Held at St. Sophia Greek Orthodox Church, at 2504 North St. Mary's.

Paul Mayo, 2504 North St. Mary's Street, San Antonio, TX 78212, (210) 735-5051, Fax: (210) 735-5649, www.sanantoniocvb.com

Waco: North Central   BluesFest

October 20, 2001

BluesFest is a giant street party featuring live music, street entertainers, food, and drinks. Held at River Square Center, downtown.

Greater Waco Chamber of Commerce. Eric Abercrombie, P.O. Box 1220, Waco, TX 76703-1220, (254) 752-6611 ext. 203, (254) 752-6551, Fax: (254) 752-6618, abercrombie@waco-chamber.com, www.waco-chamber.com

Whitesboro: North Central   Peanut Festival

October 20, 2001   **3rd Saturday in October**

Whitesboro salutes the peanut farmer by enjoying a peanut shelling contest, a peanut spitting contest (graded on distance and style), and a jalapeño eating contest. Miss West Texoma is also crowned during the parade. A classic car show is one of the many things to see. chamber@rtex.net, www.whitesborotx.com

Hutto: Hill Country   Olde Tyme Days & Street Dance
October 20, 2001

Hutto Olde Tyme Days & Street Dance features a street dance with live country music, entertainment all day and night, arts and crafts, and an assortment of great food. Held in downtown Hutto.

Hutto Chamber of Commerce, Debbie Holland, P.O. Box 99, Hutto, TX 78634, (512) 759-4881

Hay Lew,
We gots Stew???

Lotsa' folks love cookoffs,
that don't ever cook!!

Corpus Christi: Gulf   Texas Music Jam
October 20, 2001

The 1st annual Texas Music Jam was October 21st from noon to 9 P.M. on Water Street in downtown Corpus Christi.

Corpus Christi Downtown Management District, Norma Urban, P.O. Box 354, Portland, TX 78374, (361) 643-2801, (361) 882-2363, signature-socials@msn.com

Llano: Hill Country   Llano Heritage Day Festival
October 20, 2001

The Llano Heritage Day Festival features living history displays, antiques, arts and crafts, live music, food, and a Wild West shootout. Held at the Llano County Courthouse Square.

Llano Chamber of Commerce, Mary Rhodes, 700 Bessemer, Llano, TX 78643, (915) 247-5354, llanococ@telstar.net, www.llanochamber.org

Needville: North Central   Harvest Festival
October 20, 2001

The festival features live polka and country music, singing contests, a street dance, talent contest, and a cookoff. Bands featured this year were the Bobby Jones Czech Band and the Dujka Brothers. Held in scenic downtown Needville.

Harvest Fest, Inc., Evan Reindl, P.O. Box 1101, Needville, TX 77461, (979) 793-4030, (281) 565-4396, Fax: (281) 565-4396, evan_cpa@prodigy.net

San Antonio: South   Cajun French Music Association Festival
October 20, 2001

Time to party Cajun style, with food and music to match. Sponsored by de Fa Tras Chapter of the CFMA. Fun all day long in air-conditioned wood floor dance hall. Held at the Martinez Social Club at 7791 St. Hedwig Road.

For information: Joe Quintana, (210) 684-3189, www.cajunfrenchmusic.org/chapters/sanantonio.htm

Carrizo Springs: South   Brush Country Days
October 20-21, 2001

Brush Country Days is a carnival featuring live tejano and country music, food and crafts booths, a talent show, and carnival. Held at the Rodeo Arena, on Highway 83 South.

Carrizo Springs Chamber of Commerce, Melissa L. Castillo, 303 South Fifth Street, Carrizo Springs, TX 78834, (830) 876-5205, Fax: (830) 876-2957

Greenville: North Central   Cotton Jubilee
October 20-21, 2001   3rd weekend in October

This annual festival salutes cotton, the fiber that weaves together our local history, and is a great weekend getaway filled with a variety of exciting events and activities for the entire family. Enjoy the arts & crafts show, business expo, health fair, Civil War encampment, cotton exhibits, children activities and entertainment, bike rally, bed races, bingo, static displays, kids product show, 42 domino tournament, and live entertainment. Held at the American Cotton Museum, located on the north frontage road, off I-30, between exits 94 and 95.

For information contact the Greenville Chamber at (903) 455-1510, visit www.greenville-chamber.org, or e-mail: jubilee@greenville-chamber.org.

Galveston: Gulf   ARToberFEST

October 20-21, 2001

Fine arts in a beautiful town. I love the shows where you get to meet the artists. This fine arts festival is held in the heart of the Postoffice Street Arts and Entertainment District. Artists have booths that showcase their talents. Well-established artists, new artists, and artists from the local schools show their talents. Whatever your tastes, there's something there for you. Held annually in October. On Postoffice Street (between 21st and 23rd Streets) in downtown Galveston.

For more information, call (409) 763-5495. www.galvestontourism.com

Copperas Cove: North Central   Ogletree Gap Heritage Festival

October 20-21, 2001

So much fun you won't even realize how much you've learned. There are exhibitions of old-fashioned butter churning, blanket weaving, musket shooting, Civil War reenactments, horses and riders in period attire. Events take place in the scenic Ogletree Gap Valley, (254) 947-9205, covechamber@n-link.com

Brownwood: Hill Country   PecanFest

October 20-21, 2001   3rd weekend in October

Go nuts in the Hill Country at PecanFest! There is plenty of live entertainment, fun for the whole family, artisans, craftsmen, antiques, a children's craft area, pecan pie contest, and pecan products. Held under the shade trees of Riverside Park beside the beautiful Pecan Bayou, off Highway 377/67 in Brownwood, Texas.

Call for more information: (915) 646-9535. www.brownwoodchamber.org

Houston: Gulf   Annual Asian-American Festival

October 20-21, 2001

The Houston's Annual Asian-American Festival is a Pan-Asian cultural arts festival featuring dance, music, martial arts, theatre, puppetry, and much more. Held at the Miller Outdoor Theatre, located at 100 Concert Drive.

1714 Tannehill Drive, Houston, TX 77008, (713) 861-8270, (713) 284-8352, Fax: (713) 861-3450

Dallas: North Central   Sammons Jazz Festival

October 20-21, 2001

This cool Jazz festival kicks off with a New Orleans-style parade. The artists being presented in the festival include both local and nationally known jazz artists. Held at the Annette Strauss Artist Square, at 1800 Leonard Street between R.L. Thornton service road and Flora St., next to Meyerson Sammons Center for the Arts.

Joanna St. Angelo, 3630 Harry Hines Blvd., Dallas, TX 75219, 1-800-484-8497, (214) 520-7789, (972) 416-4417, www.sammonsartcenter.org/jazz.htm

Richmond: Gulf   Texan Market Days

October 20-21, 2001

This is a festival of living history that provides visitors with colorful and exciting live reenactments of significant historical events from Texas's past. There is a rodeo, and more than 100 exhibitors and vendors offer a variety of arts and crafts, food, and activities. Storytellers, singers, dancers, and other entertainers offer bluegrass, country, and pop music. Held at George Ranch Historical Park, at 10215 FM 762.

Susan A. Hanson, P.O. Box 1248, Richmond, TX 77406, (281) 545-9212, Fax: (281) 343-9316, www.georgeranch.org

Arlington: North Central   Texas Guitar Show

October 20-21, 2001

The Texas Guitar Show in Arlington centers around the buying, selling, and trading of stringed instruments. Jam sessions take place Friday and Saturday nights and include bluegrass, blues, jazz, and rock music. Held at the Arlington Convention Center, at 1200 Ballpark Way.

Texas Guitar Shows, John Brinkmann, 920 North Main Street, Mansfield, TX 76063, (817) 473-6059

Houston: Gulf   The Westheimer Street Festival

October 20-21, 2001

The Westheimer Street Festival is the largest free music festival in Houston. The biannual event features eight stages with a variety of local acts. In the past it has also included diverse events such as carnivals, volleyball tournaments, and firefighting exhibitions. Held on Westheimer Street, between the 200 and 1000 blocks.

Westheimer Street Festival Corporation, John Florez, 419 Westheimer, No. 4, Houston, TX 77006, (713) 522-6548, Fax: (713) 522-1920, westfest@wt.net, www.westheimerfestival.com

Austin: Hill Country — Big Stinkin' International Improv & Sketch Comedy Festival

October 22-27, 2001

Lots of laughs. This comedy festival takes place at over twenty different locations during a full week of belly laughs. Affectionately abbreviated, BS5 will bring the most diverse and fascinating comedy troupes from all over the world to Austin, in addition to the most respected comedy troupes from the United States. Think you're funny? Give them a call at (512) 912-7837. bsoffice@bigstinkin.com, www.bigstinkin.com

Dobbel Barrel Harroll!!!!

"You gots Some Fast Drinkers Round Here!!"

Texarkana: East — Pickin' Around the Campfire - Boo Grass

October 23-28

Pickin' Around the Campfire features fun, food, crafts, bluegrass jamming, jamming, and more jamming, and a Halloween party on Saturday night. Held at the Strange Family Bluegrass/RV Park, on Highway 59 South to 3244, then just follow the signs to park.

Sam and Sharon Strange, Route 2, Box 327 B-2, Texarkana, TX 75501, (903) 791-0342, (903) 792-2481, sfbgtxk@juno.com

Austin: Hill Country   Country Music Association of Texas Awards Show

October 26, 2001

Drop by and watch the stars come out. The Country Music Association of Texas Awards Show features various awards related to country music and multimedia. This year's show featured a band, four to eight individual performers, award winners, and Hall of Fame Inductions. Held at the Broken Spoke, at 3201 South Lamar Blvd.

Austin Country Music Association of Texas, Bud Fisher, P.O. Box 549, Troy, TX 76579, (254) 938-2454, Fax: (254) 774-7093

Spring: Gulf   Spring Creek Bluegrass Festival

October 26-28, 2001

Spring Creek Bluegrass Festival is an outdoor event for the entire family with as many as a dozen live bluegrass and gospel bands performing. No alcohol is allowed. The event features great food vendors and arts and crafts. Camper hookups are available. Held at the Coushatta Recreation Ranch outside of Bellville.

Spring Creek Bluegrass Club Festival, Carolyn Brockett, 9410 Dundalk Street, Spring, TX 77379-4340, (281) 376-2959, bluegrass22@juno.com

Flatonia: North Central   Czhilispiel XXVIII

October 26-28, 2001

This is the 2nd largest chili cookoff in Texas, which is saying quite a bit. Czhilispiel is fun for the whole family. It features a carnival, a petting zoo, czhili cookoff, BBQ cookoff, arts and crafts, a parade, tricycle races, jalapeno eating contest, car and truck show, pie baking contest, cow chip throw, and egg toss. Held in downtown Flatonia.

Flatonia Chamber of Commerce. David Urban, P.O. Box 610, Flatonia, TX 78941-0561, (361) 865-3920, Fax: (361) 865-2451, flatcofc@fais.net, www.flatonia-tx.com/czhilispiel.htm

Fort Worth: North Central   Red Steagall Cowboy Gathering and Western Swing Festival

October 26-28, 2001

The Cowboy Gathering and Western Swing Festival is hosted by Red Steagall, the official Cowboy Poet of Texas. Held at the Fort Worth Stockyards.

Hub Baker, P.O. Box 4507, Fort Worth, TX 76164, (817) 625-1025, Fax: (817) 625-1148, ww.redsteagall.com/Itinerary.htm

The historic Fort Worth Stock Yards play host to several great events.

Fredericksburg: Hill Country   Food and Wine Fest
October 26-28, 2001

Come and enjoy a day with the very best Texas made food and wine. Live music all day. Auction, games, and more entertain thousands as they sample wine and food. Enjoy the best jazz and blues in the hill country. Held on the Market Square at 100 East Main Street.

Creative Marketing, Debbie Farquhar, 703 North Llano, Fredericksburg, TX 78624, (830) 997-8515, Fax: (830) 997-9628, creative@ktc.com, www.fredericksburg-texas.com

Elgin: North Central   Hogeye Festival
October 27

The Sausage Capital of Texas hosts the Hogeye Festival, with outstanding musicians, original arts and crafts, creative children's activities, a costume children's pet parade, hog calling contests, cow patty bingo, pork cookoff, and antique car show. Cow patty bingo offers a $1,500 jackpot. Live music all day provides a variety of harmonies. The festival is held in our historic downtown on Main Street.

Amy Stallard Miller, P.O. Box 591, Elgin, TX 78621, (512) 285-5721, Fax: (512) 285-5962, economic@totalaccess.net

Palestine: North Central   Hot Pepper Festival
October 27, 2001   4th Saturday in October

Often called "Texas' Hottest Festival," the Hot Pepper Festival features a parade, street dance, bicycle tour, children's games, four stages with entertainment, arts and crafts, chili cookoff, and gunfight reenactments. The music includes blues, Christian, country, and rock. It all happens in downtown Palestine.

Ava Harmon, P.O. Box 2828, Palestine, TX 75802, (903) 723-3014, (800) 659-3484, Fax: (903) 729-6067, www.palestinechamber.org/calendar.html, www.vastcity.com/palestinetexas/gallery.html

Houston: Gulf   Houston Women's Festival

October 27, 2001

The annual Houston Women's Festival is a celebration of music, art, culture, and community and is one of the largest annual events for the women's community in Houston, drawing people from across Texas and from other states. Held at the Garden in the Heights, at 3926 Feagan.

Houston Women's Festival, Shirley Knight, P.O. Box 70102, Houston, TX 77270, (713) 861-3316, (713) 861-3316, hwfestival@earthlink.net, www.hwfestival.org

Corpus Christi: Gulf   Lone Star Texas Music Jam

October 27, 2001

The Lone Star Texas Music Jam is held from 11 A.M.-9 P.M. There is always plenty of great music. Events are held on Water Street, downtown.

Stephën Miessner, Convention & Visitors Bureau, 1201 North Shoreline, Corpus Christi, TX 78401, (361) 883-8833, Fax: (361) 883-4329, smiessner@usdm.net, www.corpuschristi-tx-vb.org/texasmusicjam.html

Fairfield: North Central   FalconFest

October 27-28, 2001   Last weekend in October

A rare close-up glimpse of some beautiful creatures. Fun and educational. See modern day falconers show the who, what, when, where, why, and how of this highly disciplined form of sport. There will be fun for all ages as you receive an overview of the more common birds of prey that inhabit Texas. Festivities begin at 9 A.M. Held at 123 State Park Road 64. Call (903) 389-4514. www.fairfieldtx.com/chamber/Events

Sour Lake: East   Old-Timers Days

October 27-28

Old-Timers Days promises plenty of music and entertainment beginning Thursday night, Friday night, and continuing all day Saturday, at the Gazebo in Lions Club Park. Country and western dancers kick up their heels at a Saturday dance in the Community Center. Carnival rides and booths reopen on Friday and Saturday. Saturday's 10 A.M. parade ends at the park. Held at the Lions Cub Park, at 500 South Ann Street.

Sour Lake Lions Club, Debbie Morgan, P.O. Box 841, Sour Lake, TX 77659, (409) 287-3573, Fax: (409) 287-2800

Salado: North Central — Fright Nights at Tablerock
October 27-31, 2001

Halloween fun for the whole family. Tablerock's half-mile-long walking trail features scenes from all the classic horror tales, The Headless Horseman, MacBeth, Wizard of Oz, the Tell-Tale Heart, the Mummy, Frankenstein, and 15 other stops. (254) 947-9205, www.allcentex.com/fright

It's Pumpkin Time in Texas, whatever your mood. Photos by Javier Cortez.

Hallettsville: North Central — Falling Leaves Polka Festival
October 28

The Falling Leaves Festival features the best in polka music with Vrazel's and Leo Majek's Orchestras. Other activities include games, a country store, auction, and a fried chicken and sausage dinner. Held at the Knights of Columbus Hall, on Highway 77 South.

Fall Festival, P.O. Box 46, Hallettsville, TX 77964, (361) 798-2311, itenhall@cvtv.net, viptx.net/~loglodge/Events.html

November

We 'bout to Run
Out of Old Time
CowBoys Round here.

Another fun month in Texas and many of the activities involve eating. Thanksgiving takes the lead, but in Texas we have a number of chili cookoffs that run it a close race. This month we also have cookoffs for spinach, wild hogs, gumbo, and syrup. Now how's that for a little diversity?

I must admit that there are times when us Texans can be a bit hardheaded about somethin' and really dig our heels in. We start off the month with an example of just such a situation. Out in the little town of Terlingua, near the Mexican border, there are two of the world's greatest chili cookoffs being held at the same time! There's a long history on why there are two. But suffice to say they didn't see eye-to-eye and have had dueling cookoffs for several years. At least they haven't had a high-noon cookoff shootout, yet.

Oh, and the Germans aren't done with celebrating Oktoberfest. The Wurstfest in New Braunfels is always fun to attend. When you're on a roll, stick with it.

Meanwhile the Scottish clans gather up for their annual festival in Salado. It's a colorful and fun time watching all the sporting events amidst the tartans, kilts, and other beautiful authentic Scottish clothes.

Always double check the dates of the events.

Terlingua & Lajitas: West

Chili Appreciation Society Terlingua International Chili Championship Cookoff

October 31 - November 3, 2001

On the Wednesday before the first Saturday of November, chili cooks and fans of a good bowl of red start gathering up. CASI holds the ultimate celebration of chili. This grandaddy of all chili cookoffs is held at Rancho CASI de los Chisos in Terlingua, Texas. Rancho CASI is located on the north side of Highway 170, eleven miles west of Study Butte and 7 miles east of Lajitas. This is the international finals for CASI.

The desert becomes a city as folks come to the Terlingua Chili Cookoffs. Photos by Buffalo Chuck.

Contact Chili Appreciation Society International, Johnye Harriman, Executive Dir, 3005 North Divis Ave., Bethany, OK 73008-4521, (806) 352-8783, (806) 355-9111, Fax: (806) 352-8599, vickiefromtx@webtv.net, www.chili.org

Terlingua: West

Original Terlingua International Championship Chili Cookoff

November 1-3, 2001

The Original Terlingua International, Frank X. Tolbert-Wick Fowler Memorial, Championship Chili Cookoff has various cooking and showmanship contests. Dance and listening music provided by Gary P. Nunn and the Sons of the Bunk House Band, Larry Joe Taylor, Ron Riley, Frank Hill, Geronimo Trevino III, and many more. Cookoff is held behind Terlingua Store, on Highway 170.

Original Terlingua International Championship Chili Cookoff, Inc., Al Hopkins, Secretary, P.O. Box 617, Corsicana, TX 75151, (903) 874-5601, Fax: (903) 874-5601 www.abowlofred.com

George West: South

George West Storyfest, Chuck Wagon Dinner & Show

November 2, 2001   **Friday before the 1st Saturday in November**

The Storytelling Capital of Texas. This festival features cowboy poetry/music/storytelling. Spend an evening on the trail. Featuring a delicious meal prepared by an authentic 1800s chuck wagon, and cowboy poetry, storytelling, and music. Held on the Live Oak County Fairgrounds, Hwy. 281 in George West, Texas.

Call (361) 449-2481 or (888) 600-3121. www.georgewest.org/storyfest.htm

New Braunfels: Hill Country Wurstfest

November 5-11, 2001   1st full week in November

Wurstfest is German for "gettin' down." This wonderful festival includes food, polka music, dancing, yodeling, arts and crafts, and a heritage exhibition. Enjoy sausage and strudel, pretzels, and potato pancakes served up by fun loving folks, polka and waltz to good ol' fashioned Oompah music. Experience a German/Texas festival rich in German culture and full of Texas fun. Events are held on the Wurstfest Grounds at Landa Park, which is located at 178 Landa Park Drive.

Wurstfest Association of New Braunfels, Suzanne Herbelin, P.O. Box 310309, New Braunfels, TX 78131-0309, (830) 625-9167, (800) 221-4369, Fax: (830) 620-1318, info@wurstfest.com, www.wurstfest.com

The Woodlands: Gulf Wildflower Festival

November 3, 2001

Held at the Cochran's Crossing Shopping Center. (281) 719-6344

Bloomburg: East Cullen Baker Country Fair and Parade

November 3, 2001

This neat fair and parade features live country music, great hickory-smoked barbecue, balloon rides, rodeo, and fiddlers contest. The events are held in downtown Bloomburg.

Bloomburg Fire Department, Norene Schumann, P.O. Box 97, Bloomburg, TX 75551, (903) 796-3296, (903) 728-5343

Woodville: East Bluegrass and Gospel Show

November 3, 2001

The Bluegrass Show jammin' begins at 5:30 P.M. with the stage show scheduled for 7 P.M. Bluegrass and gospel music. Held at the Woodville Heritage Village Museum, on Highway 190 West.

Ofeira A. Gazzaway, P.O. Box 888, Woodville, TX 75979, (409) 283-2272, (800) 323-0389, Fax: (409) 283-2194

Houston: Gulf Houston Downtown Street Festival

November 3-4, 2001

This music festival features live entertainment and benefits the Endangered Species Media Project. Held at Roots Memorial Square Park, near downtown Houston.

Don Schwarzkopf, P.O. Box 8305, Houston, TX 77219-0445, (713) 688-3773, (713) 688-3773, Fax: (713) 688-9617, earthwrks@juno.com

Salado: North Central   Gathering of the Scottish Clans of Texas
November 9-11, 2001

Liz Carpenter first introduced me to the Scottish Clans in Salado. This colorful musical and dancing event is a great deal of fun for all. I particularly enjoyed the storytelling. The festival takes place on College Hill and includes dance competitions, bagpipe playing, a traditional Scotch Ceilidh, and Kirkin' O' the Tartans ceremony. Panels of Scot experts judge contests in Highland dancing, piping, drumming, and pipe bands. In addition, visitors will want to take in the athletic events, a tattoo, which is an exchange of melodies between pipe bands, other Scottish music, and performances by some of the day's competitors in a sundown setting. Special events include a storytelling contest, a Scottish longboat shoot, a golf tournament, and a genealogy seminar. Held at the Central Texas Area Museum, 1 Main Street.

Central Texas Area Museum, Inc. P.O. Box 36, Salado, TX 76571, (254) 947-5232, www.salado.com

Crystal City: South   Spinach Festival
November 9-11, 2001   **2nd week in November**

This South Texas Plains town provides free live music all 3 days. Parade on Saturday. Carnival all 3 days. All kinds of food booths, variety booths. Softball tournament, car show, 5K run, walk-a-thon, basketball tournament. Call (830) 374-3161 ask for Mary. Held in downtown Crystal City.

Henderson: East   Heritage Syrup Festival
November 10, 2001   **2nd Saturday in November**

Sweet times in the Piney Woods. The Heritage Syrup Festival promotes old-time syrup making in Rusk County. The event features folk artists, blacksmiths, craft show, food booths, and live bluegrass music. The events are held in the Syrup Making Museum and downtown square, 514 North High Street.

The cooks at the Heritage Syrup Festival in Henderson are making their magic happen, turning sap to syrup. Photo courtesy of Henderson Chamber of Commerce.

Henderson Tourist Development Department, Suzanne Cross, 201 North Main Street, Henderson, TX 75652, (903) 657-5528, Fax:

(903) 657-9454, Susan Weavaer, tourism@ballistic.com, (903) 657-5528, www.depotmuseum.com/syrup.html hendersontx.com

Fort Worth: North Central   National Cowgirl Hall of Fame Induction Ceremony

November 10, 2001

The National Cowgirl Hall of Fame and Western Heritage Center has honored 120 Western women. The following women were inducted in 1995: Dale Evans, Barbara Van Cleve, Linda Mitchell Davis, and Marlene Eddleman McRae. Activities and various events include auctions, live entertainment, and dancing.

National Cowgirl Hall of Fame, Shelly Burmeister, 111 West Fourth Street, Suite 300, Fort Worth, TX 76102, (817) 336-4475, (806) 364-5252, Fax: (817) 336-2470, www.cowgirl.net

Crowell: Panhandle   World Championship Wild Hog Cookoff

November 10-11, 2001

The cookin' is done on the square, around Foard County Courthouse, in scenic downtown Crowell.

Donnie Miller, Crowell Chamber of Commerce, P.O. Box 79, Crowell, TX 79227, (940) 684-1670, www.ribman.com

Rockport: Gulf   Music of the Sea Festival

November 10-11, 2001

The Museum hosted the 1st Sea Music Festival November 4 and 5, 2000, and featured Texas-based musicians who perform sea music, as well as traditional Mexican, Vietnamese, and French songs. Held at the Texas Maritime Museum.

Allison Lakin, 1202 Navigation Circle, Rockport, TX 78382, (361) 729-1271, Fax: (361) 729-9938, tmm@2fords.net

Palestine: North Central   The Texas Toot (was the Texas Early Music Festival)

November 16-18, 2001   Weekend before Thanksgiving
Held twice a year. Also held the 1st or 2nd week in June.

The Texas Toot is a friendly, student-centered workshop that features outstanding musicians on a wide variety of instruments. Instruction is offered in lute, early harp, viola da gamba, violin band, renaissance double reeds, percussion, and, of course, the recorder. A classical music concert is held on Saturday night. Events are held at the Lakeview Conference Center in Palestine, TX.

David and Susan Barton, P.O. Box 751061, Dallas, TX 75357-1061, (214) 826-8721, Fax: (214) 327-5879, info@toot.org

Houston: Gulf   Backyard Chicken & Sausage Gumbo Judging
November 17, 2001

Held at the C&M Ice House in Houston. For information: (713) 946-9688, www.ribman.com

Everywhere   Tellabration
November 17, 2001   Saturday night before Thanksgiving

An annual event where storytelling takes place the world over at the same time. Some events, however, may be at an alternate time during the same weekend. This last year there were nine Texas events in Austin, Houston, Burnet, Frankston, San Antonio, and Grapevine. To learn more about the whens and wheres, check out members.aol.com/tellabrate.

National Storytelling Week (NSW) is a long-range plan under development by the Program Committee of the National Storytelling Network (NSN) Board of Directors. Their goal is to promote NSW, which became part of the USA's official calendar last year, in conjunction with Tellabration. www.tellabration.org

Austin: Hill Country   Texas Book Festival
November 17-18, 2001

A wonderful event, readers and writers get a chance to meet while wandering the beautiful grounds of the Texas State Capitol. Meet some of the finest authors in the world, one on one. Nuthin' like it! www.austin360.com

Bandera: Hill Country   Old West Fest 'N Trade Show
November 17-18, 2001   3rd weekend in November

Cowboy fun in a beautiful town. Family-fun, cowboy style with music, poetry, western trade show, cowboy side shows, chuck wagon cooking, children's attractions. Mustache and costume contests, stick horse riding, chicken bingo, old-timers hour, and shoot-'em-ups. Take the scenic ride to Bandera, only 50 miles NW of San Antonio. Sat. 10 A.M.-7 P.M., Sun 11 A.M.-7 P.M. Events are held at the Mansfield Park Jr. Livestock Show Barn - Hwy. 16, three miles north of town. Call (830) 796-7871. www.banderatexas.com/calendar.htm

McKinney: North Central   Dickens of a Christmas
November 22-23, 2001   Weekend after Thanksgiving

On the town square Dickens meets Texas, now that's special. Don't miss this award-winning Victorian extravaganza!! Live reindeer and over 100 merchants in Victorian costume reflect scenes from a "Norman Rockwell" Christmas card. Call the McKinney Convention & Visitors Bureau at (972) 562-8660. www.mckinneytexas.com

Marshall: East   Wonderland of Lights

November 22 - December 31, 2001 Held annually from Thanksgiving to New Year's

Cool evenings and beautiful lights. Get a glimpse of an old-fashioned Christmas beyond your childhood dreams. 7,000,000 tiny white lights turn Marshall into a dreamland, with the historic courthouse as its crown jewel. Santa—the real one!—is on hand, a lighted nighttime parade, candle-lit home tours, carriage rides, the "Living Christmas Tree" with caroling on the square.

Phyllis Prince (903) 935-7868, www.tourtexas.com/marshall

Lufkin: East   Holiday On The Square

November 24, 2001   1st Saturday after Thanksgiving

Come on downtown and join the fun. There are carriage rides, food booths, caroling, lighting of the courthouse, and Santa Claus. For information contact the Lufkin Convention & Visitors Bureau, 1615 S. Chestnut, Lufkin, TX 75901, (800) 409-5659, lufkintx@lcc.net

Austin: Hill Country   Victorian Christmas Festival

November 24-25, 2001

A Victorian Christmas Festival on Sixth Street includes arts and crafts, food, beverages, street performers, and lots more to kick off the holiday season. Events take place on Sixth Street, between Brazos & Red River Streets.

French Smith, 1710 South Lamar Blvd., No. B-C, Austin, TX 78704-8963, (512) 441-9015, Fax: (512) 441-9016, pop@mail.roadstarproductions.com, www.roadstarproductions.com

Dallas: North Central   Young Country Christmas Fireworks to Music

November 24, 2001

The annual Young Country Christmas Fireworks to Music creates one of the largest pyrotechnic displays in Texas. Afternoon and evening pre-fireworks activities include a carnival of rides and a festival of food, games, and entertainment. After the fireworks show, attendees are treated to a top country band. Fireworks festivities take place at the Ball Park in Arlington.

Stephen Miller, 2200 North Lamar, Suite 104, Dallas, TX 75202, (214) 855-1881, (972) 716-7800, Fax: (214) 855-1882, mei@meifestivals.com, www.meifestivals.com

Denton: North Central   Denton Holiday Lighting Festival

November 29, 2001   Held the Thursday after Thanksgiving

A traditional holiday lighting of the Christmas tree at the courthouse on the square. Live entertainment, wagon rides with Santa, Wassail Fest, and crafts for kids. Held on the courthouse square, downtown at 110 W. Hickory.

Denton Holiday Festival Association, Yvonne Jenkins, (940) 464-7273, www.discoverdenton.com

Salado: North Central   **A Christmas Carol at Tablerock Amphitheater**
November 30 - December 2, 2001

A Christmas classic at the legendary Tablerock Amphitheater. Don't miss it. (254) 947-9205, www.allcentex.com/carol

December

Cowboy Santa

Who needs them smelly ol' reindeer?

Well here we are at the end of another fun year. I hope you paced yourself, so that you have a little energy left for the Christmas related events, because there are a bunch of them. Texans embrace a wide variety of religions, and December is a significant month in most.

There are several parades and Christmas tree lightings, but compared with other months, there aren't a lot of December events here, because I've chosen only community-wide events. In December most events aren't community-wide, but rather take place at individual churches.

So, don't let it fool you, there are thousands nativity scenes, concerts, and groups of carolers all over this state. Watch your local media for information on when and where these church events will occur.

Always double check the dates of the events.

Marshall: East   Wonderland of Lights
November 22 - December 31, 2001 Thanksgiving to New Year's

Cool evenings and beautiful lights. Get a glimpse of an old-fashioned Christmas beyond your childhood dreams. 7,000,000 tiny white lights turn Marshall into a dreamland, with the historic courthouse as its crown jewel. Santa—the real one!—is on hand, a lighted nighttime parade, candlelit home tours, carriage rides, the "Living Christmas Tree" with caroling on the square.

For information call Phyllis Prince at (903) 935-7868, www.tourtexas.com/ marshall.

Salado: North Central   A Christmas Carol at Tablerock Amphitheater
November 30 - December 2, 2001

A Christmas classic at the legendary Tablerock Amphitheater. Don't miss it. (254) 947-9205 www.allcentex.com/carol

Stonewall: Hill Country   Christmas Tree Lighting and Tours of the LBJ Ranch
Starts Thanksgiving weekend and ends January 1

Join members of the Johnson family and enjoy festive choir music and light a beautiful tree to usher in the Christmas season. Then hop on a tour bus to see the Sauer-Beckman Farm, all decked out for a German Christmas, circa 1915. The tour continues through the LBJ Ranch for lighting displays around the historic buildings where Lyndon Johnson was born, attended school, and had his "Texas White House." The event begins at LBJ State Historical Park, one mile east of Stonewall.

For more information, (830) 644-2420, www.fredericksburg-texas.com/events.htm

Texas Hill Country: Regional Christmas Lighting Trail
Thanksgiving Weekend thru January 1

Blanco, Bulverde, Burnet, Dripping Springs, Fredericksburg, Goldthwaite, Johnson City, Llano, Marble Falls, Mason, Round Mountain:

Beginning Thanksgiving weekend, millions of lights will make miles of memories for families who follow the Hill Country's elaborate Regional Christmas Lighting Trail this holiday season. Eleven towns are set to dazzle visitors with breathtaking holiday extravaganza's between Thanksgiving and New Year's. Santa parades, Christmas tree lightings, carriage rides, shopping, festivals, worship services, food, dances, and chorus concerts.

Regional Christmas Headquarters, 703 N. Llano, Fredericksburg, TX 78624, (830) 997-8515. For information call (830)-997-8515.

Boerne: Hill Country   Weinachts Fest
Early December

Parade and Lighting of the Tree. For more information, (830) 816-2176, www.ci.boerne.tx.us

Canyon Lake: Hill Country   Old-Fashioned Christmas
Early December

Enjoy the lights and holiday music around the beautiful lake. For more information, clcc@gvtc.com, (830) 964-2223, www.canyonlakechamber.com

Cleburne: North Central   Christmas Parade
Early December

The parade winds from Hulen Park through downtown and back to the park.

For more information, info@cleburnechamber.com, (817) 645-2455, www.ci.cleburne.tx.us

Edinburg: South   Noche de Luces "Night of Lights"
Early December

Holiday fireworks, music, food, and Santa. University of Texas Pan American, (956) 381-2500, www.edinburg.com

Greenville: North Central   Christmas Parade

Early December

Parade and floats go through downtown. pjust@aol.com, (903) 450-8626, www.greenville-chamber.org

Harlingen: Gulf   Christmas Parade

Early December

Floats, bands, and a wide variety of family-style entertainment. The parade winds through downtown on Jackson Street. (956) 797-3227, www.harlingen.com

Harlingen: Gulf   Pinata Festival

Early December

Following the Christmas parade, includes music, food booths, piñatas, and more. Held in Gutierez Park. (956) 430-6692, www.harlingen.com

New Braunfels: Hill Country   Christmas Festival

Early December

A variety of events including an auction of fully decorated Christmas trees. Held on West San Antonio Street, across from the Brauntex Theatre. (830) 625-6291, www.nbcham.org

Longview: East   Annual Christmas Parade

December 1, 2001

Parade is held downtown, with a wide variety of participants. (903) 237-4000, www.longviewtx.com

Odessa: Panhandle   Brand New Opree

Early December

Local and area talent perform gospel and country & western. Globe of the Great Southwest, (915) 332-1586

Alpine: West   Christmas Parade

December 1, 2001

A colorful parade down the main street. For more information about this event, contact the Alpine Chamber of Commerce, 1-800-561-3735, chamber@alpinetexas.com, www.alpinetexas.com

Nocona: North Central   Christmas in Nocona

December 1, 2001

Parade featuring the arrival of Santa, church choirs, a fish fry, and lots of other entertainment. (940) 825-3254, texasturf@juno.com

Alvarado: North Central   Light Up The Square
December 1, 2001

Downtown Alvarado is transformed into a Christmas delight with thousands and thousand of lights. Hundreds of stuffed animals add to the fun. Santa will be on hand to greet the children as well as Christmas music for your enjoyment. A parade will kick off the activities at 6 P.M. (817) 790-3779

Clifton: North Central   Norwegian Home Tour
December 1, 2001

Beautiful homes in a beautiful town that was designated by the Texas Legislature as the Norwegian Capital of Texas. A tour of homes, art, and history. Arts & crafts, artisan demonstrators, storytelling, carriage rides, authentic foods, and gift shop.

Clifton Chamber of Commerce, 115 N. Avenue D, Clifton, TX 76634. Trudy Sheffield, (800) 344-3720, clifton.chamber@htcomp.net, clifton.centraltx.com

Lubbock: Panhandle   Lights on Broadway Holiday Festival
December 1, 2001

Lights on Broadway is a holiday festival for the South Plains area featuring live music, a street fair, parade, carriage rides in conjunction with the Carol of Lights Ceremony at Texas Tech University. It is located on historic Broadway Avenue with hundreds of lighted buildings. Held on Broadway Avenue, between University Avenue and Avenue X.

Broadway Festivals, Stephanie Allison, P.O. Box 1643, Lubbock, TX 79408, (806) 749-2929, (800) 687-7393, Fax: (806) 749-3237, sallison@hub.ofthe.net, www.broadwayfestivals.com

Brookshire: Gulf   Christmas Festival
December 1, 2001

Brookshire Christmas Festival features community entertainment beginning at 6 P.M. with the traditional tree and museum lighting, along with a surprise visit by Santa Claus followed by a dance in the convention center. Saturday's activities begin at 10 A.M. and include arts and crafts booths, food, games, carnival, train rides, continuous live entertainment, a petting zoo, along with the hourly Silver Bell Raffle. Held in Downtown Brookshire, between Fifth and Cooper Streets.

Diane Peterek, P.O. Box 459, Brookshire, TX 77423, (281) 934-2465, (281) 375-5298, www.dwebc.com/bpcoc

Dallas: North Central   Candlelight at Old City Park

December 1-2, 8-9, 2001

Candlelight offers a step back in time to glimpse the way the holidays were celebrated at the turn of the century. Historic homes are decorated in their time period, while candlelit paths and horse-drawn carriages create an unforgettable atmosphere. Community bands, choirs, and dance groups provide continuous holiday music. There is something for everyone in the family. Held at the Old City Park, at 1717 Gano.

Heritage Society, Jennifer Bransam, 1717 Gano, Dallas, TX 75215, (214) 421-5141, Fax: (214) 428-5361

Levelland: Panhandle   Country Fest, Rock Fest, R&B Fest and Bluegrass Fest

December 1-8, 2001

The Country Fest on the evening of the 1st at 6 P.M. kicks off the show. Rock Fest is on the 2nd and the R&B Fest on the 3rd keeps the beat going. Saturday evening on the 8th, three of the world's best bluegrass instructors take the stage with their ensembles to perform bluegrass favorites.

Chamber of Commerce, Sandy Parker, 1101 Avenue H, Levelland, TX 79336, (806) 894-3157, (806) 894-2228, Fax: (806) 894-4284, levelland-coc@door.net, www.levelland.com

Port Arthur: Gulf   International Holiday Exhibit and Festival Evening

December 2

The month-long Heritage Holiday Exhibit includes a heritage reception with holiday taste treats from 14 heritage groups and entertainment. Held at the Port Arthur Public Library, at 4615 Ninth Avenue.

Library/American Heritage Society, Marilyn Moseley, 4615 Ninth Avenue, Port Arthur, TX 77642-5818, (409) 985-8838, Fax: (409) 985-5969

Ellinger: North Central   Polka Fest

December 3

The Polka Fest activities include a polka mass, fried chicken dinner, live music, dancing, good food, and cold drinks.

Chamber of Commerce Hall, Highway 71 and FM 2503.

Ellinger Chamber of Commerce, Nancy Hoelscher, 105 East Colorado Sky, Ellinger, TX 78938, (979) 378-2315

Galveston: Gulf   Dickens on the Strand

December 4-5, 2001

Dickens on the Strand features a re-creation of a 19th-century London Christmas market. Festivities include handbell choirs, arts and crafts, food, live period entertainment, costume contest, and parades. Held on Strand and Mechanic Streets, 21st-25th Streets.

Galveston Historical Foundation, Gina Spagnola, 502 20th Street, Galveston, TX 77550-2014, (409) 765-7834, Fax: (409) 765-7851, shirley.bilotta@galvestonhistory.org, www.galvestonhistory.org, www.dickensonthestrand.org

Belton: North Central   Christmas on the Chisholm Trail

December 6, 2001

Take a glimpse back to slower times as you tour the downtown shops while choral groups and troops of carolers stroll through downtown Belton. (254) 773-2105, www.beltontxchamber.com

Lockhart: Hill Country   A Dickens Christmas in Lockhart

December 7, 2002   1st Saturday in December

Family fun on the courthouse square in a beautiful little Texas town. Join the folks for an old-fashioned Victorian Christmas festival in and around the oldest continuously operating Public Library in the state of Texas. Turn-of-the-century costumes, arts & crafts, children's events, Lighting of the Yule Log, homes tour. The courthouse (built 1894) and the surrounding historic Victorian buildings of the square are the perfect setting for a start to a special Christmas season. Jugglers, bagpipers, and horse-drawn carriage rides. (512) 398-3223, lockhart@jump.net, www.library.ci.lockhart.tx.us

Buda: Hill Country   Budafest

December 7-8, 2002   1st weekend in December

This is a beautiful little town and a fun event. Arts/crafts, antiques, collectibles, kids' rides, books, food & drink & live music, plenty of fun and much, much more!! 10 A.M. till dusk both days, parade Saturday 10 A.M. Held in scenic downtown Buda, just off of IH-35, south of Austin.

For information: Thomas Crouse, 1-800-99-4-BUDA (994-2832), tom@budatx.com, www.budatx.com/BudaCalendar.htm

Nacogdoches: East   Nine Flags Festival

December 7-8 & 14-15, 2002   1st two weekends in December

Each year this wonderful festival honors one of the nine flags that have flown over the oldest town in Texas. The event features historical reenactments, live entertainment, tour of homes, lighted holiday parade, fireworks, arts and crafts, storytelling, and much more! AND THEY GUARANTEE SNOW! Held at 200 East Main Street, Nacogdoches, TX 75961. Call (888) 564-7351.

Johnson City: Hill Country   A Timeless Christmas in Johnson City

December 8, 2001   **2nd Saturday in December**

Turn the clock back to Christmas 1920, in Lyndon Johnson's boyhood home. The glow of oil lamps brings to life memories of a special time in small town Texas. At the cabin of Johnson's grandparents, decorated for an 1860s holiday, costumed National Park rangers depict a simple frontier celebration by fire and candlelight. Visit both to experience firsthand the history of rural electrification, LBJ's gift to his home place. Lyndon B. Johnson National Historical Park. Call (830) 868-7128, ext 244.

Austin: Hill Country   Armadillo Christmas Bazaar

December 8-24, 2002

This last entry is one of my favorite events. It is a Christmas shopping opportunity with a uniquely Texas twist. There are hundreds of glass blowers, weavers, woodcarvers, leather workers, painters, and sculptors showing their wares. But their wares aren't the usual tourist/boring stuff. Nope, these folks were selected to appear because of their uniqueness. All the while, there is live music from some of the biggest names in Texas music. Go and check it out at the Austin Music Hall, located at Third and Neches, in downtown Austin. Belinda Bowers (512) 263-4238, www.armadillobazaar.com

Now you-all have a Good Christmas.

Jim heads off to find more fun fairs and festivals to put in the next book. Photo by Sally Gramon.

Well folks, I certainly do hope you enjoyed the tour of Texas Festivals and Events. I'm just bettin' you found out about some goin's on that you'd never heard of. Remember to drop me a line if you have any suggestions.

Happy Trails,
Jim

Webliography

Texas Websites

I've never heard of a webliography, but I needed a word that describes what this section is.

Austin Convention & Visitors Bureau Events, a great collection of Austin's diverse activities. www.austin360.com/acvb/events/events.htm

Texas Barbecue & Chili Cookoffs Lists many of the events in Texas. texana.texascooking.com/cookoffs.htm

Barbecue Judges Chambers Nothing is more Texas, or more fun, than a BBQ cookoff. It should be no surprise that there are dozens of sanctioning organizations nationally. There are three in Texas alone (Central Texas Barbecue Society, Lone Star Barbecue Society, and the International Barbecue Cookers Association). This website lets you look at cookoffs across the world, or by state, or all the events approved by a particular sanctioning organization. www.bbqjudge.com/webpages/events.htm

Bureau of Land Management, Wild Horse and Burro Program This website contains a number of references to publications dealing with horses and burros in the west. www.blm.gov/whb

CASI, Chili Appreciation Society International, list of sanctioned chili cookoffs. www.chili.org/cookoffs.html

Central Texas Bluegrass Association maintains a calendar of all of their events on this site. www.zilker.net/~ctbg/festival.html

CollectibleShopping.com, a listing of collectibles shows. www.collectibleclassifieds.com/texas1.htm

Commerce Connection, a website that provides links to the Chambers of Commerce in a couple of hundred Texas cities. www.lnstar.com/mall/main-areas/chamber/chambers.htm

Dyanne Fry Cortez. *Hot Jams & Cold Showers*, **Scenes from the Kerrville Folk Festival** A neat book by a neat lady I just recently had the pleasure of meeting. It's about what it's like to attend this wonderful festival over the years. Printed by Dos Puertas Publishing, 2000. www.dospuertas.com

Central Texas Bluebonnet Travel Council, a website with links to many Central Texas cities, including an events calendar. www.rtis.com/reg

Cultural Crossroads, Regional & Historical Perspectives This is an interesting website that provides short stories and links into a variety of interesting directions. www.geocities.com/~lostdutchman/roads.html

Doctor Duck's Events and Shows, an interesting listing of a wide variety of guitar related events. www.ducksdeluxe.com/ddevents.html

East Texas Vacation Guide A website that focuses on what goes on in the many towns of East Texas. www.easttexasguide.com

El Paso Convention and Visitors Bureau www.elpasocvb.com

ElSurfo - Things to Do In Texas A nice website with lots of links to many Texas websites. www.elsurfo.com/todo/tx.htm

Festivals Of Texas A great site with lots of good information. www.festivalsoftexas.com

Festivals USA A listing for numerous festivals nationwide. This address takes you straight to Texas events. www.festivalusa.com/states/txfest.htm

Festivals and Fiestas A cool website devoted to guess what...Texas festivals and fiestas. www.texas-on-line.com/graphic/festivals.html

Festivals & Events for the USA A calendar of events taking place across the United States, by state and month. www.fulltiming-america.com/festivals

The Handbook of Texas Online Provided as a joint effort of the Texas State Historical Society and the University of Texas. I heartily recommend it as an excellent resource on many aspects of Texas. www.tsha.utexas.edu/handbook/online/articles/view/

Hill Country and Central Texas Events A neat website that has dozens of websites that tie to these portions of Texas. pw2.netcom.com/~wandaron/hillroads.html

Horse Web, devoted to horse related events and festivals. www.horseweb.com/links/Events_Shows_Clinics_Etc

Houston Livestock Show & Rodeo A spectacular annual event. www.hlsr.com

The Institute of Texan Cultures at the University of Texas at San Antonio www.utsa.edu/

International Folk Culture Center - San Antonio, TX has information and links dealing with folklore, folk dances, and folk music. www.n-link.com/ ~ifccsa

Kerrville Folk Festival, the home website for one of Texas's greatest festivals. www.festivalusa.com/states/txfest.htm

La Peña, Latino Arts in Austin La Peña is a community-based organization dedicated to the preservation, development, and promotion of Latino artistic expression in all its forms. The board of directors and staff of La Peña believe that cultural expression and knowledge is crucial to the survival of the community. www.hyperweb.com/LaPena

RibMan.com This is a cool site that keeps a pretty current list of BBQ cookoffs. www.ribman.com/events.html

North and North Central Texas, a website focusing on the towns and events in this vast portion of Texas. pw2.netcom.com/~wandaron/notxroads.html

Old Settlers Music Festival Dripping Springs' spring bluegrass, blues, folk, and acoustic jazz festival. www.bluegrassfestival.com

Panhandle and Northwest Texas, a website focusing on the towns and events in this vast portion of Texas. pw2.netcom.com/~wandaron/pantx.html

PRCA (Professional Rodeo Cowboys Association) The PRCA is one of the leading sanctioning bodies for the rodeo circuit. They keep information posted on all the events they sanction. www.csarodeo.com/PRCA_rodeos.html

The Rio Grande Folklore Archive is situated in the University of Texas-Pan American Library, and is one of the largest collections of Mexican American folklore. It is the major depository for the folklore of the Lower Rio Grande Valley of Texas and Northern Tamaulipas, Mexico. www.panam.edu/dept/folklore

Roadstar Productions, a firm that puts together festivals. They maintain a calendar of their events at www.roadstarproductions.com

Round Top Festival Institute, a wonderful center for a wide variety of classical and orchestral music events. Check out the Calendar of Events. festivalhill.org/index.htm

Running Events Calendar The Road Runners Club of America is the national association of not-for-profit running clubs dedicated to promoting long distance running as a competitive sport and as healthful exercise. They maintain this cool website that has most of the races in Texas. www.rrca.org/clubs/tx/calendar.html

SearchFrog.com, a resource for a wide variety of information. www.webguidetexas.com

South By Southwest, SXSW 9 days of films, 5 days of live music, 11 days of panels, parties, awards, and trade shows. austin360.com/entertainment/features/sxsw

Star Arabian Horse, shows and events. members.aol.com/_ht_a/modelapage/index.html

State Fair of Texas, one of the largest events in the nation, which includes numerous musical, livestock, car, appliance, and art exhibits. www.flash.net/~threei/sfot/index.html

Tejas Storytellers Association Their mission is to foster the appreciation of storytelling as an oral tradition and a performing art. Their goal is to influence the values of the citizens of our region by promoting and supporting the art, craft, and history of storytelling so as to ensure the continuation of the tradition. www.tejasstorytelling.com

Texas AreaGuides.net Want to know something about a Texas town? Check out this site. It provides dozens of links to local establishments in many towns. www.areaguides.net/TX.html

Texas Association of Businesses & Chambers of Commerce, a website linking to dozens of firms and cities. www.tabcc.org

Texas Barbecue and Chili Cookoffs, texana.texascooking.com/cookoffs.htm

Texas & Oklahoma Car Shows, a private website listing of shows. members.aol.com/_ht_a/modelapage/index.html

TexasEscapes.com Cool site with lots of good information. I like their description of themselves: Romancing the legend that is Texas. Texas travel, Texas towns, Texas architecture, Texas history, Texas personalities, and nothing about Louisiana (for now). www.TexasEscapes.com

Texas Communities Online This website is a cooperative effort between numerous communities to showcase their events. rtis.com/reg/comcal

Texas Food and Wine Festivals, a website with links to dozens of wonderful events. www.texascooking.com/festivals.htm

Texas Fun Travel Guide, a collection of information about a wide variety of Texas towns. Click on the Events button. www.texasfun.com

Texas Happenings is a cool website that describes itself as "the electronic newspaper of What, When and Where events that are happening in Texas." www.texashappenings.com

Texas Highways Fun Forecast This wonderful website allows you to check out what's going on by town or by region. www.texashighways.com/forecast.html

Texas Monthly, Events & Promotions website. One of my favorite magazines is *Texas Monthly*, and they maintain a website that features various events going on across the state. www.texasmonthly.com/events

Texas Mountain Bike Racing Association has a calendar of their events at www.tmbra.org

Texas Music Office, Events Calendar A MUST for your Favorites list. The Texas Music Office, which is an office of the state of Texas, serves as the information clearinghouse and promotion office for the Texas music industry. Find out what's going on musically. What type of music do you like? Country, folk, rock, jazz, bluegrass, tejano, they have information on what's going on. www.governor.state.tx.us/MUSIC/tmec.main.htm

Texas Parks & Wildlife Department, the home website for a wonderful organization. This site contains tons of valuable information and dozens of links to websites. www.tpwd.state.tx.us

Texas Rodeos, Let's Rodeo! This neat website will point you towards all the rodeos going on across the state. www.sage.net/~txrodeo/rodeos.html

Texas State Government Information website, this is another official state site. Information here focuses on doing business, traveling, and which government agencies perform which functions and how to contact them. There is also information about all of the state symbols. www.texas.gov/ TEXAS_homepage.html

The Texas Heritage Music Foundation was established in 1987 to preserve and perpetuate the traditions of Texas music, to examine the background of Texas music, to trace influences and patterns in Texas music, and to document the role Texas music has played in society. Be sure to check out their Calendar of Events. www.texasheritagemusic.org

Texas State Official website This site is the central site for the state. There are areas of particular interest including a calendar of events, state symbols, legends, and landmarks. www.state.tx.us

Texas Travel - @Texas This is a great website, offering valuable information about a wide variety of destinations and attractions taking place in the Lone Star State. This site is jointly sponsored by the Texas Festivals & Events Association, Texas Travel Industry Association, and @ction Travel Group. www.tourtexas.com

@round Texas - Clicking on this icon will take you to a section of this site that is quite handy for locating upcoming events. It offers three different ways to search their database of events. You can search by *Date*, by geographic *Region*, or the *Type of Event*. www.tourtexas.com/ @round-texas.html

Texas State Historical Association Organized on March 2, 1897, the Texas State Historical Association is the oldest learned society in the state. Its mission is to foster the appreciation, understanding, and teaching of the rich and unique history of Texas and by example and through programs and activities encourage and promote research, preservation, and publication of historical material affecting the state of Texas. www.tsha.utexas.edu/

University of Texas Friends of the Library Calendar of Events This site lists a number of events throughout Texas. www.lib.utexas.edu/About/ friends/friends.calendar.html

Utopia Animal Rescue Ranch Founded by a group headed by Kinky Friedman, this organization cares for neglected and deserted animals. Annually Kinky and his friends put on a "Bone-i-fit" to help fund the Ranch's activities (normally in March). Be sure and watch this site to see who will be appearing. And be sure to donate to this very worthy group. www.utopiarescue.com

VirtualTexan.com is a site devoted to the state of Texas. It is sponsored by the *Fort Worth Star-Telegram*. www.virtualtexan.com

WebguideTexas.com is a neat website containing information on many major Texas cities, an events calendar, and much more information www.webguidetexas.com

West Texas Productions produces comedy wild west shows and other types of comedy related shows. www.wtpshows.com

yeeHaa! Cities & Towns Directory Down-home Texas information, just a click away. http://www.yeeha.net/directory/C5600.html

City & Chamber of Commerce Websites

Abilene Chamber of Commerce
P.O. Box 2281
Abilene, Texas 79604
www.abilene.com/chamber
Phone: (915) 673-7241
Fax: (915) 677-0622

Alice Chamber of Commerce
P.O. Box 1609
Alice, Texas 78333
www.alicetx.org
Phone: (512) 664-3454
Fax: (512) 664-2291

Allen Chamber of Commerce
210 W. McDermott
Allen, Texas 75013
www.allenchamber.org
Phone: (972) 727-5585
Fax: (972) 727-9000

Alpine Chamber of Commerce
106 N. 3rd Street
Alpine, Texas 79830
www.alpinetexas.com/
Phone: (915) 837-2326
Fax: (915) 837-3638

Alvin-Manvel Area Chamber of
Commerce
P.O. Box 2028
Alvin, Texas 77512
www.alvintexas.org
Phone: (281) 331-3944
Fax: (281) 585-8662

Amarillo Chamber of Commerce
P.O. Box 9480
Amarillo, Texas 79105
www.amarillo-chamber.org/
Phone: (806) 373-7800
Fax: (806) 373-3909

Angleton Chamber of Commerce
445 East Mulberry
Angleton, Texas 77515
Phone: (409) 849-6443
Fax: (409) 849-4520

Aransas Pass Chamber of Commerce
P.O. Box 1947
Aransas Pass, Texas 78335
www.info@aransaspass.org
Phone: (512) 758-2750
Fax: (512) 758-8320

Arlington Chamber, The
316 West Main Street
Arlington, Texas 76004-1486
www.chamber@arlintontx.com
Phone: (817) 275-2613
Fax: (817) 261-7535

Athens Chamber of Commerce
P.O. Box 2600
Athens, Texas 75751
www.athenscc.org
Phone: (903) 675-5181
Fax: (903) 675-5183

Austin Chamber of Commerce,
Greater
P.O. Box 1967
Austin, Texas 78767
www.austin-chamber.org
Phone: (512) 478-9383
Fax: (512) 478-9615

Ballinger Chamber of Commerce
P.O. Box 577
Ballinger, Texas 76821
www.ballingertx.org
Phone: (915) 365-2333
Fax: (915) 365-3445

Bay City Chamber of Commerce
P.O. Box 768
Bay City, Texas 77404-0768
www.baycity.com
Phone: (409) 245-8333
Fax: (409) 245-1622

Baytown Chamber of Commerce
P.O. Box 330
Baytown, Texas 77522
www.baytowncc.com
Phone: (281) 422-8359
Fax: (281) 422-8359

Beaumont Chamber of Commerce
P.O. Box 3150
Beaumont, Texas 77704
www.bmtcoc.org
Phone: (409) 838-6581
Fax: (409) 833-6718

Belton Area Chamber of Commerce
P.O. Box 659
Belton, Texas 76513
www.beltontxchamber.com
Phone: (254) 939-3551
Fax: (254) 939-1061

Benbrook Area Chamber of
Commerce
8507 Hwy 377 S.
Benbrook, Texas 76126
www.mesh.nt/~benbrook
Phone: (817) 249-4451
Fax: (817) 249-3307

Big Spring Area Chamber of
Commerce
P.O. Box 1391
Big Spring, Texas 79720
www.bigspringtx.com
Phone: (915) 263-7641
Fax: (915) 264-9111

Boerne Chamber of Commerce,
Greater
One Main Plaza
Boerne, Texas 78006
www.boerne.com
Phone: (830) 249-8000
Fax: (830) 249-9639

Borger Chamber of Commerce
P.O. Box 490
Borger, Texas 79008
www.borger.com
Phone: (806) 274-2211
Fax: (806) 273-3488

Brady/McCulloch County Chamber
101 E. 1st Street
Brady, Texas 76825
www.bradytx.com
Phone: (915) 597-3491
Fax: (915) 597-2420

Brazosport Area Chamber of
Commerce
420 Highway 332 West
Brazosport, Texas 77531
www.brazosport.org
Phone: (409) 265-2505
Fax: (409) 265-4246

Breckenridge Chamber of Commerce
P.O. Box 1466
Breckenridge, Texas 76424
www.breckenridgetx.com
Phone: (254) 554-2301
Fax: (254) 559-7104

Bridgeport Chamber of Commerce
P.O. Box 1104
Bridgeport, Texas 76426
www.bridgeport-tx.com
Phone: (940) 683-2076
Fax: (940) 683-3969

Brownsville Chamber of Commerce
1600 East Elizabeth Street
Brownsville, Texas 78520-4999
www.brownsvillechamber.com
Phone: (956) 542-4341
Fax: (956) 504-3348

Brownwood Area Chamber of
Commerce
521 E. Baker
Brownwood, Texas 76801
www.brownwoodchamber.org
Phone: (915) 646-9535
Fax: (915) 643-6686

Bryan-College Station Chamber of
Commerce
P.O. Box 3579
Bryan, Texas 7805-3579
www.b-cs.com
Phone: (409) 260-5200
Fax: (409) 260-5208

Burkburnett Chamber of Commerce
104 W. Third
Burkburnett, Texas 76354
www.seekon.com/L/US/TX/
Burkburnett/
Phone: (940) 569-3304
Fax: (940) 569-3306

Burleson Chamber of Commerce
P.O. Box 9
Burleson, Texas 76028
www.burleson.org
Phone: (817) 295-6121
Fax: (817) 295-6192

Burleson County Chamber of
Commerce
Somerville Chamber of Commerce
P.O. Drawer 87
Caldwell, Texas 77836
www.rtis.com/reg/somerville
Phone: (409) 567-3218
Fax: (409) 567-0818

Burnet Chamber of Commerce
703 Buchanan Drive
Burnet, Texas 78611
www.burnetchamber.org
Phone: (512) 756-4297
Fax: (512) 756-2548

Canyon Chamber of Commerce
P.O. Box 8
Canyon, Texas 79015
www.canyonchamber.org
Phone: (806) 655-1183
Fax: (806) 655-4608

Capital City Chamber of Commerce
5407 N. IH-35, Ste. 304
Austin, Texas 78723
www.main.org/busi-
ness/ccchamb.html
Phone: (512) 449-1181
Fax: (512) 459-1183

Cedar Creek Lake Chamber
100 Causeway Beach
Seven Points, Texas 75143
www.cclake.net
Phone: (903) 432-3152
Fax: (903) 432-3641

Cedar Park Chamber of Commerce
350 Discovery Blvd., Ste 207
Cedar Park, Texas 78613
www.cedarparkchamber.org
Phone: (512) 260-4260
Fax: (512) 260-4265

Clear Lake Area Chamber of
Commerce
1201 NASA Road 1
Houston, Texas 77058
www.clearlakearea.com
Phone: (281) 488-7676
Fax: (281) 488-8981

Cleburne Chamber of Commerce
P.O. Box 701
Cleburne, Texas 76033-0701
www.cleburnetexas.net
Phone: (817) 645-2455
Fax: (817) 641-3069

Coleman Chamber of Commerce
P.O. Box 796
Coleman, Texas 76834
www.colemantx.org
Phone: (915) 625-2163
Fax: (915) 625-2164

Colleyville Area Chamber
6700 Colleyville Blvd.
Colleyville, Texas 76034
www.colleyvillechamber.org
Phone: (817) 488-7148
Fax: (817) 488-4242

Colorado City Area Chamber
P.O. Box 242
Colorado City, Texas 79512
www.ccitytx.com
Phone: (915) 728-3403
Fax: (915) 728-2911

Comanche Chamber of Commerce
P.O. Box 65
Comanche, Texas 76442
www2.itexas.net/~chamber.edc
Phone: (915) 356-3233
Fax: (915) 356-2940

Conroe/Lake Area Chamber
505 West Davis
Conroe, Texas 77301
www.chamber.montgomery.tx.us
Phone: (409) 756-6644
Fax: (409) 756-6462

Coppell Chamber of Commerce
P.O. Box 452
Coppell, Texas 75019
www.ci.coppell.tx.us/chamber.htm
Phone: (972) 393-2829
Fax: (972) 393-7485

Copperas Cove Chamber of
Commerce
204 E. Robertson Avenue
Copperas Cove, Texas 76522
www.copperascove.com
Phone: (254) 547-7571
Fax: (254) 547-5015

Corpus Christi Chamber of
Commerce
1201 N. Shoreline Blvd.
Corpus Christi, Texas 78401
www.corpuschristichamber.org/
Phone: (361) 881-1800
Fax: (361) 888-5627

Corsicana Area Chamber
120 N. 12th Street
Corsicana, Texas 75110
www.corsicana.org/index3.htm
Phone: (903) 874-4731
Fax: (903) 874-4187

Crowley Area Chamber of Commerce
P.O. Box 299
Crowley, Texas 76036
Phone: (817) 297-4211
Fax: (817) 297-7334

Cuero Chamber of Commerce
124 E. Church
Cuero, Texas 77954
www.cuero.org/
Phone: (512) 275-2212
Fax: (512) 275-6351

Cy-Fair Houston Chamber
11050 FM 1960 West, Ste. 100
Houston, Texas 77065
www.cyfairhoustonchamber.com/
Phone: (281) 955-1100
Fax: (281) 955-0138

Dalhart Area Chamber of Commerce
P.O. Box 967
Dalhart, Texas 79022
www.dalhart.org
Phone: (806) 244-5646
Fax: (806) 244-4945

Dallas Chamber of Commerce,
Greater
1201 Elm Street, Suite 2000
Dallas, Texas 75270
www.gdc.org
Phone: (214) 746-6600
Fax: (214) 746-6799

Dallas Northeast Chamber of
Commerce
718 N. Buckner Blvd. #332
Dallas, Texas 75218
www.metro.com/dncc
Phone: (214) 321-6446
Fax: (214) 321-2100

Decatur Chamber Of Commerce
P.O. Box 474
Decatur, Texas 76234
www.decaturtx.com
Phone: (940) 627-3107
Fax: (940) 627-3771

Deer Park Chamber of Commerce
110 Center
Deer Park, Texas 77536
www.deerpark.org
Phone: (281) 479-1559
Fax: (281) 476-4041

Del Rio Chamber of Commerce
1915 Avenue F
Del Rio, Texas 78840
www.chamber.delrio.com
Phone: (830) 775-3551
Fax: (830) 774-1813

Denison Area Chamber of Commerce
P.O. Box 325
Denison, Texas 75020
www.denissontexas.com
Phone: (903) 465-1551
Fax: (903) 465-8443

Denton Chamber of Commerce
P.O. Box Drawer P
Denton, Texas 76202
www.denton-chamber.org
Phone: (940) 382-7151
Fax: (940) 982-0040

Denver City Chamber of Commerce
104 West Third Street
Denver City, Texas 79323
www.hiplains.net/dccofc/
Phone: (806) 592-5424
Fax: (806) 592-7613

Dumas/Moore County Chamber
P.O. Box 735
Dumas, Texas 79029
www.dumascofc.org
Phone: (806) 935-2123
Fax: (806) 935-2124

Duncanville Chamber of Commerce
P.O. Box 380036
Duncanville, Texas 75138
www.ci.duncanville.tx.us/cham-ber.html
Phone: (972) 780-4990
Fax: (972) 298-9370

Eagle Pass Chamber of Commerce
P.O. Box 1188
Eagle Pass, Texas 78853
www.eaglepasstexas.com
Phone: (830) 773-3224
Fax: (830) 773-8844

East End Area Chamber of
Commerce
4600 Gulf Freeway, Ste. 620
Houston, Texas 77023
Phone: (713) 923-3201
Fax: (713) 923-3740

Edinburg Chamber of Commerce
P.O. Box 85
Edinburg, Texas 78540
www.edinburg.com/2000/
Phone: (956) 383-4974
Fax: (956) 380-3621

El Campo Chamber of Commerce and
Agriculture
P.O. Box 1400
El Campo, Texas 77437
www.intertex.net/users/elcampo
www.el-campo.tx.us/
Phone: (409) 543-2713
Fax: (409) 543-5495

El Paso Chamber of Commerce,
Greater
10 Civic Center Plaza
El Paso, Texas 79901
www.elpaso.org
Phone: (915) 534-0500
Fax: (915) 534-0513

Everman Area Chamber of
Commerce
410 W. Enon, Suite 104
Everman, Texas 76140
Phone: (817) 293-3957
Fax: (817) 293-7698

Farmers Branch Chamber of
Commerce
12875 Josey Lane, Ste. 150
Farmers Branch, Texas 75234
www.farmersbranchchamber.org/
Phone: (972) 243-8966
Fax: (972) 243-8968

Flower Mound Chamber of
Commerce
2631 Cross Timbers Rd., Ste. 205
Flower Mound, Texas 75028
www.themetro.com/fmchamber/
Phone: (972) 539-0500
Fax: (972) 539-4307

Forney Area Chamber of Commerce
P.O. Box 570
Forney, Texas 75126
www.forney-texas.com/
Phone: (972) 564-2233
Fax: (972) 564-3677

Fort Bend Chamber of Commerce
445 Commerce Green Blvd.
Sugar Land, Texas 77478
www.ftbendcc.org/
Phone: (281) 491-0800
Fax: (281) 491-0112

Fort Worth Chamber of Commerce
777 Taylor Street, Suite 900
Fort Worth, Texas 76102-4997
www.fortworthchamber.com/
Phone: (817) 336-2491
Fax: (817) 877-4034

Fredericksburg Chamber of
Commerce
106 North Adams
Fredericksburg, Texas 78624
www.fredericksburg-texas.com/
Phone: (830) 997-6523
Fax: (830) 997-8588

Friona Chamber of Commerce
P.O. Box 905
Friona, Texas 79035
www.highground.org/friona.htm
Phone: (806) 250-3491
Fax: (806) 250-2348

Frisco Chamber of Commerce
P.O. Box 1074
Frisco, Texas 75034
www.friscochamber.com/
Phone: (972) 335-9522
Fax: (972) 335-6654

Gainesville Area Chamber of
Commerce
2700 Post Oak Blvd, Suite 2425
Houston, Texas 77056
www.gainesville.tx.us/
Phone: (713) 629-5555
Fax: (713) 629-6403

Galleria Chamber of Commerce
2700 Post Oak Blvd., Suite 2425
Houston, Texas 77056
www.galleriachamber.com/
Phone: (713) 629-5555
Fax: (713) 629-6403

Galveston Chamber of Commerce
621 Moody, #300
Galveston, Texas 77550
www.galvestoncc.com
Phone: (409) 763-5326
Fax: (409) 763-8271

Garland Chamber of Commerce
914 South Garland Avenue
Garland, Texas 75040
www.garlandchamber.org
www.dallas.net/~ktpub/gcc.html
Phone: (972) 272-7551
Fax: (972) 276-9261

Georgetown Chamber of Commerce
P.O. Box 346
Georgetown, Texas 78627
www.georgetownchamber.org/
Phone: (512) 930-3535
Fax: (512) 930-3587

Giddings Area Chamber of Commerce
171 E. Hempstead
Giddings, Texas 78942
www.giddingstx.com/
Phone: (409) 542-3455
Fax: (409) 542-7060

Gonzales Chamber of Commerce
P.O. Box 134
Gonzales, Texas 78629
www.gonzalestexas.com/
Phone: (830) 672-6532
Fax: (830) 672-6533

Graham Chamber of Commerce
608 Elm Street
Graham, Texas 76450
www.wf.net/~streetin
grahamtx.areaguides.net/
Phone: (940) 549-3355
Fax: (940) 549-6391

Grand Prairie Chamber of Commerce
P.O. Box 531227
Grand Prairie, Texas 75053
www.ci.grand-prairie.tx.us./
Phone: (972) 264-1558
Fax: (972) 264-3419

Grapevine Chamber of Commerce
P.O. Box 368
Grapevine, Texas 76051
www.grapevinechamber.com/
Phone: (817) 481-1522
Fax: (817) 424-5208

Greenville Chamber of Commerce
P.O. Box 1055
Greenville, Texas 75402
www.greenville-chamber.org/
Phone: (903) 455-1510
Fax: (903) 455-1736

Harker Heights Chamber of
Commerce
100 W Central Texas Expwy, #206
Harker Heights, Texas 76548
www.harkerheights.com/
chamber.htm
Phone: (254) 699-4999
Fax: (254) 699-5197

Harlingen Area Chamber of
Commerce
311 East Tyler St.
Harlingen, Texas 78550
www.harlingen.com/
Phone: (956) 423-5565
Fax: (956) 425-3870

Heights Area Chamber of Commerce,
Greater
545 West 19th Street
Houston, Texas 77008
www.heightschamber.com/
Phone: (713) 861-6735
Fax: (713) 861-9310

Hillsboro Chamber of Commerce
P.O. Box 358
Hillsboro, Texas 76645
www.hillsboro.net/busi-
ness/chamberofcommerce/
Phone: (254) 582-2481
Fax: (254) 582-0465

Hondo Area Chamber of Commerce
1802 Avenue M
Hondo, Texas 78861
www.rtis.com/reg/hondo/
Phone: (830) 426-3037
Fax: (830) 426-5357

Hopkins County Chamber of
Commerce
P.O. Box 347
Sulphur Springs, Texas 75483
www.sulphurspringstx.com/
Phone: (903) 885-6515
Fax: (903) 885-6516

Houston County Chamber of
Commerce
P.O. Box 307
Crockett, Texas 75835
www.crockett.org/
Phone: (409) 544-2359
Fax: (409) 544-4355

Houston Northwest Chamber of
Commerce
14511 Falling Creek, Ste. 205
Houston, Texas 77014
www.usachamber.com/houston/
Phone: (281) 440-4160
Fax: (281) 440-5229

Houston Partnership, Greater
1200 Smith, Ste. 700
Houston, Texas 77002
www.houston.org/
Phone: (713) 844-3600
Fax: (713) 651-2299

Houston West Chamber of Commerce
10777 Westheimer, Ste. 916
Houston, Texas 77042
www.houstonwestchamber.org/ie/
main_ie.htm
Phone: (713) 785-4922
Fax: (713) 785-4944

Humble Area Chamber of Commerce
P.O. Box 3337
Humble, Texas 77347
www.humbleareachamber.com
www.humblearea.com/
Phone: (281) 446-2128
Fax: (281) 446-7483

Huntsville-Walker County Chamber
of Commerce
P.O. Box 538
Huntsville, Texas 77342-0538
www.chamber.huntsville.tx.us/
Phone: (409) 295-8113
Fax: (409) 295-0571

Hurst Euless Bedford Chamber of
Commerce
P.O. Box 969
Bedford, Texas 76021
www.heb.org/
Phone: (817) 283-1521
Fax: (817) 267-5111

Irving-Las Colinas Chamber of Commerce, Greater
3333 N. MacArthur Blvd., #100
Irving, Texas 75062
www.irving.net/chamber
www.irvingchamber.com/
Phone: (972) 252-8484
Fax: (972) 252-6710

Jacksonville Chamber of Commerce
P.O. Box 1231
Jacksonville, Texas 75766
www.jacksonvilletexas.com/

Phone: (903) 586-2217
Fax: (903) 586-6944

Jasper Chamber of Commerce
246 East Milam
Jasper, Texas 75951
www.jaspercoc.org/
Phone: (409) 384-2762
Fax: (409) 384-4733

Katy Area Chamber, Greater
6001 Highway Blvd., Ste 6
Katy, Texas 77494
www.katypage.com/Chamber/
Phone: (281) 391-2422
Fax: (281) 391-3297

Kerrville Area Chamber of
Commerce
1700 Sidney Baker St., Ste. 100
Kerrville, Texas 78028
kerrvilletx.com/
Phone: (830) 896-1155
Fax: (830) 896-1175

Keller Chamber of Commerce,
Greater
P.O. Box 761
Keller, Texas 76244
www.kellerchamber.com/
Phone: (817) 431-2169
Fax: (817) 431-3789

Kilgore Chamber of Commerce
P.O. Box 1582
Kilgore, Texas 75663
www.ci.kilgore.tx.us/cham-
ber/home/content.html
Phone: (903) 984-5022
Fax: (903) 984-4975

Killeen Chamber of Commerce,
Greater
P.O. Box 548
Killeen, Texas 76540

www.gkcc.com/
Phone: (254) 526-9551
Fax: (254) 526-6090

Kingsville Chamber of Commerce
P.O. Box 1030
Kingsville, Texas 78363
www.kingsville.org/
Phone: (361) 592-6438
Fax: (361) 592-0866

La Grange Area Chamber of
Commerce
171 South Main
La Grange, Texas 78945
www.lagrangetx.org/
Phone: (800) LAGRANG
Fax: (409) 968-8000

La Porte-Bayshore Chamber of
Commerce
P.O. Box 996
LaPorte, Texas 77572
www.nwwin.com/laporte.tx/chamber.html
Phone: (281) 471-1123
Fax: (281) 471-1710

Lake Granbury Area Chamber of
Commerce
416 South Morgan Street
Granbury, Texas 76048
www.lakegranbury.org/chamber/
Phone: (817) 573-1622
Fax: (817) 573-0805

Lamar County Chamber
1651 Clarksville Street
Paris, Texas 754600
www.paristexas.com/chamberofcommerce.html
Phone: (903) 784-2501
Fax: (903) 784-2503

Lamesa Area Chamber of Commerce
P.O. Box 880
Lamesa, Texas 79331
www.pics.net/~lamesaedc/location.html
Phone: (806) 872-2181
Fax: (806) 872-5700

Lewisville Chamber of Commerce
P.O. Box 293805
Lewisville, Texas 75029-3805
www.lewisville.com
Phone: (972) 436-9571
Fax: (972) 436-5949

Liberty-Dayton Area Chamber
P.O. Box 77575
Liberty, Texas 77575
www.imswebs.com/chamber/
Phone: (409) 336-5736
Fax: (409) 336-1159

Lockhart Chamber of Commerce
P.O. Box 840
Lockhart, Texas 78644
www.lockhart-tx.org/
Phone: (512) 398-2818
Fax: (512) 376-2632

Longview Partnership
P.O. Box 472
Longview, Texas 75606
www.longviewtx.com/
Phone: (903) 237-4000
Fax: (903) 237-4049

Lubbock Chamber of Commerce
P.O. Box 561
Lubbock, Texas 79408
www.lubbock.org/
Phone: (806) 761-7000
Fax: (806) 761-7010

Lufkin/Angelina County Chamber
P.O. Box 1606
Lufkin, Texas 75901
www.lufkintexas.org/
Phone: (409) 634-6644
Fax: (409) 634-8726

Mansfield Chamber of Commerce
116 N. Main Street
Mansfield, Texas 76063
home.flash.net/~mcofc/
Phone: (817) 473-0507
Fax: (817) 473-8687

Marble Falls/Lake LBJ Chamber of
Commerce
801 Highway 281
Marble Falls, Texas 78654
www.marblefalls.org/
Phone: (830) 693-4449
Fax: (830) 693-7594

Marshall Chamber of Commerce
P.O. Box 520
Marshall, Texas 75671
www.marshalltxchamber.com/
Phone: (903) 935-7868
Fax: (903) 935-9982

McAllen Chamber of Commerce
P.O. Box 790
McAllen, Texas 78505-0790
www.mcallenchamberusa.com/
Phone: (956) 682-2871
Fax: (956) 631-8571

McKinney Chamber of Commerce
P.O. Box 621
McKinney, Texas 75070
www.mckinneytx.org/
Phone: (972) 542-0163
Fax: (972) 548-0876

Mesquite Chamber of Commerce
P.O. Box 850115
Mesquite, Texas 75185
www.mesquitechamber.com/
Phone: (972) 285-0211
Fax: (972) 285-3535

Metrocrest Chamber of Commerce
1204 Metrocrest Drive
Carrollton, Texas 75006
www.metrocrestchamber.com/
Phone: (972) 416-6600
Fax: (972) 416-7874

Midland Chamber of Commerce
109 North Main
Midland, Texas 79701
www.midlandtxchamber.com/
Phone: (915) 683-3381
Fax: (915) 682-9205

Midlothian Chamber of Commerce
P.O. Box 609
Midlothian, Texas 76065
www.midlothianchamber.org/
Phone: (972) 723-8600
Fax: (972) 723-9300

Mineral Wells Area Chamber of
Commerce
P.O. Box 1408
Mineral Wells, Texas 76068-1408
www.mineralwellstx.com
Phone: (940) 325-2557
Fax: (940) 328-0850

Mission Area Chamber of Commerce
220 E. 9th Street
Mission, Texas 78572
www.missionchamber.com/
Phone: (956) 585-2727
Fax: (956) 585-3044

Mt. Pleasant/Titus County Chamber
of Commerce
P.O. Box 1237
Mt. Pleasant, Texas 75456-1237
www.mtpleasant-tx.com/
Phone: (903) 572-8567
Fax: (903) 572-0613

North Houston Greenspoint Chamber
of Commerce
16825 Northchase-Suite 140
Houston, Texas 77060
www.nhmccd.cc.tx.us/con-
tracts/chambers/alliance/
greenspoint/gpindex.html
Phone: (281) 872-8700
Fax: (281) 872-8095

Nacogdoches County Chamber of
Commerce
513 North Street
Nacogdoches, Texas 75961
www.nacogdoches.org/
Phone: (409) 560-5533
Fax: (409) 560-3920

Nederland Chamber of Commerce
P.O. Box 891
Nederland, Texas 77627
www.nederlandtx.com/
Phone: (409) 722-0279
Fax: (409) 722-0615

New Boston Chamber of Commerce
220 A Highway 82 West
New Boston, Texas 75570-2810
www.seekon.com/L/US/TX/
New_Boston/
Phone: (903) 628-2581
Fax: (903) 628-2581

New Braunfels Chamber, Greater
P.O. Box 311417
New Braunfels, Texas 78131-1417
www.nbcham.org/

Phone: (830) 625-2385
Fax: (830) 625-7918

North Dallas Chamber of Commerce
10707 Preston Road
Dallas, Texas 75230
www.ndcc.org/
Phone: (214) 368-6485
Fax: (214) 691-5584

North San Antonio Chamber of
Commere
45 N.E. Loop 410, Ste. 100
San Antonio, Texas 78216
mc2.comsite.net/northsachamber/
index.asp
Phone: (210) 344-4848
Fax: (210) 525-8207

Northeast Tarrant Chamber of
Commerce
5001 Denton Highway
Haltom City, Texas 76117
www.netarrant.org/
Phone: (817) 281-9376
Fax: (817) 281-9379

Northwest Tarrant Chamber of
Commerce
P.O. Box 136333
Fort Worth, Texas 76136-6333
Phone: (817) 237-0060
Fax: (817) 237-2365

Odessa Chamber of Commerce
P.O. Box 3626
Odessa, Texas 79760
www.odessachamber.com/
Phone: (915) 332-9111
Fax: (915) 333-7858

Orange Area Chamber, Greater
1012 Green Avenue
Orange, Texas 77630
www.org-tx.com/chamber/

Phone: (409) 883-3536
Fax: (409) 886-3247

Palestine Area Chamber of
Commerce
P.O. Box 1177
Palestine, Texas 75802
www.palestinechamber.org/
Phone: (903) 729-6066
Fax: (903) 729-2083

Pampa Chamber of Commerce
P.O. Box 1942
Pampa, Texas 79066
Phone: (806) 669-3241
Fax: (806) 669-3244
The chamber doesn't have a website,
but check out www.pampa.com/

Pasadena Chamber of Commerce
4334 Fairmont Parkway
Pasadena, Texas 77504-3306
www.pasadena-tx-chamber.com/
Phone: (281) 487-7871
Fax: (281) 487-5530

Pearland/Hobby Area Chamber of
Commerce
3501 Liberty Drive
Pearland, Texas 77581
www.pearlandchamber.com/
Phone: (281) 485-3634
Fax: (281) 485-2420

Pecos Chamber of Commerce
P.O. Box 27
Pecos, Texas 79772
www.pecostx.com/
Phone: (915) 445-2406
Fax: (915) 445-2407

Perryton-Ochiltree Chamber of
Commerce
P.O. Box 789
Perryton, Texas 79070

www.perryton.com/
Phone: (806) 435-6575
Fax: (806) 435-9821

Pharr Chamber of Commerce
P.O. Box 1341
Pharr, Texas 78577
Phone: (956) 787-1481
Fax: (956) 787-7972
The chamber has no website, but
check out
www.seekon.com/L/US/TX/Pharr/

Plano Chamber of Commerce
P.O. Drawer 940287
Plano, Texas 75094
www.planocc.org/
Phone: (972) 424-7547
Fax: (972) 422-5182

Port Aransas Chamber
421 W. Cotter
Port Aransas, Texas 78373
www.portaransas.org/
Phone: (512) 749-5919
Fax: (512) 749-4672

Port Arthur Chamber, Greater
4749 Twin City Hwy, Ste. 300N
Port Arthur, Texas 77642
www.portarthurtexas.com/
Phone: (409) 963-1107
Fax: (409) 963-3322

Port Isabel Chamber of Commerce
421 E. Queen Isabella Blvd.
Port Isabel, Texas 78578
www.portisabel.org/index.html
Phone: (956) 943-2262
Fax: (956) 943-4001

Port Lavaca-Calhoun Chamber
P.O. Box 528
Port Lavaca, Texas 77979
www.calhountx.org/

Phone: (512) 552-2959
Fax: (512) 552-1288

Portland Chamber of Commerce
P.O. Box 388
Portland, Texas 78374
www.portlandtx.org/
Phone: (361) 643-2475
Fax: (361) 643-7377

Randolph Metrocom Chamber of
Commerce
12702 Toepperwein Rd., Ste. 112
Live Oak, Texas 78233-3282
www.rmcc.net/
Phone: (210) 590-2037
Fax: (210) 657-2048

Richardson Chamber of Commerce
411 Belle Grove Drive
Richardson, Texas 75080
Phone: (972) 234-4141
Fax: (972) 680-9103
no website, but check out
www.ci.richardson.tx.us/

Rockdale Chamber of Commerce
1203 W. Cameron Avenue
Rockdale, Texas 76567
www.rtis.com/reg/rockdale/
Phone: (512) 446-2030
Fax: (512) 446-5969

Rockport-Fulton Area Chamber of
Commerce
404 Broadway
Rockport, Texas 78382
www.rockport-fulton.org/
Phone: (361) 729-6445
Fax: (361) 729-7681

Rockwall Chamber of Commerce
P.O. Box 92
Rockwall, Texas 75087
www.rockwallchamber.org/

Phone: (972) 771-5733
Fax: (972) 772-3642

Rosenberg/Richmond Area Chamber
of Commerce
4120 Avenue H
Rosenberg, Texas 77471
Phone: (281) 342-5464
Fax: (281) 342-2990

Round Rock Chamber of Commerce
212 E. Main Street
Round Rock, Texas 78664
www.roundrockchamber.ioffice.com/
www.ci.round-rock.tx.us/
Phone: (512) 255-3345
Fax: (512) 255-5805

Rowlett Chamber of Commerce
P.O. Box 610
Rowlett, Texas 75030
www.rowlett.com/
Phone: (972) 475-3200
Fax: (972) 463-1699

Rusk Chamber of Commerce
201 North Main
Henderson, Texas 75652
www.hendersontx.com/
Phone: (903) 657-5528
Fax: (903) 657-9454

San Angelo Chamber of Commerce
500 Rio Concho Drive
San Angelo, Texas 76903
www.sanangelo-tx.com/
Phone: (915) 655-4136
Fax: (915) 658-1110

San Antonio Chamber of Commerce,
Greater
P.O. Box 1628
San Antonio, Texas 78296
www.sachamber.org/

Phone: (210) 229-2100
Fax: (210) 229-2140

San Augustine County Chamber of
Commerce
611 West Columbia
San Augustine, Texas 75972
www.sanaugustinetx.com/
Phone: (409) 275-3610
Fax: (409) 275-0054

San Marcos Chamber of Commerce
P.O. Box 2310
San Marcos, Texas 78667
www.sanmarcostexas.com/
Phone: (512) 393-5900
Fax: (512) 393-5912

Schulenburg Chamber of Commerce
P.O. Box 65
Schulenburg, Texas 78956
Phone: (409) 743-4514
Fax: (409) 743-4839
no website, but check out
www.pe.net/~rksnow/txcounty-
schulenburg.htm

Sealy Chamber of Commerce
P.O. Box 586
Sealy, Texas 77474
www.sealy-tx.com/
Phone: (409) 885-3222
Fax: (409) 885-7184

Seguin Area Chamber of Commerce
P.O. Box 710
Seguin, Texas 78156
www.seguintx.org/
Phone: (830) 379-6382
Fax: (830) 379-6971

Shelby County Chamber of
Commerce
100 Courthouse Square A-101
Center, Texas 75939

Phone: (409) 598-3682
Fax: (409) 598-8163

Sherman Chamber of Commerce
P.O. Box 1029
Sherman, Texas 75091
www.shermantexas.com/index-
frames.htm
Phone: (903) 893-1184
Fax: (903) 593-4266

Sinton Chamber of Commerce
218 W. Sinton Street
Sinton, Texas 78387
Phone: (512) 364-2307
Fax: (512) 364-3538
no website, but try
www.pe.net/~rksnow/txcounty-
sinton.htm

Sonora Chamber of Commerce
P.O. Box 1172
Sonora, Texas 76950
www.sonoratx-chamber.com/
Phone: (915) 387-2880
Fax: (915) 387-5357

South Montgomery County Chamber
of Commerce
1400 Woodloch Forest Dr., #500
The Woodlands, Texas 77380
www.smcwcc.org/
Phone: (281) 367-5777
Fax: (281) 292-1655

South Padre Island Chamber of
Commerce
600 Padre Blvd.
South Pardre Island, Texas 78597
www.sopadre.com/
Phone: (956) 761-4412
Fax: (956) 761-2739

South Wise County Chamber of
Commerce
P.O. Box 108
Rhome, Texas 76078-0108
Phone: (817) 489-2589
Fax: (817) 489-2202

Southlake Chamber of Commerce
P.O. Box 92668
Southlake, Texas 76092
Phone: (817) 481-8200
Fax: (817) 329-7497
no website, but check out
www.comercis.com/cybermovers/
southlake/community.html

Southwest Houston Chamber of
Commerce, Greater
P.O. Box 788
Bellaire, Texas 77402
www.gswhcc.org/
Phone: (713) 666-1521
Fax: (713) 666-1523

Stamford Chamber of Commerce
P.O. Box 1206
Stamford, Texas 79553
www.sunsetpass.com/scoc/
Phone: (915) 773-2411
Fax: (915) 773-5594

Taylor Chamber of Commerce
P.O. Box 231
Taylor, Texas 76574
www.ci.taylor.tx.us/
Phone: (512) 365-8485
Fax: (512) 352-6366

Temple Chamber of Commerce
P.O. Box 158
Temple, Texas 76503
www.temple-tx.org/
Phone: (254) 773-2105
Fax: (254) 773-0661

Terrell Chamber of Commerce
P.O. Box 97
Terrell, Texas 75160
www.terrelltexas.com/
Phone: (972) 563-5703
Fax: (972) 563-2363

Texarkana Chamber of Commerce
P.O. Box 1468
Texarkana, Texas 75504
www.texarkana.org/
Phone: (903) 792-7191
Fax: (903) 793-4304

Texas City-La Marque Chamber of
Commerce
P.O. Box 1717
Texas City, Texas 77592-1717
www.texascitychamber.org/
Phone: (409) 935-1408
Fax: (409) 935-5186

Timpson Chamber of Commerce
P.O. Box 989
Timpson, Texas 75975
Phone: (409) 254-3500
no website, but check out
www.timpsontexas.com/

Tomball Area Chamber of Commerce
P.O. Box 516
Tomball, Texas 77375
www.tomballtexas.com/index.htm
Phone: (281) 351-7222
Fax: (281) 351-7223

Tulia Chamber of Commerce
P.O. Box 267
Tulia, Texas 79088
Phone: (806) 995-2296
Fax: (806) 995-4426
no website, but check out
tuliatx.areaguides.net/

Tyler Texas
www.tyler.com

Tyler Area Chamber of Commerce
P.O. Box 390
Tyler, Texas 75710
www.tylertexas.com
Phone: (903) 592-1061
Fax: (903) 593-2746

Tyler Economic Development
Council
P.O. Box 2004
Tyler, Texas 75710
www.tedc.org
Phone: (903) 593-2004

Utopia Texas
www.utopiatexas.com

Uvalde Area Chamber of Commerce
300 East Main Street
Uvalde, Texas 78801
www.uvaldetx.com/
Phone: (830) 278-3361
Fax: (830) 278-3363

Vernon Chamber of Commerce
1614 Main Street
Vernon, Texas 76385
www.vernontx.com
Phone: (940) 552-2564
Fax: (940) 552-0654

Victoria Area Chamber, Greater
P.O. Box 2465
Victoria, Texas 77902
www.visitvictoria.org
Phone: (361) 573-5277
Fax: (361) 573-0460

Waco Chamber of Commerce,
Greater
P.O. Box 1220
Waco, Texas 76703
www.waco-chamber.org

Phone: (254) 752-6551
Fax: (254) 752-6618

Washington County Chamber of
Commerce
314 S. Austin Street
Brenham, Texas 77833
www.brenhamtexas.com
Phone: (409) 836-3695
Fax: (409) 836-2540

Waxahachie Chamber of Commerce
P.O. Box 187
Waxahachie, Texas 75168
www.wacahachie.com
Phone: (972) 937-2390
Fax: (972) 938-9237

Weatherford Chamber of Commerce
P.O. Box 310
Weatherford, Texas 76086
www.weatherford-chamber.com
Phone: (817) 594-3801
Fax: (817) 594-1623

Weslaco Chamber of Commerce
P.O. Box 8398
Weslaco, Texas 78599
www.weslaco.com
Phone: (409) 532-1862
Fax: (409) 532-0102

Wharton Chamber of Commerce
P.O. Box 868
Wharton, Texas 77488
www.wharton.com
Phone: (409) 532-1862
Fax: (409) 532-0102

White Settlement Area Chamber of
Commerce
201 Meadow Park Drive
White Settlement, Texas 76108
www.whitesettlement-tx.com

Phone: (817) 246-1121
Fax: (817) 246-1121

Wichita Falls BCI
P.O. Box 1860
Wichita Falls, Texas 76307
www.bci.wf.net
Phone: (940) 723-2741
Fax: (940) 723-8773

Wylie Chamber of Commerce
108 A Marble
Wylie, Texas 75098
www.wylie.tx.us/chamber
Phone: (972) 442-2804
Fax: (972) 429-0139

Texas Towns by Region

Abilene	Dumas	Panhandle
Albany	Eastland	Perryton
Amarillo	Eola	Plainview
Andrews	Floydada	Post
Anson	Fort Griffin	Quanah
Archer City	Friona	Quitaque
Baird	Fritch	Ralls
Ballinger	Gail	Ranger
Benjamin	Graham	Rising Star
Big Spring	Groom	Roaring Springs
Borger	Hale Center	Robert Lee
Boys Ranch	Happy	San Saba
Breckenridge	Haskell	Santa Anna
Bronte	Hereford	Seagraves
Brownfield	Knox City	Seminole
Brownwood	Lamesa	Shamrock
Buffalo Gap	Levelland	Silverton
Burkburnett	Littlefield	Slaton
Caddo	Lubbock	Snyder
Caldwell	Matador	Spearman
Canadian	McLean	Stamford
Canyon	Memphis	Stanton
Childress	Miami	State Park
Cisco	Miles	Stinnett
Clarendon	Moran	Stratford
Claude	Morton	Sweetwater
Coleman	Muleshoe	Tahoka
Colorado City	Newcastle	Tulia
Crosbyton	O'Donnell	Turkey
Crowell	Odessa	Vernon
Dalhart	Olney	Wellington
Denver City	Paducah	Wheeler
Dickens	Paint Rock	Wichita Falls
Dimmitt	Pampa	Winters

West

Alpine
Anthony
Balmorhea
Big Bend National
  Park
Big Spring
Del Rio
El Paso
Fort Davis
Fort Stockton

Iraan
Kermit
Lajitas
Langtry
Marathon
Marfa
McCamey
Midland
Monahans
Odessa

Pecos
Pine Springs
Presidio
Salt Flat
Sanderson
Sierra Blanca
Study Butte
Terlingua
Van Horn
Wink

Hill Country

Austin
Bandera
Bastrop
Bertram
Big Lake
Blanco
Boerne
Brackettville
Brady
Brownwood
Buda
Buchanan Dam
Burnet
Camp Verde
Camp Wood
Canyon Lake
Castroville
Cedar Park
Comfort
Concan
Devine
Dripping Springs
Early
Eldorado
Elgin
Fort Bend
Fort McKavett

Fredericksburg
Georgetown
Goldthwaite
Gruene
Hare
Harper
Hondo
Hutto
Ingram
Johnson City
Junction
Kerrville
Kingsland
Kyle
Lago Vista
Lakehills
Lampasas
Leakey
Liberty Hill
Llano
Lockhart
Lometa
Luckenbach
Luling
Manchaca
Marble Falls
Mason

Medina
Menard
Mertzon
Mountain Home
Natalia
New Braunfels
Ozona
Pflugerville
Rio Frio
Rocksprings
Round Rock
Sabinal
San Angelo
San Marcos
San Saba
Smithville
Sonora
Stonewall
Taylor
Titus
Utopia
Uvalde
Village of San
  Leanna
Wimberley

North Central

Addison	Decatur	Holland
Alleyton	DeLeon	Honey Grove
Alvarado	Denison	Howe
Anderson	Denton	Hubbard
Arlington	Dew	Independence
Athens	Dublin	Irving
Bartlett	Duncanville	Itasca
Bedford	Eagle Lake	Jacksboro
Bellville	Edgewood	Kaufman
Belton	Electra	Killeen
Bonham	Elgin	Ladonia
Bowie	Ellinger	La Grange
Boyd	Ennis	Lake Lewisville
Bremond	Fairfield	Lancaster
Brenham	Farmers Branch	Ledbetter
Bridgeport	Fayetteville	Lewisville
Bryan	Flatonia	Lexington
Buckholts	Forney	Mansfield
Burton	Fort Worth	Marlin
Cameron	Franklin	May
Canton	Gainesville	McGregor
Carrollton	Garland	McKinney
Cedar Hill	Gatesville	Meridian
Centerville	Giddings	Mesquite
Chappell Hill	Glen Rose	Mexia
Clarksville	Granbury	Midlothian
Clay County	Grand Prairie	Mineral Wells
Cleburne	Grand Saline	Montague
Clifton	Grapeland	Moody
College Station	Grapevine	Mount Vernon
Columbus	Greenville	Muenster
Comanche	Groesbeck	Navasota
Commerce	Hallettsville	Needville
Cooper	Hamilton	New Ulm
Copperas Cove	Harker Heights	Nocona
Corsicana	Harlandale	North Richland Hills
Cotulla	Hearne	Oakland
Cresson	Helotes	Palestine
Crockett	Henrietta	Paris
Cumby	Hico	Pilot Point
Dallas	Hillsboro	Plano

Plantersville
Rainbow
Rankin
Richardson
Roanoke
Rockwall
Rogers
Round Top
Rowlett
Saint Jo
Salado
San Felipe
Sanger
Schulenburg
Sealy

Serbin
Seymour
Sherman
Snook
Somerville
Springtown
Stephenville
Sulphur Springs
Teague
Temple
Terrell
Thurber
Troy
Van Alstyne
Vernon

Waco
Walnut Springs
Washington
Watauga
Waxahachie
Weatherford
Weches
Weimar
West
Whitney
Wills Point
Winedale
Wortham

South Plains

Alamo
Alice
Beeville
Brenham
Carrizo Springs
Crystal City
Cuero
Donna
Eagle Pass
Edinburg
Falfurrias
Fannin
Floresville
Freer
George West

Goliad
Gonzales
Helena
Hidalgo
Jourdanton
Laredo
Mercedes
McAllen
Mission
Moulton
Panna Maria
Pearsall
Pharr
Pleasanton
Poteet

Rio Grande City
Roma
San Antonio
San Juan
Seguin
Selma
Shiner
Three Rivers
Vanderpool
Victoria
Weslaco
Wallis
Yoakum
Yorktown
Zapata

East Piney Woods

Alto	Jefferson	Orange
Atlanta	Karnack	Overton
Bloomburg	Kilgore	Pine Mills
Buna	Kirbyville	Pittsburg
Camden	Kountze	Quitman
Carthage	Liberty	Rusk
Center	Livingston	San Augustine
Cleveland	Longview	Saratoga
Coldspring	Lovelady	Silsbee
Conroe	Lufkin	Sour Lake
Daingerfield	Lumberton	Tatum
Dayton	Magnolia	Texarkana
Easton	Marietta	Trinity
Gilmer	Marshall	Tyler
Gladewater	Mauriceville	Uncertain
Hallsville	Mineola	Waskom
Hemphill	Montgomery	Whitehouse
Henderson	Moscow	Winnsboro
Hughes Springs	Mount Pleasant	Woodville
Huntsville	Nacogdoches	Zavalla
Jacksonville	New Boston	
Jasper	Newton	

Gulf Coast

Alvin	Corpus Christi	Harlingen
Anahuac	Crosby	Hempstead
Angleton	Crystal Beach	Hitchcock
Aransas Pass	Deer Park	Houston
Bay City	East Bernard	Humble
Baytown	Edna	Indianola
Beaumont	El Campo	Ingleside
Ben Bolt	Freeport	Katy
Brazosport Area	Friendswood	Kingsville
Bridge City	Fulton	La Marque
Brookshire	Galveston	La Porte
Brownsville	Glen Flora	Lake Jackson
Clear Lake Area	Goldthwaite	League City
Clute	Groves	Los Fresnos

Mathis
Nederland
Old Town Spring
Olmito
Palacios
Pasadena
Port Aransas
Port Arthur
Port Isabel
Port Lavaca
Port Mansfield
Port Neches
Port O'Connor

Portland
Prairie View
Raymondville
Refugio
Richmond
Rio Hondo
Rockport
Rosenberg
San Benito
Sinton
Santa Fe
Seabrook
South Padre Island

Spring
Sugar Land
Taft
Texas City
The Woodlands
Tomball
Tynan
Victoria
Vidor
West Columbia
Wharton
Winnie

Index of Events

Accordion Kings Camp and Festival, 160

AirSho 2001, 202

Alabama-Coushatta Indian Powwow, 109

Alamo Irish Festival, 29

Algerita Jam and Arts Festival, 172

All-American Cowboy Get-Together, 171

Alley Oop Day, 72, 106

AlleyFest, 110

American Cancer Society Cowboy Ball, 160

Andrews Bluegrass Festival, 168

Angelina Benefit Rodeo, 67

Annual Asian-American Festival, 225

Annual Austin Rugby Tournament, The, 61

Annual Charity Bar-B-Que Cookoff, 146

Annual Christmas Parade, 244

Annual Colonial Texas Heritage Festival, 20

Annual Crossroad Championship BBQ, 172

Annual Electra Goat Cookoff, 86

Annual Fair and Rodeo, 115

Annual Fiestas del Llano, 187

Annual Fishing Fiesta, 134

Annual 4th of July Parade and Picnic, 133

Annual Goliad Massacre Reenactment, 20

Annual Hare BBQ, 144

Annual Houston Pod Chili Cookoff, 69

Annual Irving Heritage Festival, 117

Annual Itasca Chamber of Commerce BBQ, 106

Annual Joy Ride Rod Run, 30

Annual Living History Day, 20

Annual Louisiana Swamp Romp and Crawfish Festival, 66

Annual Mayfest, 87

Annual Migration Celebration, 44

Annual O. Henry Pun-Off World Championships, 94

Annual Octoberfest & Barbecue Cookoff, 212

Annual Old-Fashioned Fair, 72

Annual Old-Time Fiddlers Contest, 115

Annual Pasadena Strawberry Festival, 90

Annual POPS Concert - Bright Lights! Broadway!, 79

Annual Riverfest, 116

Annual Rogers Roundup Barbecue Cookoff, 116

Annual Southwestern Bell Plano Balloon Festival, 186

Annual Star Fest, 207

Annual Texas Cowboy Poetry Gathering, The, 24

Annual Texas Western Swing Fiddling Showcase, 36

Annual Tri-State Fair, 183

Annual Wild Horse Prairie Days Barbecue Cookoff, 106

Annual World Championship
    Bar-B-Que Cookoff, 11
Aqua-boom Celebration, 131
Arbor Daze, 65
Armadillo Christmas Bazaar, 248
Art Car Ball, 62
Artfest, 98
ARToberFEST, 225
Arts & Crafts Fair, 202
Arts Festival, 131
Arts, Antiques & Autos
    Extravaganza, 202
Asian Music Festival, 96
August Lights Arts Festival, 155
Austin Blues Family Tree Project,
    16
Austin Blues Festival, 222
Austin Bob Marley Festival, 208
Austin County Fair, 211
Austin Film Festival & Heart of Film
    Screenwriters Conference, 212
Austin Fine Arts Festival, 48
Austin Jazz and Arts Festival, 182
Austin Music Awards, 24
Austin Record Convention, 208
Austin Salsa Music Festival, 170
Austin Songwriters Conference, 146
Austin Summer Chamber Music
    Festival, 126
Azalea Festival, 34

Backyard Chicken & Sausage
    Gumbo Judging, 238
Balloon Rally of Alpine, 169
Bay Jammin' Summer Concert
    Series, 113, 129, 153
Bayfest, 197
Bayou City Art Festival -
    Downtown, 28, 216
BBQ Cookoff, 77
Beaumont Cinco de Mayo Festival at
    Riverfront Park, 74

Bedford Blues Festival & Arts Fair,
    165
Best of Texas International Music
    Awards, 211
Big Boo Halloween Festival, 216
Big Stinkin' International Improv &
    Sketch Comedy Festival, 227
Black-Eyed Pea Fall Harvest, 216
Blanco County Fair and Rodeo, 157
Bluebonnet Ball, 53
Bluebonnet Fair, 46
Bluebonnet Festival (Chappell Hill),
    48
Bluebonnet Festival (Natalia), 38
Bluegrass and Gospel, 24, 83, 130,
    167
Bluegrass and Gospel Show, 235
Bluegrass Festival, Antique Tractor,
    and Gas Engine Show, 215
Bluegrass Jamboree, 38
Bluegrass Summerfest, 113
Blues Festival, 184
BluesFest, 222
Bob Wills Day, 65
Bocktoberfest, 216
Bois D'Arc Bash, 190
Bois D'Arc Festival, 90
Bond's Alley Arts and Crafts
    Festival, 87
BorderFest, 21
Bowie Street Blues, 69
Boys Haven Crawfish Festival, 81
Brand New Opree, 244
Brazoria County Fair, 180, 201
Brazos Nights, 111
Brazosport Run for the Arts, 3
BreastFest, 63
Brush Country Days, 224
Bryan Bluegrass Music Festival, 107
Buccaneer Days, 50
Bud Otto Open Fiddle Contest, 49
Buda Country Fair, 44
Budafest, 247

Buffalo Soldier Heritage Day, 16
Burleson County Cinco de Mayo
  Celebration, 79
Burleson County Fair, 193
Burnet Bluebonnet Festival, 50
Burton Cotton Gin Festival, 57
Butterfield Stage Days, 144

Cactus Jazz and Blues Festival, 171
Cactus Pear Music Festival, 131
Cajun French Music Association
  Festival, 224
Calhoun County Fair, 219
Candlelight at Old City Park, 246
Capital 10,000, The, 43
Castro County Harvest Days, 172
Cedar Chopper Festival, 77
Celebrate Texas Independence Day,
  21
Celebration of the Arts, 94
Celtic Festival and Craft Faire, 197
Celtic Harvest Festival and
  Highland Games: Lughnassadh,
  154
Celtic Midsummer Festival, 130
Central Texas Barbecue Association
  Cookoff (Bartlett), 178
Central Texas Barbecue Association
  Cookoff (McGregor), 176
Central Texas State Fair, 161
Charles Goodnight's Chuck Wagon
  Cookoff, 191
Charro Days Festival, 15
Cherokee Rose Festival, 95
Chili Appreciation Society Terlingua
  International Chili Championship
  Cookoff, 234
ChiliFest, 47
"Chilly" BBQ & Chili, 13
Chisholm Trail Blazer, 120
Chisholm Trail Roundup "Old-Time
  Fiddlers" Contest, 118
Chisholm Trail Roundup, 121

Christmas Carol at Tablerock
  Amphitheater, A, 240, 242
Christmas Festival (New Braunfels),
  244
Christmas Festival (Brookshire),
  245
Christmas in Nocona, 244
Christmas on the Chisholm Trail,
  247
Christmas Parade (Cleburne), 243
Christmas Parade (Greenville), 244
Christmas Parade (Harlingen), 244
Christmas Parade (Alpine), 244
Christmas Tree Lighting and Tours
  of the LBJ Ranch, 242
Cinco de Mayo (Brookshire), 80
Cinco de Mayo Celebration (Dallas),
  75
Cinco de Mayo Celebration
  (Denton), 79
Cinco de Mayo Celebration (Fort
  Stockton), 80
Cinco de Mayo Celebration
  (Lubbock), 81
Cinco de Mayo Celebration
  (Sanderson), 82
Cinco de Mayo Festival (Goliad), 74
Cinco de Mayo Festival: Lo Nuestro
  (Austin), 77
City of Bedford 4thFest, 132
Claiborne Kyle Day, 193
Clear Lake Greek Festival, 86
Cleburne Springfest BBQ, 65
Colorado County Fair, 176
Comal County Fair, 192
Comanche County Powwow &
  Barnie McBee Memorial Brisket
  Cookoff, 188
"Come and Take It" Days
  Celebration, 202
Conjunto Shootout, 145
Conroe Cajun Catfish Festival, 214
Corn Festival, 120

Cotton Festival Cookoff, 107
Cotton Jubilee, 224
Cottonwood Art Festival, 77
Country Fair and Barbecue Cookoff, 182
Country Fest, Rock Fest, R&B Fest and Bluegrass Fest, 78, 246
Country Livin' Festival, 46
Country Music Association of Texas Awards Show, 228
Countryfest, 217
Cow Camp Cookoff, 80
Cowboy Artists of America Roundup, 72
Cowboy Homecoming Celebration, 158
Cowboy Roundup USA, 117
Cowboy Songs and Poetry, 45, 214
Cowtown Cinco de Mayo, 88
Crawfish Open, 53
Crazy Water Festival, 217
Cullen Baker Country Fair and Parade, 235
Czech Fest, 79
Czech Heritage Day, 184
Czech Heritage Festival, 32
Czechfest, 206
Czhilispiel XXVIII, 228

Dallas International Festival, 122
Dallas Video Festival, 34
Dalton Days, 190
Day of the Scots, 198
Dayton Old Tyme Days, 60
De Fa Tras Chapter Cajun Music Festival, 173
Deep Ellum Arts Festival, 47
Denton Arts and Jazz Festival, 64
Denton Holiday Lighting Festival, 239
Depot Day (Magnolia), 52
Depot Days (Gainesville), 90
Depot Jazz and Blues Series, 205

Deutschen Fest, 91
Dewberry Festival, 62
Dickens Christmas in Lockhart, A, 247
Dickens of a Christmas, 238
Dickens on the Strand, 247
Diez y Seis de Septiembre, 182
Diez y Seis Guadalupe Street Parade & Festival, 184
Do Dat Barbecue, 185
Doan's May Picnic, 76
Dog Days of Summer Celebration, The, 115
Double Extravaganza, 111
Downtown Hoe Down, 56

Early Day Tractor and Engine Association Annual Show, 203
Early Music at Round Top, 99
Early Settlers Festival, 142
East Texas Gusher Days, 76
East Texas Pinetop Blues Festival, 205
East Texas Poultry Festival, 204
East Texas Yamboree, 219
Easter Festival and Chili Cookoff, 50
Easter Fires Pageant, 52
Easter Pageant, 52
Eastland Old Rip Fest & Parade, 185
Eeyore's Birthday Party, 62
8th Annual Wimberley Jazz at Cypress Creek Café, The, 8
El Grito: Celebration of Mexican Independence Day, 182
Escape to Chili Island - Chili Cookoff & Junkanoo BBQ, 203

FalconFest, 230
Fall Bluegrass, 192
Fall Creek Grape Stomp, 155
Fall Festival, 190
Fall Polka Festival, 191
Fall, Fun, Food, Fest, 201

Falling Leaves Polka Festival, 231
FallsFest, 198
Family Festival in the Park, 109
Family Fun Fair, 137
Farmer Stockman Show, 210
Father's Day Celebration, 122
Fayette County Country Fair, 161
Festa Italiana, 179
Festival Chicano, 213
Festival in the Park, 81
Festival of Arts & Jazz, 108
Festival of Flags and Rodeo, 98
Festival of Freedom, 125
Festival of Quilts 2001, 189
Festival on Nolan Creek, 137
Festival on the Square, 186
Fiesta (Arts and Crafts Show and
    Festival), 91
Fiesta Amistad (Ben Bolt), 161
Fiesta Amistad (Round Rock), 99
Fiesta Around the World, 69
Fiesta Bandana City Celebration, 73
Fiesta de las Flores, 170
Fiesta del Campo, 211
Fiesta Diez y Seis, 186
Fiesta Edinburg, 15
Fiesta en la Playa, 168
Fiesta Patrias, 187
Fiesta Ranchera, 75
Fiesta San Antonio, 55
5th Annual Day Powwow Festival,
    90
Fire Ant Festival (Marshall), 215
Fire Ant Festival Barbecue Cookoff
    (Montague), 172
Fire on the Strings Bluegrass
    Festival, 95
Fish Day, 82
Folklife Celebration, 49
Folklife Festival and Frontier
    Jubilee, 67
Food and Wine Fest, 229

Forney Jackrabbit Stampede and
    Festival, 173
Fort Bend County Fair, 196
Fort Bend Czechfest, 76
Fort Griffin Fandangle, 124
Fort Worth Music Festival, 221
Founder's Day (Howe), 74
Founder's Day and Chicken Cookoff
    (Dripping Springs), 59
Founders Day Festival
    (Fredericksburg), 85
Four States Fair and Rodeo, 184
Fourth Fest (Deer Park), 137
Fourth Fest and Fireworks
    (Mesquite), 137
Fourth of July Celebration on the
    Neches River, 138
Fourth of July Celebration (Alvin),
    137
Fourth of July Celebration
    (Brownfield), 138
Fourth of July Celebration (Del Rio),
    138
Fourth of July Celebration
    (Friendswood), 140
Fourth of July Celebration (Snyder),
    132
Fourth of July Celebration
    (Wheeler), 138
4th of July Festival, 132
Fourth of July Fireworks Display,
    139
Fourth of July Freedom Celebration,
    132
Fourth of July Jubilee, 139
Fourth of July Parade and
    Celebration, 139
4th on Broadway Celebration, 132
4th on the Brazos, 142
Freedom Fest (San Antonio), 126
Freedom Festival (Orange), 139
Freedom Fiesta (Seguin), 129
Freer Rattlesnake Roundup, 68

Freestone County Benefit BBQ
    Cookoff, 106
Friendship Fest and Bartlett VFD
    Barbecue Cookoff, 181
Fright Nights at Tablerock, 231
Frontier Days and Rodeo, 168
Frontier Days (Breckenridge), 81
Frontier Days (Ladonia), 142
Frontier Days (Old Town Spring), 14
Frontier Days (Round Rock), 144,
    207
Fry Street Fair, 61
Fulton Oysterfest, 21
Fun-Fest & BBQ Cookoff, 55
Fun-tier Days (Santa Anna), 86
Funtier Days (Bandera), 97

Galveston Caribbean Carnival
    Festival, 116
Galveston County Fair and Rodeo,
    39
Gathering of the Scottish Clans of
    Texas, 236
General Granbury's Birthday Party
    and Bean Cookoff, 34
General Sam Houston Folk Festival,
    54
George West Storyfest, Chuck
    Wagon Dinner & Show, 234
Germanfest, 66
Gillespie County Fair, 159
Glen Rose Bluegrass Reunion, 197
Go Texan Cotton Pickin' Fair, 175
Go Texan Days, 8
God and Country Concert, 131
Good Oil Days, 57
Good Ole Days Barbecue Cookoff
    and Festival, 155
Gospel Festival, 67
Gospel Music Festival, 213
Go-Texan BBQ, 172
Gran Fiesta de Fort Worth, 147
GrapeFest, 177

Grayson County Fire Fiddlers
    Contest, 217
Great Texas Balloon Race, 145
Great Texas Birding Classic, The, 58
Great Texas Mosquito Festival, 148
Greater Southwest Guitar Shows -
    The Dallas Guitar Show, 37
Greater Southwest Music Festival,
    78
Greek Festival, 187
Greek Funstival, 222
Gregg County Fair and Expo, 176
Groesbeck Barbecue Cookoff, 91
Gruene Musicfest, 212
Guadalupe County Fair, 211
Gulf Coast Jam, 109

Hamilton County Dove Festival, 169
Happy Days and Rodeo, 158
Harlandale Festival, 87
Harley Davidson Chili Cookoff, 3
Harris County Fair, 210
Harvest Fest (Fort Stockton), 156
Harvest Festival (Needville), 224
Harvestfest & The Great McKinney
    Bed Races, 194
Hawkwood Medieval Fantasy Faire,
    165, 201
Hearne Chamber of Commerce &
    Robertson County Go-Texan
    Cookoff & Sunflower Festival,
    196
Heart O' Texas Fair and Rodeo, 204
Helotes Cornyval, 73
Heritage Crafts Day, 215
Heritage Day, 46
Heritage Holiday, 194
Heritage Syrup Festival, 236
Heritage Turnip Greens Festival,
    107
Highland Lakes Bluebonnet Trail,
    39, 45

Hockley County Early Settlers Reunion, 143
Hogeye Festival, 229
Holiday On The Square, 239
Hopkins County Fall Festival, 179
Hopkins County Independence Day and Fireworks Show, 133
Hot Pepper Festival, 229
Houston Caribbean Festival, 188
Houston Children's Festival, 32
Houston Downtown Street Festival, 99, 235
Houston Heritage Chapter Cajun Music Festival, 83
Houston Hot Sauce Festival, 189
Houston International Festival, 58
Houston International Jazz Festival, 62
Houston Livestock Show and Rodeo, 12
Houston Women's Festival, 230
Howard County Fair, 159
HUG-IN, 12
Hunt County Fair, 117

Independence Day Parade / Tractor Pull, 133
Independence Day Symphony On The Square, 130
Indian Summer Festival, 218
International Accordion Festival, 194
International Gumbo Cookoff, 76
International Holiday Exhibit and Festival Evening, 246
International Kite Fest, 66
International Piano Competition for Outstanding Amateurs, The, 112
International Young Performers Musical Competition and Isabel Sconti Piano Solo Competition, 38

Iron Horse Heritage Days Festival, 218

Janis Joplin Birthday Bash, 4
Jasper Fall Fest, 206
Jasper Rodeo, 84
Jaycee Jubilee, 168
Jaycee Roundup Weekend, 143
Jaycees Annual Rattlesnake Roundup, 26
Jazz'SALive, 183
Jefferson Salutes America Fourth of July Celebration, 140
Jerry Jeff Walker Birthday Weekend, 36
Jim Bowie Days, 121
John Lennon Birthday Jam, 207
Jourdanton Days Kactus Kick (formerly Dairy Days), 93
Juice Anniversary Celebration, 3
July Fourth Celebration (Grand Prairie), 133
July Fourth Celebration (Lamesa), 140
July Fourth Celebration (Lufkin), 140
July Fourth Old-timers Reunion, 134
July Homecoming, 140
July Jubilee (Leakey), 134
July Jubilee Celebration (Brady), 134
June Bug Jamboree, 121
Juneteenth Celebration (Fort Worth), 122
Juneteenth Celebration (Waco), 123

Kaleidoscope Creative Arts Festival, 86
Kendall County Fair, 162
Kerr County Fair, 212
Kerrville Folk Festival, 96, 105
Kerrville Wine and Music Festival, 162
Kickback Country Weekend, 119

Killeen Festival, 40
Kimble Kounty Kow Kick, 170
Kingsland Bluebonnet Festival, 45
Kiwanis Fireworks Show, 141
Kolache Fest (Hallettsville), 198
Kolache Festival (Caldwell), 173
Kolache-Klobase Festival, 115
Kueckelhan Rodeo, 148

La Salle County Fair and Wild Hog
    Cookoff, 27
Labor Day Square Dance Festival,
    166
Ladies State Chili Bust, 206
Land of Leather Days, 9
Larry Joe Taylor's 4th of July Island
    Time Festival, 142
League of Celtic Nations Festival &
    Highland Games, 195
Lee County Fair Charcoal
    Challenge, 91
Liberty Hill Festival, 63
Liberty Jubilee, 38
Light Up The Square, 245
Lights on Broadway Holiday
    Festival, 245
Living History Day, 174
Llano Heritage Day Festival, 224
Lobsterfest, 201
Lometa Diamondback Jubilee, 33
Lone Star Texas Music Jam, 230
Lone Stars and Stripes, 136
Lonesome Dove Days, 74
Lovefest, 10
Lubbock Arts Festival, 60
Lubbock Summer Jazz Festival, 125
Luling Watermelon Thump, 123

Magnolia Festival, 59
Magnolia Homes Tour and Live Oak
    Arts and Crafts Show, 90
Maifest, 84

Main St. Fort Worth Arts Festival,
    55
Main Street Arts & Crafts Show,
    189
Main Street Days Festival, 92
Maize Days, 175
Mansfield Hometown Festival, 189
Mardi Gras Galveston, 14
Mardi Gras of Southeast Texas, 22
Mardi Gras Upriver, 23
Marlin Festival Days, 77
Martin Luther King Parade, 3
Mauriceville Crawfish Festival, 59
May Festival, 98
May Fun-Fest, 76
Mayfair, 72
Mayfair Art Festival, 89
Mayfest, 73
Mays' Bluegrass, 145
McLennan County Go-Texan
    Cookoff, 188
MDA Benefit Rodeo, 159
Medina County Fair, 188
Medina Lake Cajun Festival, 191
Mediterranean Festival, 213
Memorial Day Fair on the Square,
    97
Memorialfest, 100
Mesquite Championship Rodeo, 43,
    71, 105, 129, 153, 165
Mexican Fiesta, 175
Mid-Winter Festival of Music, 4
Mills County Youth Fair and
    Livestock Show, 3
Mineola May Days Bean Fest, 78
Mobeetie Bluegrass Festival, 149
Montalba Outdoor Music
    Celebration, 167
Montgomery County Fair, 30
Montgomery County PRCA Pro
    Rodeo, 154
Montgomery Old West Festival, 117
Motorola Marathon, 11

Moulton Polka Waltz Celebration, 31
Moulton Town & Country Jamboree, 148
Mud Dauber Festival, 32
Music Crossroads of Texas Festival, The, 169
Music in the Park at Fullerton-Garrity Amphitheater, 123
Music of the Sea Festival, 237

Nacogdoches Heritage Festival, 102
National Accordion Convention, 30
National Championship Barbecue Cook-off, 159
National Cowboy Symposium and Celebration – The National Championship Chuck Wagon Cookoff and The American Cowboy Culture Awards Show, The, 171
National Cowgirl Hall of Fame Induction Ceremony, 237
National Polka Festival, 75
Navasota Blues Festival, 124
Neches River Festival, 54
Neches River Rendezvous, 106
Nederland Heritage Festival, 33
New Dimensions Festival, 221
New Ulm Art Festival, 51
Newton County Fair, 72
Night in Old Fredericksburg, A, 146
Night in Old Pecos/Cantaloupe Festival, 126
Nine Flags Festival, 247
Noche de Luces "Night of Lights," 243
Noches Norteñas, 112
North By Northgate Music Festival, 33
North Texas Irish Festival, 23
North Texas Longhorn Show, 19
North Texas New Music Festival, 210

North Texas State Fair and Rodeo, 157
Norwegian Home Tour, 245
Nostalgia Days, 75

Oakland Fireman's Festival, 110
Oatmeal Festival, 169
Ogletree Gap Folklife Festival & Barbecue Cookoff, 221
Ogletree Gap Heritage Festival, 225
Oktoberfest (Addison), 179
Oktoberfest (Fredericksburg), 203
Oktoberfest (Winedale), 209
Old Depot Arts Fest, 188
Old Gruene Market Days, 13
Old Pecan Street Fall Arts Festival, 198
Old Pecan Street Spring Arts Festival, 82
Old Settlers Music Festival, 47
Old Settlers Reunion, 153
Old Sorehead Trade Days, 46
Old West Fest 'N Trade Show, 238
Olde Tyme Days & Street Dance, 223
Old-Fashioned Christmas, 243
Old-Fashioned Fourth of July, 141
Old-Time Fun Festival, 150
Old-Timers Days, 230
Onion Festival, 93
Original Terlingua International Championship Chili Cookoff, 234
Overton Bluegrass Music Festival, 143

Pacific Islander Watauga Fest, 40
Panhandle South Plains Fair, 190
Parker County Peach Festival, 145
Pasadena Livestock Show, Rodeo and Fair, 214
Peach and Melon Festival, 154
Peanut Festival, 222
Pecan Street Fall Arts Festival, 182

PecanFest, 225
Permian Basin Fair and Exposition, 180
Pickin' Around the Campfire, 29
   Boo Grass, 227
   Trade Days, 54
Pickin' in the Pines (Mineola), 183
Pickin' in the Pines (Pine Mills), 95
Picnic in the Park, 119, 154
Pinata Festival, 244
Piney Woods Fair, 210
Pineywoods Purgatory, 212
Pioneer Day (New Boston), 157
Pioneer Day (Temple), 125
Pioneer Days (Whitney), 201
Pioneer-Chickfest, 181
Pioneers and Old Settlers Reunion, 156
Pleasure Island Music Festival, 66
Plum Creek Bluegrass Music Festival, 51
Polk Street Block Party, 160
Polka Fest, 246
Polski Dzien - Polish Day, 120
Port Lavaca - Calhoun County Bay Days, 91
Portland Pioneer Days, 61
Poteet Strawberry Festival, 48
Prazka Pout and Praha Feast, 156
PRCA Stampede Rodeo, 62
Prickly Pear Pachanga, 204

Quadrangle Craft and Music Festival, 174
Quanah Falls Festival, 173

Rabbit Fest, 89
Rattlesnake Hunt, 25
Red HOT & Blue Festival, 136
Red River Rodeo, 114
Red River Valley Fair, 161
Red Steagall Cowboy Gathering and Western Swing Festival, 228

Redbud Festival, 28
Refugio County Fair & PRCA Rodeo, 26
Refugio's Festival of the Flags, 202
Regional Christmas Lighting Trail, 243
Renaissance Polyphony Weekend, 8
Republic of Texas Chilympiad, 183
Ribolympics at Heartland Mall, 97
Rice and Crawfest, 49
Rice Harvest Festival, 218
Rio Grande Valley International Music Festival, 4
Rio Grande Valley Livestock Show, 29
RioFest, 58
Riverfest, 19
Robert Earl Keen's Texas Uprising, 100
Rockin' 50's Day and Car Show, 57
Roughneck Chili and Barbecue Cookoffs, 45
Round Top Festival, 120
Roundup Days, 72
Roundup Rodeo, 114
Roy Orbison Festival, 116
S.A.L.T. Fishing Rodeo, 101
Sabinal Lions Wild Hog Festival and Craft Fair, 37
Sacred Harp Singing Convention, 156
Sahawe Indian Dancer's Summer Ceremonials, 148
Saint Patrick Festival, 28
Saints Roost Celebration, 131
Salado Legends-Outdoor Musical Drama, 147
Salmon Lake Park Bluegrass Festival, 165
Salt Festival and Rodeo, 112
Sammons Jazz Festival, 226
San Antonio Stock Show and Rodeo, 9

San Jacinto Festival, 59
Sanger Heritage Celebration, 178
Santa Rosa Roundup, 89
Scarborough Renaissance Faire, 53
Schulenburg Festival, 154
Scurry County Fair, 179
Seabrook Music Festival, 207
Seafair, 209
Septemberfest, 174
Shakespeare Festival, 11
Sherman Arts Festival, 181
Shivaree, 109
Shrimpfest, 159
Shrimporee, 178
Siglo De Oro Drama Festival, 16
Silver Dollar Downs Crawfish Race
    and Festival, 83
Sixteenth of September Celebration,
    176
Smithville Jamboree, 61
Snaketales, 19
Snookfest, 57
Sombrero Festival, 15
Somervell County PRCA Rodeo, 22
Songwriters Festival, 89
Sounds of Summer Music Series,
    113
South by Southwest Music and
    Media Conference, 26
South Padre Island Jazz and Latin
    Music Festival, The, 167
South Plains Opry Celebration, 112
South Texas Music Fest and Texas
    International Bull Chip Throwing
    Contest, 12
South Texas Music Festival, 15
South Texas Polka and Sausage
    Festival, 35
South Texas Ranching Heritage
    Festival, 13
South Texas State Fair, 221
South Texas Youth Stockshow, 10

Southern Gospel & Bluegrass
    Gospel Singing, 101
Southwest Guitar Festival & Guitar
    Foundation of America
    Convention, 219
Southwestern Exposition, Livestock
    Show & Rodeo, 3, 8
Southwestern International
    Livestock Show & Rodeo, 9
Space City U.S.A. Guitar Show and
    Music Expo, 87
Spamarama, 43
Spicy Food and Music Festival, 94
Spikefest, 146
Spinach Festival, 236
Spring Bluegrass and Gospel
    Festival (Glen Rose), 64, 176
Spring Bluegrass Music Festival
    (Atlanta), 92
Spring Break at South Padre Island,
    16
Spring Creek Bluegrass Festival,
    228
Spring Fest (Marble Falls), 85
Spring Fest (Old Town Spring), 35
Spring Festival (Somerville), 59
Spring Fling - A Flower and Garden
    Show, 36
Spring Ho Festival, 133
Spring Polka Festival, 23
Spring Roundup Celebration in
    Aransas County, 20
Springfest Barbecue Cookoff, 69
Squatty Pines Storytelling Festival,
    13
St. Patrick's Day Celebration, 32
St. Patrick's Day Festival, 30
St. Patrick's Day Parade and Irish
    Festival, 28
St. Patrick's River of Green, 31
Stagecoach Days, 92
Stampede Rodeo, 100
Star of Texas Fair & Rodeo, 19

Starr County Fair, 22
Star-Spangled Fourth, 134
State Fair of Texas, 196, 200
Steel Guitar Jamboree, 27
Stonewall Peach Jamboree, 121
Strange Family Bluegrass Festival, 97, 162
String Fling, 11
Sugar Festival, The, 166
Summer Festival (Littlefield), 107
Summer Polka Festival, 125
SummerBlast, 110
Summerfest (San Marcos), 141
Sutton County Days and PRCA Rodeo, 158
Swisher County Picnic Celebration, 144
Sylvan Beach Festival, 68

Tablerock Spring Festival, 93
Tamuk Jazz Festival, 35
Taste Addison, 94
Taylor International Barbecue Cookoff and Rodeo, 157
Taylor Jaycees National Rattlesnake Sacking Championship, 21
Tejano Conjunto Festival, 83
Tejano Fest (San Antonio), 110
Tejano Fest (San Marcos), 206
Tejano Music Awards, 29
Tejano Thursdays Concert Series in San Antonio, 115
Tejano Wednesdays Concert Series in Dallas, 114
Tejas (Texas) Storytelling Festival, 19
Tejas Storytellers Summer Conference, 129
Tellabration, 238
Temple Jazz Festival, 39
Terrell Heritage Jubilee, 53
Texan Market Days, 226

Texas - A Musical Romance of Panhandle History, 114
Texas Bach Festival, 27
Texas Bar-B-Q Festival, 93
Texas Beer Festival, 40
Texas Blueberry Festival, 116
Texas Blues Festival, 49
Texas Book Festival, 238
Texas Butterfly Festival, 220
Texas Cactus Festival, 23
Texas Christian University Jazz Festival, 48
Texas Citrus Fiesta, 5
Texas Cowboy Poetry Gathering, 23
Texas Cowboy Reunion, 135
Texas Crab Festival, 67
Texas Crawfish Festival, 78
Texas Dogwood Trails, 33
Texas Electronic Music Festival, 95
Texas Fiddlers Contest and Reunion, 98
Texas Folklife Festival, 113
Texas Gatorfest, 178
Texas Gospel Singing Convention, 52
Texas Guitar Show (Austin), 11
Texas Guitar Show (Arlington), 226
Texas Heritage Music Jazz Festival, 122
Texas Independence Celebration (Luckenbach), 25
Texas Independence Day Celebration and Parade (Alamo), 14
Texas Indian Market and Southwest Showcase, 36
Texas Interactive Music Conference and Bar-B-Que, 220
Texas International Apple Festival, 149
Texas Ladies State Chili Championship, 61

Texas Mountain Western Heritage Weekend, 56
Texas Music Awards, 117
Texas Music Educators Association Annual Convention, 14
Texas Music Festival and Chili Cook-Off, 55
Texas Music Jam, 223
Texas Natural Festival Weekend, 88
Texas Open Chili Cookoff, 155
Texas Pecan Festival, 187
Texas Polka Music Awards Festival, 29
Texas Relays, The, 44
Texas Renaissance Festival, 194
Texas Rice Festival, 203
Texas Rose Festival, 220
Texas Scottish Festival & Highland Games, 107
Texas Shakespeare Festival, 123
Texas State Arts and Crafts Fair, 98
Texas State Bluegrass Festival, 122
Texas State Championship Fiddlers Frolic, 63
Texas State Forest Festival, 193
Texas Storytelling Festival, 21
Texas Summerfest, 97
Texas Swing Evening, 118
Texas Tech Jazz Band Festival, 24
Texas Toot, The (was Texas Early Music Festival), 111, 237
Texas Train Festival, 187
Texas Woodcarver's Guild Fall Roundup, 192
Texaspride Celebration, 20
Texomaland Junior Fiddlers Contest, 34
3rd Coast Music Conference, 197Titus County Fair, 193
Timeless Christmas in Johnson City, A, 248
Tom Tom Festival, 108
Tomato Fest, 119

Tops in Texas Rodeo, 144
Totally Texas, 52
Town and Country Jamboree (Moulton), 150
Town and Country Jubilee (Hereford), 118
Trader's Village BBQ, 214
TRCA Stampede Rodeo, 64
Trinity Community Fair, 195
Trinity Valley Expo, 218
Tri-State Fair, 184
True Value/Jimmy Dean Country Showdown, 108
Tule Creek Bluegrass Festival, 96
Turkeyfest Parade and Festival, 213
Tynan Rec. Club Festival & BBQ, 212

Uncle Fletch Davis Hamburger Cookoff American Music Festival & Operation Rainbow Chili Cookoff, 88

Valentine's Day Oldies Dance, 12
Very Special Arts Festival, 15
Victoria Bach Festival, 120
Victoria County Czech Heritage Festival, 191
Victoria Livestock Show & Auction, 25
Victorian Christmas Festival, 239
Viva! Cinco de Mayo Celebration, 73
VIVA! El Paso!, 106, 129, 153

Walker County Fair, 39
Washington County Fair, 186
Washington's Birthday Celebration, 9
Watermelon Festival, 149
Waylon's West Texas BBQ, 167
Weimar Gedenke Country Fun Festival, 85
Weinachts Fest, 243

Wendish Festival, 191
West End's Taste of Dallas, The, 143
West Texas "Roots" Music Festival, 99
West Texas Fair and Rodeo, 172
Western Days (Elgin), 146
Western Days (Yorktown), 221
Western Heritage Classic, 85
Western Swing Weekend, 108
Westfest, 166
Westheimer Street Festival, The, 226
Wharton County Freedom Festival, 136
Wharton County: Youth Fair and Exposition, 64
Wheel Roundup, 43
White Buffalo Festival, 208
Wild Azalea Days, 33
Wild Horse Prairie Days, 108
Wild West Extravaganza, 9
Wild West Festival BBQ Cookoff, 178
Wildflower Day in the Spring, 58
Wildflower Festival, 235
Wildflower Trails of Texas, 65
Wildflower! Arts and Music Festival, 86
Wildflowers Days Festival, 50
Williamson County Old Settlers Celebration, 111
Willie Nelson's Fourth of July Picnic, 141
Windfest, 60
Winedale Spring Festival and Texas Crafts Exhibition, 44

Winter Jazz Concert Series, 10
Wise County Old Settlers Reunion, 148
Wonderland of Lights, 239, 242
World Championship Barbecue Goat Cookoff and Arts and Crafts Fair, 167
World Championship Cowboy Campfire Cooking & Pasture Roping, 100
World Championship Fiddler's Festival, 158
World Championship Wild Hog Cookoff, 237
World of Texas Championship BBQ, 124
Wortham Blind Lemon Jefferson Blues Festival, The, 175
Wurstfest, 235

XIT Bluegrass Festival, 63
XIT Rodeo and Reunion, Rita Blanca Park, 153

Y.O. Social Club Party, 181
Yamboree Fiddlers Contest, 219
Yesterfest and the Salinas Art Festival, 56
Yesteryear Festival & Celebration, 125
Young Country Christmas Fireworks to Music, 239

Zapata County Fair, 27
Zilker Kite Festival, 26
Zilker Summer Musical, 142

Looking for more?

Check out these and other great titles from Republic of Texas Press

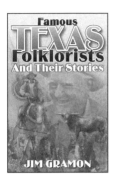

Famous Texas Folklorists and Their Stories
Jim Gramon
1-55622-825-2 • $18.95
310 pages • 5½ x 8½ •
paper

Lone Star Ladies: A Travel Guide to Women's History in Texas
Melinda Rice
1-55622-847-3 • $18.95
248 pages • 5½ x 8½ •
paper

Texas Old-Time Restaurants and Cafes
Sheryl Smith-Rodgers
1-55622-733-7 • $18.95
288 pages • 7½ x 9¼ •
paper

Barbecuing Around Texas
Richard K. Troxell
1-55622-697-7 • $18.95
312 pages • 5½ x 8½ •
paper

Exploring Texas with Children
Sharry Buckner
1-55622-624-1 • $18.95
288 pages • 5½ x 8½ •
paper

Counter Culture Texas
Susie Kelly Flateau and Mark Dean
1-55622-737-X • $24.95
272 pages • 7½ x 9¼ •
paper